LAST SHOT

LAST SHOT

*A coming-of-age memoir of addiction,
ambition and redemption*

JOCK ZONFRILLO

**SIMON &
SCHUSTER**

London · New York · Sydney · Toronto · New Delhi

Aboriginal and Torres Strait Islander readers are warned that this book contains images of people who are deceased or who may now be deceased.

LAST SHOT
First published in Australia in 2021 by
Simon & Schuster (Australia) Pty Limited
Suite 19A, Level 1, Building C, 450 Miller Street, Cammeray, NSW 2062

10 9 8 7 6 5 4 3 2

Sydney New York London Toronto New Delhi
Visit our website at www.simonandschuster.com.au

 A catalogue record for this book is available from the National Library of Australia

Author's note: Some names have been changed in this memoir to protect people's privacy.

ISBN: 9781761101915

Cover design: Meng Koach
Jacket images: Tina Smigielski
Author photo: Kelly Gardner
Typeset by Midland Typesetters, Australia
Printed and bound by CPI Group (UK) Ltd, Croydon CR0 4YY

This book is dedicated to everybody who's ever felt unworthy. You are worth more than you know . . . it's just that nobody understands you yet. They will come along, I promise.

For me, that's my four beautiful children, Ava, Sofia, Alfie and Isla. I love you all more than I could ever explain.

My Loz, who not only found me but unwound me, rewired me and made my life richer than I ever could have imagined. I most certainly never truly felt worthy until I met you, gorgeous. Thank you.

My mum and dad, on whom I blame nothing: I own each and every one of my bad decisions.

Finally, to food: without you I would be behind bars or in a pine box six feet under.

FOREWORD

by
Jimmy Barnes

As I sat reading my good mate Jock's book there were a few things I noticed immediately. Jock and I are great friends and we even refer to each other as brothers. But it wasn't until I started reading this that I realised how close that bond really is. We came from different parts of Scotland, totally different upbringings and from different times, and I am a wee bit older than him, but we are similar in many ways. Turning these pages felt like I was taking a peek into what my life might have been like if my family had stayed in Glasgow and stayed together. I know now it still wouldn't have been enough to save me the pain I had to feel.

Jock came from a loving home but it wasn't enough. Nothing would be enough for him for a long time. There was something in him that I see in myself; something that drove him to want more. He needed to see and feel everything. He felt more at home outside his comfort zone, breaking the rules and living on the edge, than he did anywhere else. There would be no easy road for Jock, a child living in a city where heroin could be bought from ice cream vans that cruised the streets playing music to attract children. A place where a life could be lost in the flash of a blade just for being in the wrong place at the wrong time. There was only one way it could go. It would be a hard ride. A life that at times would feel like a roller-coaster. Jock would have to feel a lot of pain, physically and emotionally. His world would crumble many times, like it did with the loss of his beloved grandfather, Nonno. But this was just the beginning. Loss would be something he would have to get used to. There was a lot more coming his way.

A lesser man would not survive the life he would lead. Pain, agony, self-hatred and fear. And all this could happen in one night while running wild on the tough streets of Glasgow. But Jock would survive and move on to not only survive but to build a life for himself that most can only dream of. Along the way he tried his best to destroy every-thing that came close to him, but his love, his passion, the light inside him burned so bright that even he couldn't put it out.

Eventually all the confusion of being a young man with his feet planted cautiously in two different worlds would come beautifully together. Jock learned that being Scottish and Italian, one of the things that brought confusion and heartache as a child, was actually a blessing. He had the depth of history and the culture of two worlds to draw on. The sense of romance and hope he inherited from his Italian side and the single-minded, never-lie-down attitude he learned from the Scots would make him a force to be reckoned with. All the highs – and believe me there were highs – and all the lows he felt growing up would become an integral part of the complex, talented, loving human being that Jock is now.

This is a story of hope. A story of perseverance and resilience. A story of passion and love. A remarkable tale of a remarkable man who took the hard, hard road and made it his own. Jock's cooking is just one part of that complicated life, but it is a huge part. It's the way that Jock shares his love with everyone he comes close to. But I know Jock: it is only one part of that love. If you watch him as he engages with strangers: searching, probing, looking for a connection. Or if you watch his eyes as he holds his babies in his arms, you will see a man who is full of love and who is still searching; still trying to make himself an even better man. His journey is just beginning. There are great times ahead for him.

If you get to see yourself in someone else's book it's a bit of a gift and it is the mark of a good storyteller. I'm sure as you read this book you will see a bit of yourself too. You don't have to come from Scotland to really know hardship and pain, but it certainly helps. I am proud to call Jock my brother. Sure, he's still a work in progress and he's not perfect, but nothing will stop him from trying to be a better man.

PROLOGUE

I'll be honest. There are people who'll tell you being on the telly isn't all it's cracked up to be – but they're lying. It's a pretty good gig, all things considered. Every day we film *MasterChef* I get up in the morning and go into a studio where teams of very talented people work absurdly hard to, quite literally, make me look good while I scoff food for a living. That's a pretty lucky place to find yourself at my stage of life – particularly when you've lived the life I have.

It's a much easier job, for example, than working twenty hours straight in a kitchen, long past the point of physical and mental exhaustion, all while some salty-mouthed sous chef screams insults about your cooking/work ethic/knife technique/genetic heritage. You're far less likely to go home with a serious knife wound or a burn. It's infinitely more rewarding than being, for example, a junkie. Or bankrupt. Or homeless. Or dangerously irresponsible. Or opening a restaurant that nobody comes to. Or being publicly shamed in the media for all of the above.

It's far better than being a pathological perfectionist and workaholic, to the point where all your relationships combust and you find yourself stranded and alone on the wrong side of the world, far from friends and family. Trust me, being on the telly is not that bad.

Every day I get to work with people who are just as passionate and excited about good food as I am, a privilege I've been looking for my whole life. To work with aspiring cooks who've put everything on the line for a shot at a career in food is something I can relate to painfully well. I can't imagine a better job than working on *MasterChef*. The money is great, and for the first time in my career I get to come home at a reasonable hour and spend time with my kids, which, as Mastercard would say, is priceless.

On reflection, there is one better job than working on *MasterChef*, and that's working on *Junior MasterChef*. That's my favourite part of the job, because when I'm away from my kids, all I think about is my kids. I know how to talk to kids, because I'm very much a kid myself. At heart, I'd say I'm a juvenile delinquent. Over the years I've learned how to adult and wear a nice suit and all that, but underneath the facade I'm just a wee lad with a ridiculous sense of immaturity.

I can see on a child's face when they're worried, scared, anxious, whatever it is, and I understand, because I go through the same thing on set. On the adult set, before we start rolling, it'll take me time to warm up and tamp down my anxiety. I'll come in early, make everyone coffee and try to ease myself into not worrying about the hundred people standing behind the studio lights waiting for me to fuck up.

That whole scenario is very intense. But when the kids are on, things aren't as serious as in the adult world – they don't have to worry about mortgages or marriages, or looking silly in front of their colleagues when the show goes to air. They can be entirely in the moment, and any chef will tell you that's when we cook at our best.

There's very little difference between the expression on the face of a globally famous Michelin star chef plating up their signature dish, and a ten year old really nailing a panna cotta they're about to serve to their mum. For me, that's what it's all about. When the kids are competing, they aren't thinking about their careers or what happens afterwards. They have nothing but excitement and focus. Every day with those kids is just a joy. There's an infectious excitement that takes me right back to the start of my career and the feeling of wonderful discovery that real cooking is all about.

If you watch that show, the pure exuberance of those kids when they take on a recipe and create a little piece of art on the plate is precisely what drew me to cooking in the first place. I've been pursuing that feeling in one way or another my whole life, for better or worse. At times, it almost destroyed me. But in the end, it saved me. Along the way, there was shame, fear, anxiety and despair, but also hope, joy and a lot of properly delicious food – and that's not a bad life to live.

CHAPTER ONE

ood, if you're doing it properly, is about so much more than
the taste. It's about a moment; a sense of place and time.
When I take a bite of *spaghetti alla carbonara* on a miserable
day, I'm immediately back in my nonno's kitchen. Nonno
cooked *carbonara* the way my dad did, and the way that
I do – properly. *Guanciale, pecorino, parmigiano*, eggs; that's
it. No white wine, no onion, no garlic, no fucking cream. If
you put cream in the sauce, you would not only disappoint
my nonno but ruin what is one of the greatest dishes in the
world, elegant in its simplicity and heritage. A forkful of
proper *carbonara* elevates the smoky fat, the sharp cheese,
the silken just-set texture of the egg into something truly
perfect. Within those layers of taste lie decades of tradition,
centuries of culture, thousands of hugs from Nonno. For
me, that's what cooking is about.

The first thing I remember about growing up in Scotland
is the smell of my Scottish grandparents' house – mothballs,
meat and mashed potatoes. Walk into their house in Prestwick
and you'd be hit in the face with the scent: browned mince

with a bit of carrot mashed in, served on boiled potato. That's a smell that will never leave me. I call up that particular scent in my memory and the chef in me has notes: a very flat, mundane flavour base with maybe undertones of offal, depending where the mince came from. You'd do well to brown the meat a little more, caramelise some shallots to cut through with some sweetness.

Not that Scottish cuisine can't be sweet. In winter Grampa's house reeked of clootie dumpling, a Scottish pudding of breadcrumbs, suet and spices that is steamed and then dried slowly in front of the oven with the door open – so that smell permeates the whole house – until it forms a tough crust on the outside.

It was proper Scottish food, cooked by Scottish farming stock. It was designed to fill you up after working in a field in the freezing rain all day, not to be lingered over on a lazy afternoon. In the winter the staples were meat and potatoes; in the warmer months, throw in tomato, cucumber, runner beans – whatever was stubborn enough to grow in a greenhouse in the northern summer.

We didn't put on flights of fancy. The food was an extension of that stoicism that comes with being Scottish. Culturally, Scots like us faced life by squaring their shoulders, raised to endure any kind of discomfort or hardship and just cop it. The food was just a way to keep you going until you got there. It was sustenance, fuel; nobody was eating for pleasure.

Contrast that to the Italian side of my family, where eating was purely for the joy of it.

My first memory of that joy is holding Nonno's hand and toddling into the beautiful chaos of Fazzi's Italian deli in Glasgow. The smell hit me before my eyes took anything in, and I can still call it up: fresh focaccia, salami, parmesan – and beneath it all the whiff of garlic, spice and briny olives. It blew my mind. Everything changed for me after that, in the best possible way.

Mum was a Scottish hairdresser, Dad an Italian barber. They worked in shops on opposite sides of an arcade, saw each other through the window, fell in love, and that was that.

This was in Ayr, a little town on the west coast of Scotland not far from Glasgow – river, rain, a haunted house, a broken-down old castle, and once home to one of the world's greatest poets, Robert Burns. In 1976 I was born there, Barry Zonfrillo – half-Italian, half-Scottish, joining my sister, Carla, who'd come along a couple of years earlier.

Grandma and Grampa on my mum's side were farmers. Nonna and Nonno on my father's side were immigrants from Scauri, in the Lazio region of Italy, sort of in between Naples and Rome. Their home was in a little mountain village, Santi Cosmae Damiano. They'd live there most of the year until it got hot. Then they'd move down to a shack on the beach for a summer of swimming and fresh fish and pasta. Then back up the mountain for the winter. Dad's family moved to Glasgow as part of a wave of Italians looking for opportunity and better lives, but retained that very Mediterranean-Italian tradition. Very steeped in the culture, very family oriented, very smartly dressed. Nonno, Dad's dad, was the most Italian man who ever lived. He wore a suit every day of his life. If he had to go down the street to buy a newspaper he'd make sure his shoes were shined. This was in Glasgow, the tracksuit capital of the UK. He looked like a million bucks until the day he died, when he had a stroke while eating a plate of spaghetti. I'm not joking. It was very sad, actually.

Nonno was at the dinner table working away at his plate of pasta, and he started moving strangely, missing the plate with his fork, suddenly not able to talk properly. He was rushed to the hospital, and we rushed after him. I remember being taken by car to Glasgow, bundled up against a miserable sleeting night in a big duffle coat and wellies. We had to park some distance from the hospital, and by the time we reached his ward I was saturated.

Nonno was lying in his hospital bed in a cramped, stuffy room heated by an old-fashioned bar radiator. I was dripping wet, so rested my wellies on the radiator to help dry them. We ended up sitting so long by Nonno's deathbed that my wellies melted onto the radiator, and I had to be prised off it to be carried off home.

That was my first experience of losing someone, but in a strange way, I've always felt that he never really left me. Nonno was such a loving, larger-than-life guy that through my whole life I've always felt him kicking around somewhere in the back of my mind. Right to the end he was so full of energy, and devoted it all to us kids. He'd catch your eye and hold it in a way that made you feel you were the most important person in the world at that moment. His kindness and sense of presence was something I could understand was extraordinary, even as a child. I remember thinking that when I was old I wanted to be just like him:

a kind, wise nonno running around with all his grandkids. I'll never forget how sad his passing made my dad.

Dad was one of three along with my uncle Leo and aunt May, who'd married a Sicilian man in Glasgow called Tony Fratta. Their family wasn't a hybrid of Scottish and Italian – it was full-on Italian in every way.

They spoke Italian around the house, and when I went around they'd batter you with the full Italian hospitality experience: brined olives, smoked meat, coppa, bresaola, pickled vegetables in bright little pools of vinegar and oil. I'd walk in and the air would be full of the salty, starchy smell of pasta on the stove, and my mouth would just start watering.

The two sides of my family were worlds apart. I remember even at four years of age thinking, 'Wow, there's such a difference between my home and theirs.' Later in life I could identify it as cultural differences, but the understanding that people were shaped by their culture and had different ways of doing things and seeing the world was there from the very beginning, even if I didn't know what 'culture' was back then.

Basically, from the time I could walk, I recognised the Italian passion for food, and that Italian life is very different from Scottish life. Naturally, I tended to gravitate more towards the Italian side; it was so much livelier. I'd walk into Nonno's house and he'd be hugging me with one hand and plating up *cacio e pepe* with the other and it was all just more exciting. The concepts are fused in my mind: parmesan, pepper, love. To me as a child, the Italian mode of affection, which involves bombarding your loved ones with carbohydrates, was very appealing. I've found that most times in life are made more joyous with the addition of lasagne, and my childhood was definitely one of them.

It was the complete opposite of the broad-shouldered, stoic Scottish side of our family, where you worked hard, lived quietly and didn't indulge in luxury or fancy food. I probably saw Mum's dad wearing a suit four or five times in his life. I've got a photo of him wearing one on his birthday and he does not look very pleased about it. Grampa's idea of dressing up was a cardigan. It was a culture where you didn't complain; you just got on with life and tried to get along with everyone.

If an Italian feels a certain way about you, you're going to know about it, and Nonno was no different. If you'd made him angry, you'd know about it. If he loved you, same story – and he loved his grandkids; doted on us as only a grandparent can. Nonno had an office in his house in Glasgow with this drawer full of toffee lollipops. He'd give us lollipops when we visited and Mum and Dad would go ballistic because we'd come home wired from having eaten too many.

It's not that our home wasn't loving; it was, absolutely, but it was also very strict. Mum was a very sensible, taciturn Scotswoman. Dad was strict too, but sort of back-up strict, there to support Mum, but marginally more laid-back. Scots of the day weren't physically demonstrative; not a great deal of kissing and cuddling went on. It's simply a different mode of affection, I suppose.

But it's possible that I was especially receptive to affection expressed through cooking, because I'd been obsessed with food as far back as I remember. As part of our primary school curriculum, we had to keep a journal: a diary of what we did in the evenings after school, what we got up to on the weekend; that sort of thing. Perhaps it was meant to encourage creative writing, but I filled mine with pages and pages of notes on food: things I'd eaten; ragus and bolognaises I'd watched being made; polpetti, lasagne, banoffee pie. Trips to the deli, the smells and sounds of the coffee machine and the joy of panettone at Christmas time.

The first thing I ever cooked was a dinner for my parents. They'd taken a bit of meat out of the freezer, and I remember looking at it defrosting on the bench and thinking to myself that I could probably make it nicer. My mum had a cookbook, *Modern French Culinary Art*, so I flicked through that until I found a recipe for sauce *Espagnole*.

'That sounds very fancy,' I said to myself, 'I'm going to cook sauce *Espagnole*.' My dad loved Spain, and here was this recipe for Spanish sauce, how could he not love it?

So, I followed the recipe: caramelised onion, roux, hot stock, tomato puree, garlic, celery; a thousand things to keep on top of. An epic undertaking, especially for a six year old. Somehow, despite following the recipe perfectly, I missed the description of what sauce *Espagnole* – a mother sauce – is, and in particular the part that explained that it is 'rarely used directly on food'.

I remember trying it, and thinking it tasted awful, and then watching Mum and Dad put it on their steak and choke it down with these big smiles on their faces, 'Oh, that's very interesting, son. Very nice.'

They were too polite to tell me otherwise, although afterwards Mum complained loudly about how much mess I made. She's still complaining about that to this day.

It was a nice, respectable middle-class sort of home in the suburbs of Ayr, and Mum and Dad worked hard to move up in the world. Mum had ambitions, and traded in hairdressing for a career in human resources in a local company. Dad was always working. By 7 am he'd be down at the barber shop, and he'd work his arse off without a break until 6.30 pm. After work he'd usually run errands or play lawn bowls, so I didn't see as much of him as I would have liked.

In order to get to spend a bit of time with him, I helped out at the shop on Saturdays. I'd drive down with him first thing in the morning then hang around all day in the barber shop, sweeping up, washing hair and listening to these middle-aged men busting each other's balls just relentlessly. Grown men who spent their entire lives winding each other up like schoolchildren – looking back, it was a weird, uniquely Scottish version of mateship: a fun, piss-taking, very male environment where the guys played practical jokes on each other constantly and there was always a bet going on in the background.

It was never really assumed that I would follow in Dad's footsteps. He was well-liked, well-respected; he cut the hair of every prominent man in town, so from the outside it seemed a good life to lead. But when I thought too hard about going into barbering, it just didn't sit right. I didn't want to just be silver-spooned into a good job and live my life that way. It was a hard job, and while I loved the camaraderie, the thought of being trapped in a shop six days a week for my entire life terrified me. I didn't know what I wanted to do with life, but it wasn't that.

Over the years, I've often looked back and wished that I'd stayed in town, taken over the shop. I would have loved nothing more than being able to work with Dad every day. I'd probably have been bored to tears as a barber but that would've been mitigated by the chance to have him with me through the years as I went through all life's ups and downs. Of which there would be many.

My mum and dad did that middle-class thing of buying a house in an area with a good comprehensive school and cadging a proper education that way. So, I went to a school that had a good reputation, as far as it went.

In my first week at primary school I was clowning around in the playground and ended up in deep trouble. I'd picked up a rock – it wasn't a boulder but, frankly, it was a fairly massive rock – and was trying to break it against a wall. It ended up going through a window and I ended up in the principal's office.

Getting tagged as 'trouble' from the get-go meant I was treated as such from then on and school was a bit of a nightmare for me. Looking back, it seems I was always in trouble, even if I didn't necessarily deserve all of it.

Every time I got into trouble at school it was very embarrassing for my mum, who worried what other people in town thought of us. She also didn't like it when Carla and I spoke with thick Glasgow accents, or used Scottish slang, so sent us to elocution lessons early on.

We attended these for a good ten years, ironing out our accents, performing Robert Burns at poetry recitals – all that kind of stuff. I was allegedly pretty good, and even got in the local paper for winning a recital competition, but it wasn't exactly the norm where we came from. My peer group was very working class: there was no way I could tell them I was in elocution classes: I'd get bullied to the ends of the earth! So I guess I played up a little in school to throw them off any idea that I was posh.

I hated primary school: hated everything around it. I hated having to go five days a week and then having to do elocution lessons and learn poems about fucking roses on the weekend. I was miserable about it for such a long time.

Then, coming out of primary school, it was Belmont Academy, again a state-run school, and again, really rough. There was a sunken passageway that ran alongside one of the school blocks, with a balustrade and a raised playground above it, which the kids called 'Grog Alley'. There was a first-day hazing tradition in which all the older kids would line up along the balustrade and run the first years through the alley while they spat on them.

So our first day of high school was not a happy experience. It was made worse because we'd been told about it in the final days of primary school so we'd been shitting ourselves for months. Then the day comes and the stoic Scottish side of you just endures it, and you're careful not to cry or tell anyone about it. It's not until later that you look back and think, 'Hang on, what the fuck? What was that about?'

A couple of cousins, Paul and Marco from Leo's side, had been at the school before me. On the first day the teacher was calling out the names from a list, got to Zonfrillo, and asked me if I was related to Paul and Marco. They'd been noted smart-arses, so I tried to convince the teacher that it was a very common Scottish surname and that I'd never heard of the other boys, but he was having none of it. That really set the tone for the next few years.

It was miserable going in, and it stayed that way. We'd got to that age where kids start to become aware of cultural difference, and that made me a target for bullies. One minute I was a white Scottish kid like everyone else, the next I was this dago – spick, wop, greasy Italian; all the names under the sun on account of my surname.

At lunchtime I'd open my sandwich and the other kids would smell the garlic and salami and would home right in on me. It's funny, later in life some of them would be laying out extortionate amounts of money for *salumi* plates in wanker restaurants in the 90s, but nobody was there to tell the kids that.

Hopefully these days parents do a better job of educating their children about cultural differences, but back then it was a free-for-all. Nobody told us that old mate from a Pakistani family has food that's different from ours, and not only that, but it's fucking amazing and you should try some. The attitude was: it looks different, it smells different, it's wrong. Biryani? What the fuck is that? It must be shit. Then it's a pile-on. Fucking cream cheese on a ciabatta was enough to make those kids go full *Lord of the Flies*, so the poor Pakistani kid didn't have a chance.

So I pushed back. I'd been the smallest kid in the class for as long as I could remember, and knew that if I let myself be bullied by the older kids it would never let up, so I fought my way through high school. I was in brawls all the time, but I couldn't let it go. Then the bullies left me alone, so I'd go after them when they picked on the weaker kids.

By a relatively early age I'd developed this real rage against the system. I put on a bit of a mask or a persona because I was always on the brink of being a target because of my cultural difference. Part of that was being the first with my fists up if there was an altercation, and part of that was being a bit of a clown and getting up to mischief. My gang of three or four kids started acting up to the older kids, throwing stuff at them and getting chased down the yard. I didn't want to bully the first years, but the culture of the place meant you had to antagonise someone, so we antagonised the bullies.

I couldn't wait to get out of school; didn't engage, didn't pay attention to the teachers. I hated school, and the teachers hated me. Every day one of them would bollock me, telling me I'd never amount to anything. I guess the way they saw it, I'd drop out of school and get a job on a fishing boat or on an oil rig, which turned out to be where most of my pals would end up. That or in jail. On the west coast of Scotland the prospects were not amazing.

Some of the teachers weren't so bad, but others were simply bullies. There was this one teacher, a horrible little man. You'd be sitting at your desk and he'd come and put his foot on it and then sort of lean over you to try and intimidate you.

So I went to class but didn't do any of the work; didn't engage with it at all. One day the teacher came around and looked in my exercise book and there was nothing in it, just drawings on the back and front covers, so he went fucking psychotic. The idea that I'd been in his class for nearly a year and done nothing made him wild.

'You're going to do the whole year's work by the end of this week!' he screamed at me, crossing to the cupboard, a walk-in closet really, where the textbooks were kept. He was in there, his voice echoing as he screamed bloody murder at me about how I wasn't leaving until all the work was done, and I thought, 'No chance'.

Next thing I knew I'd run across the room, slammed the door of the cupboard and locked him behind it. Then it was just silence. The whole class was staring at me goggle-eyed. They couldn't believe I'd just done that, and neither could I, but now that I had it was too late to take it back.

Then the bell rang and we scarpered. It wasn't long after that I got collared and taken to the headmaster's office. But it was worth it.

I was always in trouble in school and it was a source of constant grief for my parents, so there'd always be a thrashing waiting for me at home. There was a big blue belt hung in the hall cupboard, and depending on how bad you'd been you either got the end with the leather or the end with the buckle and, you know, the buckle end was pretty fucking nasty – but corporal punishment was normal back then, just a fact of life for me and my mates.

Back in the day in Scotland, child-rearing was fairly free-range, even for strict parents like mine. As long as you were home before dark in the summer, people assumed you were off playing football.

My mates and I would break into an old haunted house up on the hill and mess around in it until we fell through a ceiling. It was good fun, but at some point you'd get caught by people walking their dog or whatever, and every time I got into trouble it was, 'I know your father, young man. I'm going to have to tell him about this.'

When I was around eleven, my three mates from school (Chris One, Chris Two and Gavin) and I got this idea that we were going to steal cars. We scoped out a local car yard and planned a heist.

We discovered the car yard always kept the keys in the ignition so customers could come, turn the engine over, check out the car and make sure it was in good working order. In the evening, the owner of the car yard would go around, take the key, lock each car and go on his way.

So we thought, right: we'll go down during the day, grab the keys and lock the car up, then wait until nightfall. Then at closing, the owner will see the car's already locked and won't worry about it.

So we snuck in there, crawling like we were in the SAS, and each of us picked a car, took the key, locked the car then disappeared to wait.

Sure enough, at closing time the guy went around, checking each car's doors were locked before moving on to the next, until he'd checked them all. Then all we had to do was wait for him to go home and nightfall, when we cut the chain on the gate, went in and picked up our cars.

It was a good plan, except ... *we were eleven*. None of us knew how to drive a motor vehicle. Chris One and

Gavin both got a car and drove them out. They immediately smashed one of them, so I went back to get another.

Chris Two kept watch while I tried to find my car. It was pitch black, and I got disoriented and couldn't work out which car I had the keys for.

By sheer bad luck, the manager of the car yard was coming back from town at that minute, passed the car yard and noticed the chain had been cut. He turned off the road, parked out the front, got out and began to search the car yard.

Chris Two, who was on lookout, started whistling and coughing, and I crouched down behind the cars, thinking, 'Fuck, what am I going to do?'

The guy was stalking between the cars, getting closer, and he could hear me scurrying about but he couldn't see me. He went into the office and I could hear him calling the cops, leaning half out of the building to keep an eye on the gate, and that's when I decided to run. He dropped the phone and started chasing me. Chris Two was on his bike and was gone instantly, leaving me alone, running down the road with the guy from the car yard right behind me.

After a couple of minutes I heard the siren coming and now my heart was pounding because I knew if I got caught by them I was absolutely fucked. I wasn't so much scared of the law as I was of my mum and dad finding out about this.

A patrol car screeched to a stop on the road in front of me, and this copper climbed out. I looked at him and he looked at me, just staring each other right in the eye in the middle of the road.

'Oh, he's pretty old,' I thought, 'I can probably outrun him.'

I started running, and the cop chased me for I don't know how long; it seemed like forever. I just could not get rid of this copper, didn't matter how old he was. Turned out I had the senior long-distance fucking champion of west Scotland on my tail.

In the end the chase ended up at a pub, the Balgarth Hotel. It had a steep driveway that went up to a car park ending in a retaining wall beneath which was a three-metre drop. I figured I was pretty nimble, could jump that distance easily and then scarper but the cop would struggle.

Sure enough, I bolted up the road and cleared the drop just fine, but when the cop jumped he landed heavily and sprained his ankle.

'Perfect,' I thought, and went back up the hill past the pub, because from there I could cut across the road and get home.

But as I was running past the pub, by sheer bad luck a bunch of firemen started piling out. They'd been having a lock in, and they were three sheets to the wind. At that moment, old mate copper dragged himself up the driveway and screamed, 'Stop that kid! He's been stealing fucking cars!'

So these firemen tackled me, picked me up and handed me to the copper.

Then I was in the back of the police car, trying to negotiate with this very angry, puffed-out, injured officer. I was pleading with him, offering him money, my bike; telling him I'd do anything if he let me go. He asked me my name.

I shut up then, because I knew that if I didn't tell the cop anything he wouldn't have anything on me. That's sort of the level I was operating on.

He looked at me in the mirror and said, 'You're Ivan Zonfrillo's boy'.

He knew my dad. Of course he did. Ayr was that kind of a place. Dad probably cut his hair. I realised I was just so, *so* fucked, and sure enough, when Mum and Dad arrived at the police station they were just vibrating with anger.

Then the cop was questioning me with my parents in the room. Dad was so angry he couldn't speak. When he was angry he'd go quiet, and I'd never seen him so dead silent. When Mum was mad she'd keep boiling over and then put a lid on it. So there was Mum with a full rage face on, screaming and yelling, but Dad didn't say a fucking word. He sat there, his face completely blank, picking fluff off his trousers.

The cop was asking me who the other boys were and saying I'd best come clean as they'd already caught them. Dad gave me a look which clearly meant *don't say a fucking word*, so I shut up and didn't say anything; just sat there until they took me out of the room.

Dad followed not long afterwards. He took me out of the police station to the car park after having a chat to the copper. I wasn't going to be charged, and would be let off with a warning.

On the car ride home, I was very aware that my dad had saved me: through his connections and good standing he'd been able to get me out of custody. But I also knew that now I was completely fucked.

It was four in the morning by then, and I was thinking that Dad had to be at work in a couple of hours, and I was supposed to be working with him. The car trip home was completely silent, not a word exchanged. The anticipation of what would happen at the end of that silence was just the worst thing I ever experienced as a kid.

When we got home, I told Dad I was going to bed.

'You're going fucking nowhere,' he said.

I don't need to tell you what happened next, but after it was over I had to limp my way to bed. By then, it was only a couple of hours before Dad and I were due at work. I wasn't even all the way asleep before Dad woke me up to go to the barber shop. On the journey in, Dad was still in this blackout rage. He didn't say a word until we got close to the shop, when he turned to me and said, 'Don't fucking mention this at work today. You just fucking smile at people, you say "hello", everything's normal. Just don't fucking talk to me.'

When we got to work the other boys in the shop saw that I'd clearly had a rough night and been thoroughly lathered. I was visibly far from normal.

'What happened to you?'

'Oh, I got jumped on the way home from school.'

'Who were they? We'll fucking get them,' they said, all the lads from the shop gearing up for a fight. Dad was standing there glaring at me so I just shrugged.

'Whatever, don't worry about it. Just some boys from another school. No idea who they were.'

And that was the longest day in the history of my life. I had to stand there smiling and sweeping up hair and shooting the breeze all the while full of the most horrible worry about what my dad thought of me and the shame I'd brought down on the family name.

On Monday I went to school and found out the two other boys who'd taken cars had been caught and charged. Chris Two, the lad who'd been keeping an eye out for me, got away with it, but the rest of us were come down on so hard by our parents we never really spoke about it again.

So that for me was probably the end of boyhood. One part of it was the realisation that things can go horrifically wrong real quick. The bigger revelation was seeing another side to my parents I hadn't seen before. Suddenly I saw this side to life that was all too fucking real.

There was a lot of anger but no attempt to understand how we came to be at that moment or why I would be out at night stealing cars. Honestly, I think Dad was more upset that I'd been caught than because I was out breaking the law. It wasn't that I'd messed up. It was that I'd messed up and been caught so visibly – the whole town would know about it.

How about a conversation about what I'd done? Looking back on it now, I think that if my son stole a fucking car at eleven years old I'd want to know why. Like, Son, what was the process by which you arrived at this decision? How were you planning to drive it? How were you going to reach the pedals with your wee little legs?

Instead, all he had for me was this blind rage that at a certain point was more about him being at his wits' end than just about what I'd done that night. It was really the climax to years of bad behaviour, and I don't think he knew what to do. I certainly didn't know what to do, or how to process the event in a way that made sense. My entire life experience was pretty much working for Dad on a Saturday and going to school.

From then on, my parents never let go of it. It was this weird sort of grudge that Mum and Dad held against me. While they didn't verbalise it, they never let go of it. It was just this thing that brought shame to the family in their eyes, and everybody knew about it. I don't think my parents ever really forgave me, but life went on.

CHAPTER TWO

About a year after the caper with the cars, we went on holiday to what was then Yugoslavia, where two important things happened. The first was that I lost my virginity beside a hotel pool.

I was twelve, she was French, and older. Much older. It was very wrong, now that I think back. My parents went for a walk or something, this girl just sort of moved in on me and that was the end of being a virgin; wouldn't be needing *that* any more. But that's not even the most memorable part of the trip.

We were staying in Budva, an ancient medieval town on the Adriatic Sea. Our hotel was back from the seawall in the newer part of town, but one day we went for a walk in the medieval old town, and I smelled something cooking.

There were these little stalls all along the seafront that sold Yugoslavian street food to all the half-cut sunburned tourists who drifted out of the bars in the old town, and the smell of garlic and grilled prawns came right down into where we were staying.

I hounded my parents to take me back there and give me a taste of whatever that was, just nagged them relentlessly, until they gave up and took me back. I handed over some money at a stall and got a handful of *cevapi*, this skinless, coarse sausage served on a crust of bread and a bed of raw onion.

I can still taste it: cascading flavours of smoke, spice and fat with a deep garlic and paprika undertone and a rude little kick from the onion. In some ways that memory is clearer in my mind than that first hotel poolside taste of romance, if you could call it that.

My parents wouldn't touch the street food. Any meat that was too spiced, or vaguely raw, or too fishy or, worst of all, a crustacean, was not for them. Mum would eat a prawn, but only if it had been stripped of legs, head, guts – any evidence that it had ever been swimming – and drowned in cocktail sauce. To this day, they'll see me eat a scallop on TV and call me: 'How could you put that thing in your mouth?' Imagine how they felt when they tuned in to watch me eat bats (Vanuatu), raw cow stomach (Ethiopia), sea snails (Belize) and mangrove worms (Arnhem Land). What can I say? I like to try new things.

When I look back to all the little food memories that formed my palate, that *cevapi* would definitely be one of them. All those intense flavours that clashed and sparked off each other and elevated that sandwich to something else altogether.

When you're given the chance to try something out of your comfort zone, you do it. I always have. Cram it into your mouth, snort it up your nose, bang it into your vein; if it doesn't kill you, you never know: it might make your life more interesting.

In 1988, about a year after that, my twelfth birthday was coming up and I had my eyes set on this bike, a fancy, special-ised brand of racing bike. *Really* fancy, and *really* expensive.

'You're having a laugh,' Dad said when I asked for it. 'No way are we buying that. If you're gonna buy that you want to get another job.'

I was working with Dad part-time already, but I started going into town after school and visiting stores on the high street asking for work: Top Shop, Marks and Spencer, Greggs bakery chain. None of them would hire me.

'You're too young, son,' they all said, and I went away a bit dejected, until one of them said to me, 'You should go to a restaurant. They often hire kids to wash dishes and that sort of a thing.'

I was like: 'Fantastic, child labour, let's go.' My sister was working part-time as a waitress in a place called North Park House, so I tried there, and the manager gave me a job washing dishes, cash in hand.

Great, washing dishes; fabulous. I started washing dishes every weeknight and on Sundays. Basically anytime I wasn't at school.

The chefs would be at one end of the kitchen and I'd be at the other, and they'd throw these pans straight off the stove into the sinks. Like, just launching these red-hot, sizzling missiles past my head. They'd hit the sink and splash all over me. It was just a very different, exciting environment to be in.

I'd been there maybe three weeks when one of the chefs had a motorcycle accident and was off work. So Davie Auchie, the head chef, came to the back of the kitchen where I was scrubbing pans.

'I need you to come and work in the kitchen for me.'

'How's that?'

'I'm down a chef and I need you to cook vegetables for service.'

'Okay yeah, on two conditions: I get a pay rise and I never have to wash dishes again.' I had only just turned twelve at this point, and Davie looked at me like, *you little shit*, but said, 'Yeah, no worries', and I got ushered into the kitchen.

I was on the veg. The first thing Davie taught me was how to get shallots in a pan with some butter and sweat them off until they were translucent. He got me to taste them then, to take note of it, and only once they had *this* certain taste and texture did you add the blanched beans, toss with salt and white pepper then tip into a copper pan, making sure the pan was polished, and put it on the pass.

I did as he told me, sent the dish off then watched the beans get matched with the meat and go off into the dining room – and I was ecstatic. One minute there was a bunch of raw, boring ingredients and within a few minutes it changed completely into this delicious restaurant dish – and *I* had done it. I remember thinking, 'Holy shit, this is what it's all about!'

All of a sudden I was a vital cog in the machine producing all this beautiful food. A docket would come in with covers – orders – for a particular table, and we'd all just move as one unit to make it happen. I'd be tossing potatoes in a pan with herbs and seasoning, the flame would be going up across the room at the meat station, and one element at a time the dish would be built on the plate as it went down the pass, culminating in the waiter taking it out to the dining room. Every plate was like this little piece of art; and I was a part of this engine for creating pure fucking excitement.

There was passion, there was drive, excited people were yelling and swearing and flames were flaring up from the pans. Customers would stick their head in the door and tell us that was the best meal they'd ever had. There was food unlike anything I'd ever tasted and all these ingredients I'd never seen before.

In the barber shop it had been this all-male energy of men busting each other's balls and having the same conversation about the weather again and again. Same barber's cape, same chat; different head on top of it.

Now for the first time I was working with women. Two of the chefs were these real tough ladies who'd get in my face and bollock me over a plate of carrots. I fucking loved it. This was in stark contrast to school, where pretty much everyone from the new students to the oldest teachers seemed miserable to be there.

People loved what they were doing, and it showed. Like all head chefs, Davie was incredibly busy and short-tempered, but he always dropped everything to devote time to show me how to get the seasoning just right or to char a bit of broccoli. If I didn't have it just right, he'd show me again, and again, until I had it down perfectly. And the women in the kitchen, while they'd bust my chops on the daily, would come over and show me a technique over and over until I got it right.

'You're a fucking chef now,' they'd tell me with a clip over the ear to make me stand up straight. 'This is how you hold yourself.'

I walked out of that first shift as a cook and knew that I wanted to be there. I was fucking hooked for the first time in my life. It was so focused and passionate and determined. That night I went home and thought, 'This is it: I'm going to be a chef.'

I worked part-time for about a year. Then one day, Dad was cutting the hair of a customer who managed a restaurant in another part of town. He mentioned that he'd just taken on two French chefs who'd worked in Michelin restaurants. I don't know if Dad knew what that meant, but he under-stood that French cuisine was considered pretty much the best in the world, so he told him I was working at North Park House as a cook and wanted to become a chef. The manager thought I might learn something different at his restaurant and suggested I come in for an interview. So I did, and they gave me a job.

I think Dad was pretty proud that I'd found something I was so passionate about, and that these people saw potential in me. He actively encouraged me to move on to the next stage of cooking. It was a big deal for me. One of several moments in life that I felt Nonno was looking after me.

I told Davie Auchie I was leaving. That was one of the hardest things I'd ever done in my thirteen years, but it didn't hit me until I told him that not only was I leaving this place that had given me something truly life-changing, but I was going to a competitor. He didn't take it well; nobody in the kitchen did. The notion of loyalty wasn't something I really understood at the time, but Davie sure did. We didn't speak again for decades.

The new restaurant was levelling up in all kinds of ways. The head chef position was shared by the two French chefs, young guys with good pedigrees who'd been poached from very well-regarded French kitchens to take over.

The French chefs had a mentality of 'work hard, party hard'. For them, living hard was a prerequisite of being an amazing chef – and they were amazing chefs. These dishes they were creating were more extravagant, more high-end, more colourful, just . . . more everything, than anything I'd seen in my first kitchen.

These chefs were at the top of their game, and on top of that they were living lives that seemed impossibly glamorous to a teenager from small-town Scotland. They'd produce all this incredible food all day, then at night go out partying. On the weekends they were out doing ecstasy and smoking weed and all that mischief. Now and again after service, they'd invite me to smoke a joint with them, then take me back into the kitchen and teach me this and that. It was an education, in every sense of the word. I had my first line of cocaine with those guys during a shift when they said, 'Do you want to do some Charlie?' That was my entry point into that whole world.

There'd been a bit of weed at school, smoking joints behind the bike sheds and all that, but for the most part I'd managed to stay away from Class As. It didn't really appeal to me, but the way these guys lived did. They had great jobs, prestige, respect from the other chefs, nice clothes, money. On the weekends they went out and had chicks hanging off them, coming into work on a Monday with all these crazy war stories. They were cool, basically; having what seemed like a great life and it just reinforced the fact that I needed to get the fuck out of school and start a career as a chef.

After that I was even less interested in school or even in working with Dad on a Saturday. I continued to work in the barber shop partly out of a sense of duty, and more because I wanted to be close to Dad, but the whole time I just wanted to be back in the kitchen. Nothing had ever grabbed me like that.

So I disengaged from school completely. I'd sit at the back of the class and go to sleep because I was tired from working late nights. The teacher would be droning on about this and that and I'd be thinking about broccoli and plucking pheasants, or wondering if the poacher would turn up that night with a venison shoulder and if I'd get to break it down with a knife.

It kept me on the straight and narrow a bit as a kid, but by the same token, it disengaged me entirely from everything else. I didn't even really care about the social groups at school or being cool or anything like that. I hung out with other kids, but the whole time I'd rather be in the kitchen. School itself was so irrelevant I couldn't wait to leave.

I'd started hanging out with a new friendship group who were a little bit rougher around the edges than my mates from school. In my mind, I was already an adult, ready to be part of that world. I was fourteen, and Ayr seemed claustrophobically small. After the debacle with the car theft, I knew that whatever mischief I got up to in town would get back to my parents instantly, so the bright lights of Glasgow called.

Glasgow was so exciting and exotic compared with Ayr. It just felt so *alive*. Scots are an amazing race of people, and Glaswegians are among the best of them. Beneath the rough, tough exterior, there's a warm underbelly to the people of Glasgow. As a rule the entire city was up for a chinwag at any moment. Even as children we'd pass a total stranger in the street, and they'd stop and strike up a conversation with us just for the pleasure of a friendly chat.

We spent so much time just hanging out in the streets and meeting new and exciting people. To this day, one of my favourite things to do is walk the streets of Glasgow. I'll get off the plane, go straight to a chippie, then walk down the street with a haddock and a serve of chips in newspaper, eating them on the hoof as I wander about. The smell of the grease and malt vinegar on the now-wet newspaper, the architecture, the accents: it all takes me right back to childhood and starts recharging my batteries.

Of course we were too young to be spending our weekends on the streets of Glasgow. But my mates and I would tell our parents we were off out to play soccer, park our bikes at the train station and off we'd go into Glasgow.

Once there, we'd run amok. We went through a stage of increasingly elaborate pranks: ringing doorbells and scarpering; leaving flaming bags of dog poo on doorsteps; the 'Grand National' – racing through every backyard in a street, jumping each fence . . . all the classics, plus a few

of our own invention. Our mate PT was fearless, but physically tiny – a really small dude – and he had a great idea
for a prank. We'd go around to the back of electrical stores
and pick up one of the carry crates a TV would come in.
We'd carry that box to a roundabout in the middle of the
road, PT would climb in, we'd close the box, then hide and
wait. Sure enough, eventually someone would drive by, see
the box, think a TV had fallen off a truck and stop to get
it. They'd get out, have a quick look around then lift up the
box, which was when PT would leap out screaming. They'd
get the fright of their life and were always angry when we
appeared from the bushes in stitches.

Booze too. We'd get some older kid to go into a bottle
shop to buy us alcohol. We weren't discerning – there
was this cheap fortified wine called Buckfast (which was
disgusting, but did the job) and this other drink, Diamond
White (also disgusting, this totally colourless fake cider), as
the goal was simply to get absolutely fucking poleaxed.

Then the drugs started creeping in. This was the late
80s, and Glasgow was absolutely awash with narcotics of
all types. Vast amounts of heroin and no shortage of party
drugs or weed. Even the ice cream vans sold drugs. There
were these ice cream vans that parked outside the tenement
flats in Glasgow that you could go and buy gear out of any
time of the day or night. In the mid-80s there were proper
turf wars between rival ice cream trucks over the lucrative
drug trade and a bunch of people got murdered. We'd pool
our money and go buy a gram of weed off the ice cream
man, plus a couple of choc-dip cones to go with it – because
when it came down to it, we were still children.

We'd smoke a joint or we'd buy a pill, which were about £25 each back then, and split it four ways. So technically we were doing class A drugs, but not in a serious way: it was a lark. That line between boyhood shit and too-real grown-man shit was barely there for us.

One night we were out in Glasgow, five of us just walking down the road late at night. It was cold out and the streets were empty except for the occasional car. A Ford Escort rolled up the street and pulled up next to us, and the driver wound the window down.

'You,' the driver said, pointing at my mate Billy. 'Give us your jacket.'

Now, Billy had just got this new jacket, a very expensive leather bomber with the name of the designer embroidered on the back. It was his pride and joy, and he simply looked at the guy and went, 'Fuck off, you're not getting my fucking jacket.'

We walked on, but we kept an eye on the car, because we were beginning to think this was going to be a fight, and generally in Glasgow a fight meant someone was going to pull a knife. It was fairly standard for blades to come out. We called them 'chibs', as in, 'I'm pure gonnae chib ye'.

We walked on, and the car went up the road real slow, then turned around and came back to us. The driver leaned out the window again.

'I *said* give us your fucking jacket!' he yelled, and Billy turned around and just started giving it to him.

'You can all fuck off! You're not getting my jacket, who the fuck do you think you are? What are you going to do . . .'

and so on, calling him every kind of shit-stain under the sun, and we were all laughing . . . until the car stopped and guys start piling out of the car and pulling knives.

There were five of them and five of us, but they were driving, so much older than we were. We might have thought that we were wee hard men running the streets of Glasgow, but we were no older than thirteen, and those boys were a lot harder than we were.

So we scarpered, legging it up the road as fast as we could, and the boys from the car took off after us. They were bigger than us, faster than us and they had blades, and this wasn't so funny any more. All of a sudden we were *not* having a fun night out on the town in Glasgow.

They were gaining on us, and someone yelled that we should split up. Three of us went one way and Billy and I the other. We ducked down a side road and peeled up the side of a church. I was in the lead, Billy was right behind me, and just behind him I could hear these five armed fucking strangers gaining on us. The churchyard ended at a big iron gate with a coil of barbed wire running across the top. There was nowhere to go but over it.

I went to leap the fence but caught the top of it. I was scrambling up over the wire and it was just mincing my hands. I looked over and the guys from the car had already reached the churchyard, just as Billy started trying to climb the fence.

Then I was sort of teetering on the fence, half tangled in the barbed wire, and I was trying to reach down and pull Billy up. My hands were ruined, just shredded, clothes ruined, blood everywhere, and I couldn't get a grip. Then the guys from the car rocketed into the fence.

The force they hit the fence with knocked me down on the other side, so I couldn't do anything but lie there, winded, as they collared Billy and dragged him back down.

They got on top of Billy and started pummelling him. There was nothing I could do but leg it and find my way back to Ayr on the train. In Glasgow, back then, it wasn't rare for a night to end in violence. People were jumped all the time, and you put it down to bad luck. If you were in a scrap, you cleaned yourself up as best you could and snuck back to the suburbs. It's not something you could tell the cops about, because that would mean your parents finding out that you were out misbehaving, and that was the worst possible outcome. Or so we believed.

A couple of days later I was at my Dad's shop killing time between haircuts when I opened the newspaper and saw Billy's photo. He was dead. Found by passers-by in a churchyard. No witnesses, no suspects. That's how I found out about it.

So I was sat there in the barber shop, holding the paper after reading that my mate had been murdered, and there was nothing I could do about it. It's not like I could tell my dad I was out causing mischief in Glasgow when I was supposed to be playing football. I wasn't about to go to the police. Even law-abiding citizens of Glasgow didn't trust the police if they had any sense. And even if I'd wanted to, I didn't know who the boys were, had no evidence, and didn't know for sure what had happened. So there was no way to talk about it. You kept your mouth shut, you got on with it. Any trouble, any trauma, you park it for later.

That was Glasgow. That was childhood. It was a hard, brutal, not very nice place for a child to be, but we didn't know any better. It wasn't all stabbings and beatings – there were plenty of good times, and wonderful people in the city, but it was also a place where it didn't take much to go off the rails.

After that, I started to get more serious about work. I knew that if I went up to Glasgow with my pals I was going to be making mistakes, and besides, I'd be missing out on the cheffing thing. It was this weird pull in two different directions. I could be a lad, eating fish and chips and stealing from shops, likely to get a chib in the back for no fucking reason – or I could hang out with these cool-as-shit French guys and learn about food, and try and absorb the lifestyle that came with it. It wasn't really a choice, when it came down to it.

The French guys told me that if I really wanted to get on with being a chef, I should do an apprenticeship. They talked me through what it was and how it worked, and said they'd vouch for me if I wanted to pursue a career as a chef.

'Fuck yeah, let's do that,' I said, and asked them to point me towards the best, most prestigious, most difficult apprenticeship a chef could do. So that's what they did.

CHAPTER THREE

In 1991, when I started looking for a position, the Turnberry Hotel was the most prestigious – and by far the hardest – apprenticeship in Scotland. Probably in all of Britain. Built in 1906, Turnberry is a very posh hotel that's been a luxury getaway for golf-playing gentry ever since. To give you an idea of the sort of place it is: Donald Trump owns it now.

Set on 324 hectares of rugged Scottish estate along the Ayrshire coast, it has famous golf courses, nature hikes and woods where deer and pheasant run wild. During the 1980s it was a Five Red Star hotel with a famous French-style kitchen with a brigade of about sixty chefs that went up to eighty in the summertime with the tourist season.

As it happened I went to school with a guy whose dad was the executive chef, so I asked him to ask his dad if they would take me on as an apprentice. (That was one benefit of still being at school, I suppose.)

Mum and Dad drove me up to Turnberry, and I had an interview and a day's trial. It was mind-blowing: just so much bigger than anything I'd encountered so far. Twenty times the size of anything I'd worked in before – twenty times the people, the covers, the energy, the stakes.

Mum and Dad were pleased when Turnberry gave me the apprenticeship. When I'd first started getting into cooking as a boy they thought it was a phase; that I would grow out of it. That changed when I became an apprentice, but they also saw it as a way to keep me out of trouble, which was just magnificently misguided of my poor parents.

The apprenticeship came with accommodation within the hotel, and I saw my ticket out of living at home. Mum and Dad were happy enough for me to leave home because it came with a job – and besides, I'd only be a half-hour drive away. Now I could earn my own money and control my own destiny. Above all, I'd have my independence: I wouldn't have to worry about going out and getting sideways and then coming home and facing my parents, or sneaking in or out of the fucking window. I got grounded constantly all through childhood, and now I'd be able to do whatever I wanted. I couldn't see a downside.

So that was it: I was offered the job, I took it and I left school early. All my mates stayed to finish and sit their finals, but I was out of there.

I was fifteen, so young I had to get an official letter declaring that I was leaving and have all my teachers sign it to show they knew I was dropping out. For years my report cards had been shocking – I misbehaved, I got bad marks, I was told I'd 'never amount to anything' – so I walked into school with the letter and this big fucking chip on my shoulder. When I took it around, I was a proper smug little shit. 'I'm out of here,

I've got a proper job in a posh hotel. I'm going to be making better money than you,' I'd grin. 'Now sign the paper.'

I felt so superior – in my mind these people who'd made my life miserable for years would go on being teachers in a shitty school forever, while *I* would be a chef, which was infinitely better. But I really had no right to think like that, because back then being a chef was no cool thing.

Everyone at school took the piss out of me when I told them I was leaving to cook. All anyone knew about cooking in those days was home economics: baking scones and ironing shirts with a pinny on. For a boy to want to cook was weird in my mates' eyes.

This was before Jamie Oliver and Nigella Lawson and rock star chefs and televised cooking competitions. It was just a blue-collar job for people who didn't mind being yelled at and having saucepans thrown at their head for twenty hours a day.

At the time, Turnberry was famously the hardest kitchen in Scotland. Now I was learning from the best chefs how to cook the best food, working my fingers to the bone through pain and injury in the pursuit of food perfection while grown men screamed in my ear about what a piece of shit I was. I was overjoyed. It was exactly what I'd been searching for.

For some reason I was never happy just turning up and doing my job reasonably well. I'd picked up this perfectionist streak from Davie Auchie, which was reinforced by the two French chefs, and now I was in a place where only the best existed within the four walls of the kitchen.

Everyone at Turnberry believed in the superiority of the kitchen 100 per cent. That it was the best food; the height of culinary achievement; that there was no other way to cook food at that level. They regarded themselves as the best. Period. And I wanted to be the best. That meant being part of the Turnberry brigade.

The brigade system of cooking is organised with a clear hierarchy to maximise efficiency. At the top of the pile is the executive chef, the most senior of the staff. Generally, they have so much clout they don't actually cook any more. The role is business-oriented and they'll look down on everything else from on high, popping out once in a while to do some marketing or PR work. Now and again an executive chef will have a hand in developing a menu.

Then you have the head chef, who's responsible for day-to-day kitchen management. Most of the time they're the only real contact between the executive staff and the rest of the kitchen, and everything more or less hinges on them. At Turnberry that was Mark Bull.

Next in rank is the sous chef, who's the second-in-command. Basically, they're the muscle the head chef deploys to keep everything running smoothly. A good sous chef is able to step in and work their way through a backed-up service, inspire the whole brigade to work harder, keep morale up and still gut an apprentice with a paring knife if they look at them funny. Normally a kitchen has one, hand-picked by the head chef, but because Turnberry was a vast operation, we had four.

Then there are the chefs de partie, who hold down one particular station. So for example you've got your *chef pâtissier*, or pastry chef, who's on all baked items including breads, desserts, ice cream and cakes, and – more important than pretty much anyone else in the kitchen – the *saucier*, who does the sautés and the sauces. Then depending on the size of your kitchen, you have the *poissonier, rôtisseur, grillardin, garde manger, entremetier* and so on and so on.

Underneath all of them are the commis chefs, the junior chefs who move around kitchens as they're needed according to what's happening on the day, who answer to the chefs de partie. And underneath *them*, and in terms of prestige about as important as the dogshite on the soles of their boots, are the apprentices.

The brigade system brings a military-type structure to the chaos in kitchens. It has been in place since the nineteenth century, and in some ways it reflects the view of human rights popular back then.

Turnberry used to take on a dozen apprentices at a time, and very seldom would any of them make it all the way through the two and a half year apprenticeship. Of the twelve in my group, only three of us completed the course – and the others never set foot in a restaurant kitchen again. One of them changed careers straight afterwards; another died of a heroin overdose.

The apprenticeship was designed to break you, the way you'd break a horse. You got drafted out of the herd, and the older chefs broke you down then built you back up as something they could use in the brigade.

The more strong-willed you were, the harder you fought and the longer they'd take to break you, but they always broke you in the end. All it meant was you had a harder time before you crumbled.

So for me it was shocking, because at this stage, I knew how to cook, to a point. I was not a great chef by any means, but I'd seen good cooking; I knew how it worked and what good food tasted like. I might not have been able to do it yet, but I knew what it was.

I'd already picked up some bad habits because I wasn't trained in the robotic military precision of the brigade. I'd trained with the French guys, who were a bit fucking freestyle: really passionate and cooking great food, and more interested in what was on the plate than the etiquette.

Working in my first jobs I'd already absorbed how a chef stood and acted, and then all of a sudden I was in this arcane old-school chef world. There's a tall chef's hat and a necktie and monogrammed jackets, and chef pants, black socks and shiny black shoes. In the morning the chefs would line up for inspection and you'd have to show your fingernails were clean and lift your trousers to prove you had the correct socks on.

If you were working and you put a knife down with the blade facing out instead of in towards your station a sous chef would appear behind you screaming their head off. It was part of the culture to keep apprentices in a state of panic and exhaustion because when you had no fight left in you they could start to make you into a chef.

As a new apprentice at Turnberry you got assigned to one of the four sous chefs, who would be responsible for you, so everything you did reflected on them. If you could acquit yourself in the kitchen and move on up through the ranks, it was a point of pride for them that they'd taken this green lump of an apprentice and carved them into a junior chef. But it couldn't happen for all of us, and sous chefs were all competing with each other so they'd try and grind down each other's apprentices until they cracked and quit.

So you've got this situation where your chef is trying to break you so he can rebuild you in his image. Meanwhile you've got three other guys just trying to break your spirit so they can get rid of you. My sous chef was an intense dude, even for a sous chef.

You'd be moving around the kitchen a fair bit, shadowing and aiding the chefs de partie as they worked their sections: veg, fish, pastry – whatever it was. Say you were on veg and there was a *pommes Anna* on the menu – finely sliced potatoes layered with butter and seasoned with thyme and garlic, then pan-fried before being baked. A classic dish, simple enough once you knew it, but learning it was a process of being shown how to hold a knife just so to produce slices (no mandolins allowed) in exactly such a way; how to arrange them, and so on. And you'd only be cutting potatoes once you'd earned the right to do so. Until then you were peeling them and picking leaves of thyme in the corner. So it was a process of learning new, highly specific techniques every day in the different sections, while the sous chef mentoring you swung by every once in a while to pepper you with abuse.

That was a cakewalk compared with the days when your sous chef wasn't in the kitchen. On my sous chef's day off, the other sous chefs would fucking descend on me like carrion birds. The result was that there was never a moment in the day when someone wasn't yelling right in my ear – and it was always a very long day.

Most prestigious restaurants don't have breakfast shifts, but Turnberry did because, being a hotel, there was a breakfast service and room service. So if you pulled a breakfast shift you'd pitch up at 5 am and work steadily until 3 pm. Most of the time there'd be a double shift, so you'd be back at your station at 5 pm ready to do the evening service, which meant you'd get out around 11. So it was a long day for a young kid to be getting reamed relentlessly by some socially maladjusted sous chef.

But I moved on up. Because I knew how to hold a knife I got elevated pretty quickly to do jobs that were beyond an apprentice. By the end of a year I was running a section, not just preparing a station. Other apprentices would spend a day picking a couple of thousand identical sprigs of thyme, and I was a little closer to the real action.

The abuse in that kitchen was extraordinary: verbal abuse, mental abuse, physical. You know, you don't realise it at the time because you just think it's the pathway to becoming a chef. Because you don't know any different. And you couldn't explain it to anyone outside the restaurant industry anyway because no one would understand. It was a weird, hermetic, fucking pressure cooker where this fucking crazy cycle of abuse was tied to the idea of excellence.

The culture of attrition was designed to get the best out of people, but for anyone who couldn't hack it, it was disastrous. It was survival of the fittest, like the Hunger Games: everyone with half an eye for an opportunity to get one over someone else.

It was a means to an end, but looking back it's clear it was a piss-poor way of going about it. There are much better ways to make a chef that aren't based on extreme, relentless violence. Verbal, mental or otherwise.

In hindsight, it was just a completely fucking dysfunctional place to be, but at the time I just didn't know any better. I remember calling Mum and Dad in tears after about six months of seventeen-hour days and endless abuse. I'd reached breaking point, and I just didn't know how I could take it any more.

'Is this it?' I sobbed down the phone. 'Is this my fucking life?'

'You've just got to stick it out son,' Dad said. 'It'll get easier.'

They had no idea what I was going through. They couldn't know the whole story. And I couldn't tell them the whole story because that would mean telling them about the drinking and the drugs and all that stuff that was wearing me out apart from the work. They would have been distraught to know I was fucking around with substances. On the odd visit home, they'd seen me come in absolutely poleaxed after pills and weed and a bottle of Jack Daniel's, but they thought I'd just had too much to drink, and would put me to bed with a nice cup of tea.

If I'd told them everything they might have tried to remove me from the situation, which was impossible. Already I couldn't imagine a future for myself where I wasn't a chef, and a chef of the level demanded at Turnberry. If I had to weather a little harm along the way, that's how it had to be.

I've got plenty of scars from those days. I was a cheeky fucker, so I was always in the shit. Turning the other cheek, being the bigger man – all that shit never wore with me, ever. After I'd settled down in the kitchen and realised I was valuable to them, I worked out I could fight back a little and get away with it.

One of the sous chefs, Greg – not my guy, one of the others who was trying to drum me out of the kitchen – was always going me. He picked on me more than any of the other apprentices, laying into me day after day for no real reason. So one day I decided to give him a reason.

It was well known around the hotel that he was seeing this girl who worked there, so one day I decided to spread a rumour that I'd seen Greg snogging another girl in the tearoom.

So I start spreading this rumour, and rumours go around a hotel in seconds flat, and it was obvious it had come from me. It was real petty, schoolyard shit, but in my defence, I was a teenager. The problem was, I was a teenager in an environment of serious, sometimes unhinged, adults.

Later that day I was flat out doing prep when I got a message to go to the freezer. Picture this big walk-in cold room where the walls are lined with meat and fish in different stages of being butchered and prepped, all frozen solid.

Swinging the door open I barrelled in, not seeing Greg waiting for me until he'd already slipped behind me and shut the door, blocking my way out.

He then started tearing me to shreds: 'What the fuck are you thinking? What the fuck's the matter with you?'

He was furious. Quite rightly, now that I think about it, but I started to answer back, which is the worst thing you could do with any of those guys. He was twice my age, twice my size, four times as loud and eight times as angry.

I was running my mouth, trying to explain what I'd done, blah, blah, blah, and he was just bellowing over the top of me. We were right in each other's faces until he got so frustrated he hit me. With a fish.

At this point you need to know about finnan haddock, a salted fish that's been cold-smoked over green wood and peat, from north-east Scotland. At Turnberry we poached it in milk for a lovely smoky, flaky, light breakfast delicacy. Very Scottish, very traditional; not a lot of fun to get slapped in the face with.

We were standing by a stack of boxes of frozen haddock and the chef just grabbed one of these great big frozen fish and clubbed me with it. The fish had been split and butterflied out so their ribcages were splayed and these sharp frozen bones caught me right under the eye and opened up my face. There was an explosion of blood all over the freezer.

So I was standing there holding my face together with my hands, spraying blood everywhere, and the sous chef was standing in front of me with his bloody haddock.

'Look at this fucking mess,' he said, dropping the fish. 'Clean this shit up.'

'Yes, chef.'

Yes, the sous chef slapped me in the face with a regional fish delicacy, but he was still my superior, and that's how Turnberry worked.

He left, shutting the door on me, and I began cleaning up my blood. It was well below freezing in there and the blood had frozen solid over everything – the floors, the walls, the produce. It took me a good hour and a half to chip off all the bloody icicles and get it all mopped up. Then I went to my section, where I was now really in the shit.

The next time I went into town to visit Dad at the barber shop the lads took a look at my face and wanted to know what happened. So I told them the whole story and they were livid.

'He gets his hair cut here, Barry,' one of the lads said. 'We'll sort it out for you.'

Sure enough, next time Greg went in they gave him a nice trim and then took him into the alley behind the store and worked him over. After that, he never touched me again and kept a respectful distance in the kitchen, but still did his duty when it was his turn to teach me kitchen techniques.

For Turnberry chefs, even an apprentice who couldn't hack it in their restaurant was better than the vast majority of cooks out there. There was a reputation to uphold. Even the guys who hated you went out of their way to make you a better chef.

There was one chef de partie in particular who introduced me to an amazing aspect of cooking, when he took me out into the woods and taught me how to hunt.

The woods surrounding the hotel were full of wild deer and game birds. Hotel guests could lay down a small fortune and take rifles out to the woods on a pheasant-shooting tour. Most of the time, though, the woods were deserted and tranquil, and once in a while staff could go out and stalk game. One day this chef de partie took me with him.

I'd been fishing with Grampa – trout, salmon – but this was something else entirely. I learned how to clean a gun, how to load and shoot it, how to stalk deer – following an animal through the forest: hoof prints, droppings, signs on trees where it had stopped to nibble on twigs or moss. He taught me how to identify the scratching ground of pheasants, and to build funnel traps to catch them.

There's nothing as real as the feeling of being out in the woods on a hunt. It's dead calm, just you and a rifle, with an intent to kill an animal to feed yourself. The fact that you've only got one shot, that you've got to wait and be patient until you can see the white of its eye – and it can sense you. By then, you and the deer have some sort of bond and only when you can make a clean job of it, ensuring the deer doesn't suffer, do you take its life.

There's something profoundly honest about it; so much more so than waiting for a delivery truck to turn up with a couple of hundred farm-raised cookie-cutter steaks.

We were also taught the really old Scottish traditions of that forest, which mosses and mushrooms you could forage and how to eat them. We'd collect dried branches to cook the deer on that would burn and smoke in a very particular way. It was an introduction to a super-local, ancient way of cooking. I loved it.

Years later that would be a whole trend in food: foraged ingredients, talking about a connection to a sense of place. All that banging on about a 'sense of place' grew annoying, to be honest. Of course you've got a sense of place: you're standing in Scotland; we all know you're standing in Scotland – everyone's swearing and the weather's fucking miserable.

For me, it was more about a sense of the moment. When I ate that venison, seared and smoky-rich from cooking on the branches it had lived among and served with the mushrooms from its *terroir*, it was a sublime experience: an encapsulation of the act of pulling the trigger, taking the life; the taste of that moment. That's what real cooking is all about.

In some ways, from a culinary point of view, that really fucked me up. Once my palate had been elevated to that level it became harder to enjoy a mediocre meal. Sometimes I can tell that the cook didn't give a shit about the food placed in front of me; had chopped together six different recipe books and rehashed ideas to try and plate up something technically interesting that misses the mark.

When someone is connected to what they're cooking, through a moment for them - whether a memory or emotion or an instinct or whatever – you can *feel* it. Like, you've got the six tastes – bitter, sweet, salty, sour, savoury, umami – and then there's this whole other element of feeling that I believe can be tasted.

It's a bit of a curse, really, that a lot of chefs have. It touches your tongue and you know exactly what the dish is, and what happened every step of the way for it to get in front of you. So if it's badly done, or plagiarised – just a pale imitation of someone else's vision – that's the worst. You've had the original so you know you've been given this loveless forgery.

Nine times out of ten, when I taste a dish I'll know exactly where it came from, how it's been prepared, and how fresh and loved the ingredients that went into it are. It's very rare that I'm perplexed and unable to discern everything about a dish by tasting it. When that happens, when I'm baffled by a particular taste or sensation in a dish, there's very little more exciting to me as a chef than that. That one meal in ten is what I'm always looking for, and it's not necessarily fine dining: more often than not, it isn't.

At the same time it gives you reverence and admiration for the greats. When you eat Pierre Koffmann's pig's trotter, for example. It's not the most beautiful-looking dish in the world. To a casual diner it's just a pig's foot on a plate with a quenelle of mash and gravy – but it is actually a masterwork executed to the point of perfection. It speaks of Koffmann as an artist and a person, and is among the most delicious things I've ever been lucky enough to eat.

A pig's trotter carefully de-boned and perfectly prepared with caramelised veal sweetbread, onions and morels, all bound together with a chicken farce so light it defies its own existence. Then served with a *pomme puree* laced with duck fat and smoother than buttercream icing. To finish it off, a mind-boggling madeira sauce made from the stock the trotters were cooked in. To be able to taste that and as a chef discern the sheer artistry that went into it: what a magnificent privilege.

The way you're trained makes that happen. You're not born with it. I was fortunate to find myself trained and mentored by, or simply working alongside, these incredibly talented chefs who woke me up to this way of experiencing food.

Whatever talent I may have been born with, I would never have been able to tap into it without the skills (and scar tissue) that I acquired as I was trained.

So, as shit as much of the apprenticeship was, it was also a wildly steep learning curve. There were chefs in that kitchen from all over – Italian, French, British – all of them with something to teach me. The kitchen was this really exciting blend of accents, with people screaming in English and French, and me trying to keep up and nobody being able to understand me.

Despite my mother's best efforts to elocute it out of me, I had a very broad Scottish accent, especially when I got drunk, or excited in the middle of service – or both – when I'd suddenly start speaking in Glaswegian slang nobody else could understand a word of.

Many of my colleagues had English as their second or third language, and even the English guys had trouble with the Glasgow accent, so they started taking the piss and calling me 'Jock'. In Euro-slang, 'Jock' is a slightly derogatory nickname for Scottish people, so that's also what people who struggled to pronounce 'Barry' started calling me.

It stuck. When you move from kitchen to kitchen there's always someone there who's either worked with you before or who knows someone you worked with who's told them that Jock's coming to join the team.

So I guess, from then on, I was Jock. I walked into my apprenticeship as Barry Zonfrillo, and would walk out as Jock, armed with the best cooking education in Scotland – and some of the worst possible habits a lad could acquire along the way.

CHAPTER FOUR

All this time, there was the whole other path I was embarking on. After work, in the staff block, we could do whatever we liked. Which for most of us was getting poleaxed.

Turnberry was a very grand hotel. The guests were very posh. My parents would have been priced out, not that they'd ever have gone there anyway. It was a very exclusive milieu; expensive and luxurious, with marble and oak everywhere. The staff quarters, less so.

Our accommodation was the pits. Picture a prison block and paint it beige – a long corridor with tiny little rooms branching off, each about 3 × 2 metres, with most of the floor space taken up by a single bed, a sink and a cupboard. Accommodation for men and women was segregated, but that didn't mean much: everyone was canoodling all over the place. The chances of walking in on a couple of stressed-out horny apprentices thrashing about were pretty good.

It was dirty, even by the standards of an adolescent boy. Skanky, crusty carpet in the dorms, creaky floorboards in the corridor. You'd creak on up to the showers, which were like something out of a Victorian mental asylum – big block showers that were absolutely rank with soap scum and human hair and all that shit. It was disgusting.

Despite it all I still loved it. For the first time I had true independence: my own home, didn't have to report to anyone outside work, could do whatever I wanted. In my mind, I was an adult living an adult life. I was certainly *living* with adults. I was surrounded by people in their thirties and forties in an environment that was pretty hard core, both in and out of the kitchen.

I was hanging around with guys who were twice my age and going out drinking and taking the same amount of drugs as they were, because in that context it seemed normal. At the same time, I had all that teenage boy shit going on: listening to Jimi Hendrix, reading about how he used to soak his sweatband in LSD and all that, and admiring the excess.

'Oh, I'm just like Hendrix,' I'd tell myself, rocking up to work on acid. 'My life is just like his life.'

The culture of drinking and drugs in the staff block was pretty real. It takes a certain kind of personality to be drawn to the restaurant industry. We didn't have a drought of mouthy, reckless extroverts, so if you put a couple dozen of them in a dormitory and factor in sleep deprivation and adrenaline from being screamed at day in day out for weeks on end, then things got pretty loose pretty quickly.

You were expected to work to excess and party to excess. It all seemed a bit rock-and-roll to us. We thought it was brilliant. And when Turnberry got too small, there were plenty of other options out there.

You could catch a train to Glasgow pretty easily, so my mates and I made the most of the days off and went clubbing. One time I met a girl in a club and convinced her to come back with me to my room in the staff block. There were two or three other lads who were after her that night, but she chose me, and off we went.

We were back at Turnberry, walking across the lawn towards my room, when I got jumped by one of the lads who'd been after the girl and who'd followed us all the way home with a baseball bat.

So I got into this fight with this guy over this chick, and his mates and my mates got involved and it turned into an all-in brawl. Suddenly there's blood and teeth flying everywhere on the lawn of this classy country hotel.

We fought them off, and afterwards we went back to the dorm to skin up some joints and rack up a few lines, and enjoy that post-brawl camaraderie. Someone passed me a joint and when I reached for it I realised my arm wasn't working right. I'd taken a bat right to the shoulder during the fight and now it was really starting to hurt.

'You all right, Jock?' my mate said. 'Your shoulder doesn't actually look all that great.'

'It doesn't feel all that good. It feels like the worst dead arm in the world.'

'Take your shirt off,' he said, and when I did, he went, 'Oh, that's not normal. Get in the car.'

They drove me to the hospital and the emergency room. By the time I got there, my arm had turned this grey colour and was flopping around at a gross angle, like I was halfway through deboning a chicken. It was only dislocated, so

I thought, 'No worries'. They popped it back in and I was at work the next day. To this day it still dislocates if I move the wrong way.

Our group were more or less all Turnberry kitchen staff, and we were a very tight unit. We'd spend close to twenty hours a day working together, and then spend every spare minute getting wasted. Pretty much the entire kitchen crew. The higher ranks, like the executive and head chefs, didn't go for that kind of life, but pretty much anyone under the sous chefs could be relied upon for a good time.

We'd get two days off and get into a car and set off from Scotland with the primary goal of getting absolutely fuck-eyed as inexpensively as possible. If there was a rave nearby we'd go there, otherwise we'd head all the way down to Liverpool to go to Cream, or Manchester and the Hacienda, or Leeds for Hard Times, or even London to go to Ministry of Sound.

Some of the parties and the raves that we went to, the sheer amount of substances we put in our bodies, I can't believe it, looking back.

I remember being very fond of this particular kind of acid, which were stamped with an X. They were just excellent, high quality acid, and I was a big fan. Then they brought out XX acid, which was twice the dose, followed by XXX acid, which was three times as strong as a single trip.

Then one night we went out to a club, the Ayr Pavilion, where there was a rumour going around that someone had brought in an innovation: XXX ecstasy, which was a strong pill with the XXX acid tab hidden inside.

'Great,' I said, 'fabulous, let's get some.'

My mates warned me off; they heard they were bad news, but I'd made my mind up. If you told me I couldn't handle a pill, I was going to drop two.

Two pills later, things had deteriorated quickly. I was flailing around the middle of the dance floor and people were melting like candle wax all around me. The club closed around 3 am, and normally we'd drop another round of pills at 2 am so we were still going strong when we emptied out on the street. Then we'd buy temazepam jellies off the guys who hung around outside. Jellies were a downer, whereas ecstasy is an upper, so between them it suspended you in this weird floating jellified state.

This time when the club closed, my mates took me outside, and I remember being mad that we hadn't taken more pills – which I really didn't need, because I could neither walk nor talk.

I ended up going to some stranger's house and at that point I was basically a poorly made terrine: all my bones had been removed and I was just sort of oozing over whatever couch they put me on.

People start shovelling cocaine up my nose to try and pull me out of whatever crazy hole I was in and then filling me with downers to bring me back down.

I came to all alone, sleeping in a back alley with the trash. Literally no idea how I'd come to be there, what city I was in or if I was even in Scotland. Still, I turned up to my shift the next day on time.

My wage was £72 a week. Of that I had to pay £30 back to Turnberry for room and board, and then another £20 for the 'social club', which was this club for staff with a pool table and beer and crisps. By the time I got a day off I had next to no money.

If you didn't have enough money to buy a pill, somebody would always shout you. A pill was £25, which was a small fortune, but a half of one was enough to get you properly trolleyed. This was the dawn of the early 90s, the British golden age of ecstasy and house music.

By the time I left Turnberry I was taking four pills in a night. Your tolerance builds up quickly when you're getting on it, and that gets expensive pretty quickly.

When you're buying pills on a regular basis, of course it's not long before the person you're buying pills from says, 'Why don't you buy ten and you'll get them cheaper?' And that way, you know, you've now got two free pills every time you buy ten and you're helping out your mates at the same time. It's basic trickle-down economics. At that point, if you're buying an acid trip it makes more sense to just invest in a whole sheet and eat it all on a Wednesday.

There was a group of us who dropped acid every Wednesday after service. Why it was Wednesdays, I couldn't tell you. Who knows how traditions get started?

On one particular Wednesday evening we wandered out of the staff block and spilled out onto the pitch and putt lawns and the path leading up to the entrance.

Turnberry is an elegant heritage building on a hilltop, accessed by a huge stairway. It's so steep that at a certain point in the ascent you lose sight of the hotel itself and you can only see the glow from all the up-lights. At that point we sort of fell about, freaking out because we were tripping so hard we'd misplaced the hotel.

No worries though: we got to the top and found the hotel again, and then we went and tried to look in the windows, knocking on the glass to get the attention of the guests. So all the posh people trying to enjoy their brandy in peace look up and see all these fucked-up, goggle-eyed chefs pressing their faces to the glass like little kids in an aquarium.

Of course, we got collared and taken into the general manager's office – where they also had security footage of us rolling down hills on the golf course and throwing flags and golf balls at each other – and were given a dressing down.

In hindsight, I'm very surprised that someone high up in the hotel didn't look at the kitchen staff and say, 'What the fuck is going on in there?'

We didn't exactly hide the fact that the kitchen was going through massive quantities of drugs every week, but I suppose nobody minded as long as we kept cooking at the level we did.

It was a point of pride to be able to go out all night, come into work on no sleep, and still hold down your section. You'd work an eighteen-hour day with maybe a break in the middle, get a quick bite to eat, then go out at night and get trolleyed. Then some days you'd be back before dawn for the breakfast service.

One time I had the breakfast shift on Thursday morning, and I was still well-broiled on LSD. I was trying to cook a fry-up but the sausages were squealing on the grill and the eggs were doing this little dance in the pan.

I'd like to see many chefs handle that. That's a proper pressure test challenge: to rock up to work on no sleep and a couple of tabs of acid and try to get a full English breakfast plated up while the eggs are trying to jump out of the fucking pan on you.

Turning up the next day was something I could manage – most of the time. On one occasion I lost four days; still have no idea where they went. I just went out clubbing one night and came to four days later in some Glasgow backstreet.

I hurried back to work, three days late for my shift, but obviously my absence had been noted. Word spread that I'd been missing for four days, and when someone in the restaurant saw me trying to sneak back onto the property through the woods leading up to the staff block, they were waiting for me.

I swung open the door to the kitchen corridor and all the chefs – every authority figure in the kitchen – were lined up along the edge of the corridor. They gave me a sarcastic round of applause as I did this walk of shame down the line of chefs into the Head Chef's office, where I got absolutely torn apart.

They didn't sack me though. I'd been told by the sous chefs that I was a very talented cook, and so they tolerated my behaviour. I was always a bit cheeky – talking back when I really shouldn't have, which the chefs hated – but at the same time I was clearly deeply passionate about becoming a chef. I was a good cook before I even got there, and from my first day in the cold larder I was really engaged with the job, totally focused on my career and absolutely single-minded in my pursuit of perfection. If I cooked a dish and it wasn't absolutely spanking I was furious with myself, and wouldn't let it go until it was. Turnberry liked that and knew that I had the potential to be a real chef, so looked the other way for behaviour that would have got any other kid booted from his apprenticeship.

The executive chef had this 'misdemeanour book' in his office. When you first arrived in the kitchen, you were told that any time you got out of line, or did something wrong, or answered back to a superior chef, you'd get written up in the misdemeanour book. The first time you'd get a verbal warning from your sous chef, and it got noted in the misdemeanour book. The second time, you were given a written warning by your sous chef, and it was logged as the second strike in the book. The third strike would be a written warning from the head chef, which was your last chance. The fourth would be an official written warning from the executive chef, which would be like the general of an army personally writing to you to get your act together because you were on your last chance. After the fifth misdemeanour, they didn't note it in the book because then you were sacked and marched out, no questions asked.

I got my first misdemeanour, then second, third, fourth. Then my fifth, sixth and seventh sailed on by and I was still apprenticed. By the time I left, I had more than a hundred misdemeanours. The head chef told me it was a record.

But I was a good cook, on my way to becoming a great one, and that meant more to the senior chefs than some bullshit idea of discipline. As long as I kept turning up and working at the level I was, I could get away with almost anything, which is a terrible lesson for a boy of fifteen to learn.

*

With the benefit of hindsight, I can understand now that the reason I was partying so hard was because I was deeply unhappy.

That whole period of my life was like taking a leap into this adult world of transcendent food and knowledge, and excellence in this craft I'd fallen in love with, and landing instead in a pool of misery and shite.

I can see now that it was a time of role models indulging the most destructive parts of my personality, and me internalising all these ways of behaving and treating other people because I was taught they were inseparable. All in all, the whole Turnberry experience was a difficult introduction to the concept of work and being an adult.

It forced me to grow up far, far too fast, and to act a lot older than I was. It was a crazy environment for an adult to be in, let alone a kid, and you began to internalise that aggression and need to break people. Guys in their forties would come into my section and I would run rings around them, this talented, energetic little gobshite making them look like dinosaurs. They'd come into the section and try to get their bearings and instead of helping them I'd been trained to humiliate them. If I could reduce a grown man to tears that'd be considered an achievement in the eyes of my superiors.

It made sense to endure abuse all day, and then in turn abuse people, and then to go home and take whatever substances you could to not think about what that meant in the larger scheme of things. Alcohol did the trick, so did pills and Charlie, but nothing worked like heroin.

I first smoked a little heroin off some foil on a weekend in Glasgow. After a bit of vomiting, the high was unlike anything I'd had before. After that, whenever it was on offer when we were out and about getting up to no good, I would always go for it. At some point I started seeking it out and, not long after that, I realised that smoking heroin was a waste of time and injecting was the faster way to the high I needed.

Heroin is very moreish, which is putting it fucking mildly. It takes a lot of H to actually become an addict. There's a widespread belief that a couple of hits is enough to form an addiction, but it takes a good couple of months of shooting up regularly before an addiction forms. I managed to make that happen though, because I couldn't get enough of the stuff.

Nothing blows your mind out and helps you forget a bad day at work like a shot of smack. Work was this full-on, relentless thing that you walked out of absolutely wired. You couldn't wait to get as far away from that as you could, and you can't get any further away than letting go of yourself. The more stressed-out and upset you were, the more heroin you could take, and the more you'd forget your misery. It would always be there in the morning, but that would be the morning's problem.

CHAPTER FIVE

By the end of the second year of my apprenticeship, I'd turned sixteen and I hated Turnberry. I'd developed a deep resentment for everything about the place.

I was getting very jaded from seeing horrific shit happen day-to-day in the kitchen. One time this new guy, a young chef de partie from another restaurant, was put on the veg section on his own on a Sunday lunch.

That's a hectic section in any kitchen, but at Turnberry on a Sunday it was a three-man section, minimum. You've got to prep four different potato dishes, six different vegetables, make hollandaise for the asparagus, polish copper pots, and a hundred other things before service even starts. Once it began, there'd be two or three hundred covers, and they had this new chef doing it on his own.

He was struggling, and there was a sous chef standing behind him screaming full tilt. By the time service started he'd fallen behind. This poor guy was trying to do three jobs on his own. He was working the deep-fryer, blanching vegetables to order, running gratins through the salamander – a dozen tasks.

We were serving onion rings that day, so he had to churn those out too – slice onions and dredge them in flour, milk, flour, milk, flour, into the deep fryer – which sounds simple but takes heaps of time when you're down to the wire and everything is chaos around you. There was no way he could do it, of course he was going to cock up, but that was likely the point. The poor guy had no doubt been set up to fail. The sous chef had probably decided to get rid of him, as this was how you made room for someone you liked better.

Despite all that he was doing okay, until a waiter brought back a meal which was missing a serve of onion rings. The chef expediting the pass had probably just forgotten to put them on the order, but that would make him look bad so he put the blame on this chef de partie. Suddenly management is in his face, screaming, 'Where's the fucking onion rings?'

The poor kid was frantic, battering these rings, rushing to the fryer and dropping them in, then pivoting back to get a serve of broccoli on. Instead, he slipped on the tiles, teetered for a minute, then lost his balance and fell straight into the deep fryer.

His arm sank all the way to his shoulder, and beneath the oil his hand got caught on the heating coil at the bottom of the fryer. Suddenly this kid is stuck, up to the shoulder in 200 degrees Celsius burning oil, trying to get free and letting out this primal fucking scream, like an animal being slaughtered, a horrific noise that pierced right through the kitchen and out into the restaurant.

The sous chef launched himself across the pass, grabbed the kid and hauled him out of the fryer and into the fish sink full of ice. The kid's arm hit the ice, sizzling. This great big cloud of steam billowed up, and the kitchen filled with the faint smell of cooked meat. We just put our heads down and kept chopping away at our prep. We didn't want to be next. When he was done screaming, they pulled him out of the sink and sent him off to the hospital. We never saw him again. He was done. They replaced him with someone else.

The brigade system is a fear-based hierarchy that teaches you not to step out of line and to work through anything, whether it's the sous chef screaming in your face or your colleague falling into a fryer and losing half his arm. The end goal is that you can turn up to work and just labour like a robot, and the end goal of a robot on a kitchen station is nothing short of perfection.

In that system, there isn't a great deal of room for creativity when you're at the bottom of the ladder. For example, at Turnberry, they wouldn't let me anywhere near the meat section or teach me how to cook meat properly until they judged me skilled enough, because it was too expensive to risk fucking up. I found this really frustrating because I wanted to know everything there was to know about food, right then, right there.

So when I pulled a graveyard shift, I'd really enjoy it, because the kitchen emptied out and you were expected to jump from section to section according to whatever work needed to be done.

I'd blitz through all my work then sneak into the meat section and pass the graveyard shift by teaching myself to cook meat. I'd 'borrow' all these steaks from the cool room – sirloin, fillet, rib eye – and cook steaks for the night porter, because he was the only other guy awake at that hour.

I'd cook us a couple of steaks and take them up to him in the lounge room of the hotel, where he'd grab us a couple of beers and we'd have a meal and chew the fat. This was something we were absolutely not allowed to do, but at that time of night the porter was in charge, so who was going to complain?

One night, I'd just brought up the meal and we were sitting down to eat when the phone rang in the reception area. The porter got up to answer it, but when he did, there was nobody there, just silence.

This happened again, the moment he sat down: the phone rang and again, no one was there. So he sat down again, cut his steak, and was just about to put the first bite in his mouth when the phone rang a third time.

Again, he jumped up and went to the phone. This time, he looked at the little code that says where the call is coming from in the hotel and said, 'Oh. That's weird.'

'What do you mean?' I jumped up, straightaway at battle stations because I thought we were busted.

'The call's coming from the library,' he said.

'So what's weird about that?'

'It's impossible: there's no phone in the library. We only plug that extension in when there's a conference.'

A shiver went down my spine, because I'd heard all sorts of spooky stories about Turnberry being haunted. It had been a hospital during the war and lots of people had died there. There'd also been suicides over the years and all sorts of other macabre shit you'd expect from an old Scottish manor house. Guests were always complaining about weird noises and footsteps in empty hallways and things like that – but this was the first time I'd encountered it myself.

The porter picked up the phone: no one there. He hung up and just as we were leaving the reception area it rang again, the call again coming from the library.

Instead of answering it, we bolted down the hall towards the library, while the phone kept ringing in reception, the sound echoing down the hall behind us. But the second we got to the library and kicked the door open, it just stopped.

Inside that room it was freezing; well below zero. There were no windows open and, sure enough, no phone plugged into the extension.

It was fucking weird and spooky, but shit like that happened all the time on the night shift. Chairs suddenly moving; a French door opening by itself. Inexplicable. I was doing a lot of drugs, but not enough to account for some of the things I saw.

I put it down to the bad vibes of the place; the culture of anxiety and dread. The established chefs were proud of that culture of fear. There was even a little lounge room where the executive chef and the sous chefs had their lunch which they called 'the Crypt'. Like a vampire's lair. Even the names in that place were disturbing.

For all the aggression, and all the abuse, I did become a better chef. I learned an extraordinary amount over such a short period of time. By fifteen I could cook; really cook. All these techniques, the palate, how to tell what a fish will taste like by the smell of it sizzling in butter, the way a knife should feel when slicing through meat; it's all there baked into your muscle memory. It gave me the thickest skin you could wrap a kid in, even one who already had a pretty tough Glasgow-childhood hide. It indoctrinated this aggressive resilience into me that doesn't let you stay down: you fall and you get up again, continuously, learning to push against the world until the world backs down instead of you.

There was a college component of the apprenticeship, so one day of the week we went to a vocational college to study a hospitality curriculum alongside all these other aspiring chefs. Some of them were just blue-collar guys who wanted a job in a kitchen with no ambition beyond a steady job and a pay cheque, and wanted to know how to throw together a decent braised beef with mashed potato for a bistro lunch menu.

Turnberry apprentices were not like that. We had the reputation to uphold, so we could be nothing but the very best. Before we went in for a lesson on, say, braised beef, even if that wasn't our station back at the restaurant we'd be taught half a dozen times how to prep a perfect piece of beef; how to sear and braise it; exactly how it should look and taste and smell. We never went to college with anything less than a perfectly executed dish in our repertoire, so we sailed through college, absolutely blitzed it.

When I was sixteen I entered a competition for the title of Young Scottish Chef of the Year. I went in with this full head of steam: I wanted to dominate and destroy the rest of the competition. My dish was perfect, a Turnberry-level bit of cuisine, and I won, but I hated it. It wasn't a competition:

there was no passion or drive or creativity, I was just winning because I was better trained and more exacting than the other kids. It seemed like bullshit to try and compare what I was doing to what they were, so I opted out of competing the next time.

I was looking for something else; something more than being the best by default, but I wasn't sure what that was yet.

One of the chefs at Turnberry, this French guy, kept banging on about *'proximité'*, how proximity to chefs who could wake you up to a certain way of eating and tasting and cooking was the most important thing you could do as a young chef. I had no idea what he was talking about, but he explained it further.

'If you want to be great, then you need to stand next to the greats. If you want "it" then you need to seek out and stand next to "it" and experience it for yourself. That's *proximité.'*

It took me going to a dictionary and looking up what the fuck he was talking about to really understand it, but then it became clear.

If only someone had identified in me what was clearly a burning passion to move forward and said, 'One day a week we're going to put you next to the guy who cooks meat so you can watch and learn'. Then I wouldn't have had to steal steaks and cook them in the middle of the night.

There's great value in that, standing next to the guy whose job you want so you can see what it's really about. My dad used to get the apprentices to shadow a barber and watch as they did haircut after haircut in order to pick up the style. So when they did finally have a pair of scissors in their hand they had some kind of idea, even though they'd never done it before. You watch something enough, you probably end up being able to have a decent crack at it.

So after that, *proximité* is something I've kept in mind my entire life. If I had to make a decision about where to go, who I wanted to work with, I always considered who I would be standing next to, whether they were someone I would become a better chef just by being close to.

In my mind, that meant a Michelin star. The *Michelin Guide* is a century-old guide to fine dining that anonymously reviews restaurants and gives them a star rating: one, for 'a very good restaurant in its category'; two, 'for excellent cooking, worth a detour'; and three, 'exceptional cuisine, worth a special journey'.

It's a big deal to win or lose a star; it can make or break a restaurant. If a celebrity or a head of state comes to town, your stars decide if they eat at your kitchen or a rival's. More than one chef have killed themselves over losing their stars. It's an august celebration of food in its most perfect form. To get three stars, each dish on the menu has to be perfect in its inspiration, execution and presentation. Back in the 90s, they only really cared about classical French haute cuisine – but to be fair, back then that was all anyone cared about. It was certainly all I cared about.

Between my mates in the kitchen, all the talk was of the *Michelin Guide*. The idea that food could matter that much appealed to me, and so did the fact that few Michelin restaurants were part of the hotel kitchen. That meant that I could cook haute cuisine without room service trolleys and people ordering club sandwiches with crisps and all the other hotel bullshit. It wasn't that I thought that was beneath me, exactly, but I didn't want to spend my life frying bacon and eggs for some stockbroker to eat while he read the paper on his mini-break.

Ever since the French guys took me under their wing back in Ayr, I'd got this idea of what a chef is, and it meant plating up these borderline works of art, and I wanted to be doing that. I wanted to send out a Frenched rack of lamb sitting on a gravy that was so rich and shiny I could see my ugly mug in it. I wanted to be around *real* food. To my mind, that meant Michelin.

One of the guys was talking about the Arkle, which was a Michelin star place inside the Grosvenor Hotel in Chester, a city in north-west England. The hotel housed both your bog-standard hotel kitchen, and the esteemed fine-dining restaurant. I figured that was the smart move, because it would get me into the action of a Michelin star restaurant and I would still get staff accommodation.

I wrote to the management of the Grosvenor Hotel – this was long enough ago that you would still write a letter asking for a job – and they told me they would take me on trial in the hotel kitchen when my apprenticeship ended. If I was good enough, I would be moved into the Michelin kitchen. They offered more money, staff accommodation and a Michelin star. I would have been there the next day if I could.

I was still only sixteen, with a year to go on my apprenticeship and college requirements, so I went to see Norman, my tutor at college.

'Listen, I need to wrap this up because I'm going to go and work in a Michelin star place,' I told him.

'That's amazing!' he said. 'Let's fast-track you through.'

Norman worked out how to cram the final twelve months of my degree into a three-month accelerated course, which meant doing extra days on top of the ninety hours a week I was doing at Turnberry. He arranged it so I got my certificate and could graduate a year early, and as a tutor he was thrilled one of his students was going to the Arkle.

The guys at Turnberry, however, were not thrilled.

'What the fuck are you talking about, you want to leave Turnberry?' they said, gobsmacked. They didn't understand at all. In their eyes there was no greater kitchen to work in, and they couldn't fathom wanting to walk away just a year out from finishing the apprenticeship and moving up.

But I needed to be gone. All I cared about was that the food at the Arkle was going to be better because it had a Michelin star, even if I didn't really understand what that meant on a practical level. My understanding was basic enough that I knew there was an arbiter of taste about what constituted good food, and in their eyes the Arkle was better than Turnberry. My mum and dad, for their part, were sorry to see me move further away, but I'd only be a short train ride away, and in a whole new world in terms of prestige, so they understood.

I had a sense of mission now, so I packed my life up in Scotland and went to Chester.

CHAPTER SIX

I said goodbye to all my mates at Turnberry and took the train down to Chester, which meant heading south into England, but moving up in every other possible sense.

Chester is a properly posh city. If you've never been, picture an English postcard scene and you get the idea. You've got the cathedral, you've got the city walls – there's this low-key Tudor grandeur everywhere you look.

The staff accommodation was right in the heart of the city, down a little cul-de-sac full of beautiful brick semi-detached houses. We were four chefs to one of these houses, but we all got our own rooms, so after the grim, haunted mental hospital vibe of the Turnberry staff block, this was a pretty sweet deal.

On the way down to Chester, I had an idea that it would be a fresh start for me. Away from the gang at Turnberry I could get a new and healthier peer group, lay off the drugs, concentrate on cooking; get on the straight and narrow a little more. I was in the mindset that I was making a fresh start, and had the purest intentions . . . right up until the moment I met Bob.

On my first day of work I turned up and this guy, about my age, walked up to me and shook my hand.

'You must be Jock. I'm Bob. Welcome to Chester.'

That afternoon, on our break, we went outside and he told me to jump in the car – he had a Vauxhall Nova, this little racer sort of a car that he'd done up with alloy wheels and all that shit – and said we'd go say hi to his sister.

So before I knew it we were driving to Blacon, a little suburb just outside Chester that back then was one of the largest – and famously the roughest – council estates in Europe.

We pulled up outside a council house with bars on the windows and this big security door.

'We'll get an eight of weed while we're here, for the weekend,' said Bob.

'From your sister?'

'From her boyfriend.'

Bob banged on the door, and after a minute a shutter opened. This face peeked out, saw it was Bob, slammed the shutter and opened the door.

The guy invited us inside, and we went through the security door, a gate into a contained porch, then another secure door. It was like going into the depths of a bank vault, passing through all these intense layers of security with this guy just calmly escorting us through, like nothing weird was going on.

Finally we reached a room behind a heavily fortified door where these men, really rough, *EastEnders*-extra types, were sitting around a kitchen table drinking beer and getting high. The air was thick with pot smoke: they were passing around a joint and sorting through a stash on the table that was just heaving under all the drugs strewn across it.

There were more drugs in that room than I'd ever seen in my life: kilos of weed in plastic bags; big bags of cocaine and smack all set out on the table like a potluck supper. There were cartons of illegally imported European beer stacked up and lining the walls, and one of the guys got up and asked if I wanted one.

So I met Bob's sister and her boyfriend, Danny, who was the dealer who owned all the gear on the table. A super-nice guy, was Danny; a solid bloke.

We hit it off straightaway. He was a Scouser, from Liverpool, and he was excited that I was from Glasgow, because we shared that sort of industrial-decay cultural background where stabbings are a rite of passage. He'd been in and out of jail his whole life.

He and his mates were very rough – there were guns all over the place – but by this point these were my sort of people. I could relate much more easily to these lads who were smoking pot and talking shit in the middle of the afternoon than I did my parents' middle-class milieu where you discussed real estate and school zones and local politics. I wasn't much interested in any of that – this scene was much more my speed. The guns, however, were a little disconcerting.

I asked Danny if I could score an eighth of weed, and he went off and got a bag, then pushed an ounce of weed over the table to me.

'Just take the bag,' he said. 'I'll give it to you on tick so you can sell a bit to make it worth your time and just bring the money back when you've got it.'

'Oh fuck it, why not?'

And that was that. I didn't have the willpower to say no, and then I was driving back to work with this giant bag of grass in my pocket and that was the end of the fresh start.

I began in the Arkle's hotel kitchen as a junior chef de partie.

Putting aside the toxicity, aggression, bullying and all the rest of it, what I was actually taught by the Turnberry chefs in terms of how to cook was fucking unbelievable. It soon became apparent that I was just so much better than anyone else my age in that kitchen. At Turnberry I'd been belittled until I thought I was a bit of a shit cook. Now came the real-isation that I could run rings around pretty much anyone in a normal kitchen.

I was obviously talented – I could cook, and I knew how to lead others, because I'd had it beaten into me at Turn-berry, where I was trained to do whatever needed to be done in a heartbeat – it was muscle memory. And now that I was in another kitchen, I began to see the value of everything I'd been taught. I'd found my way to the one-star pretty quick, and was chuffed: I was talented, fast, inspired – and a 24-carat gobshite.

My temper was out of control. I didn't know how to curb myself as a chef because I was emulating the behaviour of my mentors, who'd been aggressive and loud – and all the rest.

I was a bit of a fucking bully, to be honest, because in my mind being unreasonable and belligerent was the only way to make brilliant food. The way I thought of a kitchen was a bit like a high-performance engine. It took every part working perfectly in its precise role to make the machine work. If any part was even slightly off, the whole thing began to fall apart, and the only solution was to rip out the part and either rebuild it or throw it away. No discussion, no compromise – not the healthiest attitude, especially as I wasn't actually working with machines but with people, with their own feelings, hopes and dreams.

My attitude didn't really fit in at the Arkle kitchen, which had a much more laidback vibe than Turnberry. My new colleagues were much more chilled out in every way, so I began to dial back my behaviour, knowing that it probably wasn't right.

The day-to-day work in the kitchen was done by the head chef, Nick, a Greek guy who was an amazing, inspiring chef. Once in a while you meet a chef whose passion for the food he cooks shines through every morsel he touches. It was magical, really, the way he could take the same dish that everyone on the line was cooking but elevate it to something truly wonderful.

He was one of the most talented chefs I've ever known, though he drank heavily, as did his sous chef.

These guys would fill tea mugs with cognac and walk around the kitchen sipping them. If the exec chef or management came by, it looked like they were having a nice afternoon cuppa, but they were secretly drinking 40 per cent strength alcohol and getting more than a little tipsy.

That was the culture of the kitchen. We would go into service and Nick inevitably was having another quiet drink. But then when he was in the kitchen, he was fucking brilliant: so focused; so talented.

Meanwhile, out of the kitchen, I was having a marvellous time. After that first trip to the council estate, Bob and I became great mates. We went out every weekend and just had the time of our lives. From Chester we had easy access to all the best clubs in England at the time, so we'd go to Hacienda or Renaissance, which was a house music party where they'd take over a manor house for the weekend and put on the most amazing couple of days.

My mentality at the time was to chase excess at every opportunity. One night we had a party and an Irish chef who'd just come back from visiting home had brought back a Coke bottle filled with moonshine. He was going on and on about how it was too strong to drink more than a few sips, and so of course I challenged him to a drinking competition.

We sat down and went shot for shot, and halfway through he vomited on himself and passed out, but I kept right on drinking until the whole bottle was gone. I had nothing to prove to anyone but myself, but I went right on doing it and blacked out for the night. In the morning I came to hanging upside down and tangled in a Hills hoist. It was snowing and so cold I developed pneumonia, but by rights I should have frozen to death out there.

Antics aside, it was an amazing time with amazing friends and we travelled all over the country. Very few people know better how to seize the day and make the most of life than chefs on their day off. Some of the best friends I've ever had came out of kitchens, as well as my first real girlfriend.

Lucy was a commis chef in the pastry section. She was seventeen, same age as me, with gorgeous ice blue eyes and a beautiful Welsh accent. It became clear that we fancied each other, and I started to strategise about how to get to know her. I ended up asking her if she wanted to go for a cup of coffee and it was only after she'd said 'yes', and we were sitting down in a cafe looking at each other did we realise how weird that was. I'd never in my life asked someone to get coffee. Don't think I ever did again, but in any case, we ended up dating.

I introduced her to my parents, who were stoked that I'd met a nice girl, and she introduced me to hers, who took me to a brawl.

On Christmas Day 1993 I'd driven to Denbigh, an old fortress town in Wales, so I could spend Boxing Day with Lucy in her hometown. We spent a very wholesome day with her parents – gifts, the tree, the works – and then Lucy and her family said they'd take me to the fight.

It transpired that there was a tradition in this town of a Boxing Day brawl. Everyone on the high street would board up their windows and then would go outside and smack each other about. From 9 am grown men would be drinking pints while waiting for a fight. As I walked down the street, some bloke came up and gave me a right hook, so I hit him back, and we started scrapping in the middle of the road. After a few solid hits, we burst out laughing, went and had a pint, and then went on to the next pub to do it again. A weird fucking tradition for a town to have, but I was that numb with booze and substances that it all made sense to me.

At the time, I was taking an industrial amount of drugs, and to make that affordable on a junior chef's wages I was also selling a stupid amount of drugs. I was getting a lot of gear from Danny and selling it to punters around Chester and pulling in far more money than I'd ever made as a chef. At one point I was making thousands of pounds a week, most of which I managed to either spend on very nice clothes or bang into a vein.

It got to the point where people in the greater Chester area knew I was a drug dealer and they would come around to the house at all hours, knocking on the door looking for gear. People were starting to notice – my flatmates in the staff accommodation included. Most of them were cool, but there was this one woman who was a real goodie two shoes. Some punter would come around and have a beer and leave with a bag of weed, and she'd watch them go down the street with this suspicious look on her face.

I was half-afraid she'd grass me out, but in the end I nearly got busted for a stupid fucking reason. A customer was going to a rave and had written out this whole shopping list of drugs he wanted: 'Jock, can you get me twelve pills, two grams of Charlie and an ounce of weed.' He'd left it on my bed for me to find, and before I got back management had done a spot check of the accommodation. They'd found the note and it had been passed on to the general manager.

So I got hauled into the office and got shown this note by the general manager, who was a big sweaty posh guy who told me he suspected me of dealing drugs.

'What are you on about?' I said.

He put the note down on the table and I read it, and my heart just stopped. Then this guy, who was a real snob and who'd never actually spoken to me before, because he wouldn't bother talking to a lowlife like me, asked, 'Who's Jock?'

Now, by this stage all my mates and anyone who actually set foot in a kitchen knew me as Jock, but on my paperwork I was still Barry Zonfrillo, and this guy didn't know that, so I shrugged.

'I don't know any Jock.'

'Well, we found this in your room, and I believe that you're dealing drugs,' he insisted, and went on to boast that he was best friends with the chief of the drug squad, and he was going to rat me out – this whole elaborate speech.

'Whatever,' I told him. 'Don't know what you're talking about, mate.'

But then I was a bit nervous about the whole thing, so I decided to lie low for a while. As it turns out, it's not that easy to just stop selling drugs in a town like Chester. People looking for drugs can be pretty determined, and they just kept turning up at my door, so I ended up having to get a mate to stand at the end of the cul-de-sac and turn people away. There was also the problem that I still had a pretty substantial amount of contraband in the house.

Nothing happened for a couple of nights. Then, on the third night, I was woken up by the sound of an engine idling right outside my window. I sat up in bed, and looked out the window, which ran right up onto the road, and the whole window was taken up with this police van. That bright orange stripe alongside the van was basically inches away from my nose, so I scarpered.

Up, out of bed, got the drugs, straight in the toilet, hit the flusher, then back to bed and pulled the covers up over my head like I was hiding from the bogeyman. I was sure this was it. I could see myself being carted away in fucking hand-cuffs, and I lay there freaking out and waiting for the door to get hammered down. Then, nothing.

No knocks on the door, no one swinging through the window on a rope. Fucking nothing. The engine idled for a few minutes and then the van trundled on up the street.

That was close enough for me. When it came down to it, I didn't want to be a fucking drug dealer, not when I had so much going on in the kitchen and this career I was in love with. I wrapped it up pretty quickly, told everyone I couldn't help them any more, and vowed to concentrate on my career.

That wasn't as straightforward as it might have been. It got to the point where some of the staff weren't in any state to run a kitchen. They turned up and started hitting the cognac, so were basically AWOL, and I ended up in charge of the kitchen by default. Which, as a seventeen-year-old chef de partie, I really shouldn't have been.

I was in way over my head. I had no idea how to run a kitchen. By now I'd been in a Michelin kitchen for less than a year, and I'd never been any kind of senior chef. I was just trying to run a Michelin star service to the best of my ability, so I was reverting to how I'd been taught to lead, which meant basically bullying people until I got my way.

When an order came in I'd berate the cooks if it wasn't ready the second it was physically possible. I'd put a plate on the pass and if it wasn't picked up, I'd tear into the waiters. If a plate went onto the pass with a fingerprint on the rim,

I would tear out the nearest throat and throw it to the side to prove a point.

In the end, the waiters got sick of the kid running the kitchen and screaming at them night after night, and they staged a revolt. One night, in the middle of service, they made a decision to deliberately crash the service, because then something would get done to fix the kitchen.

So they hung back and dawdled, just chilling out in the dining room while the orders rolled in. They weren't coming in to pick up the food that was stacking up on the pass, and I started losing my fucking mind.

Picture me standing on the pass just screaming at them, full-head-of-steam Glasgow boy blowing his lid, cursing the day those rotten fuckers crawled out into the world. I was calling them every name under the sun and using the foulest language, and of course my voice carried out all over the restaurant. The posh customers had probably never even heard some of the adjectives I was deploying before – the kind that would make the roughest heads on the housing estates of Chester blush – so they were rightfully horrified. The restaurant had to send complimentary champagne out to the tables to apologise.

Nick gave me a call the next day and gave me the heads up.

'They're going to sack you, Jock,' he warned. 'All that shit that went down last night, they're going to call you in and give you the arse.'

So when I was hauled into the office I knew what was coming. The assistant HR manager spelled it out for me. She was very sorry, but my behaviour was unreasonable and unacceptable, and all the rest, and she gave me a P45 pink slip to terminate my employment.

I thought this was completely unreasonable on a number of levels. It was galling to me that I'd been left this impossible task and then hung out to dry.

'What did you want me to do?' I tried to argue. 'I was left to run the place when I shouldn't have been near that position for years!'

The thing that pissed me off the most was that management sent the assistant HR manager. They didn't even send the actual HR manager, who I could see through the window of his office pretending that I wasn't standing just outside.

So I tried to reason with her, but there wasn't much I could do without shopping some of the others, and venting to this poor young woman wasn't going to fix it, so that was that.

I was picking my shit up to vacate the staff accommodation when I got a message from management: I'd never work in a Michelin star kitchen again. They'd see to it personally that as far as high-end fine dining went, my career was over.

So I moved out of the lovely Tudor townhouse, got a room in a weird share house next to the zoo, and a job in a hotel across the road from the Arkle that served regular, non-haute cuisine dining. It was a shit kitchen, which was a bit of a revelation to me.

It had never occurred to me that there were kitchens that just didn't care about food. Worse, they seemed to actively hate it; to hold a grudge against the idea of good taste. They were taking frozen crumbed chicken breasts, deep-frying them and serving them with noodles as a meal. Heartbreaking; a fucking insult to everything I was passionate about.

I worked there for as long as I could, which wasn't long. Life was miserable, pretty much. Every day I'd catch the bus to work in this kitchen that was just shit. I was broke, at this point quite badly addicted to heroin, which was not a cheap pursuit; any money I had went straight to the pushers. A really profound addiction is like trying to fill a bucket with a hole in it. No matter how much money you pour into it, your habit will find room for it. If I wasn't shooting up at least twice a day I'd get sick with the first symptoms of withdrawal: shakes, muscle pain, nausea. Worse, my pride was hurt.

The whole time I was seething, just stewing on management telling me I'd never work for another Michelin star place in my life.

I knew I had to get on with life, for my own peace of mind, but I also knew I had to prove that place wrong. I had to get a job in another Michelin star place, and it had to be a three-star place. I would take only the best of the best. Anything else would mean I'd failed.

The more I thought about it, the more convinced I was that I'd been wasting my time in a one-star when I could be in a three-star. That would mean leaving Chester, which would mean time away from Lucy, which made us both a little sad, but we were ambitious young chefs so understood that travel was part of any real career.

From there it was an easy decision. Most of the three-stars were in France, and I thought that was an option, because my French was okay, but my preference was to stay in the UK. There were only a few three-star places in the country, but one of them was talked about by those who knew as the hottest kitchen in the world.

I started asking all the older chefs I knew what the best Michelin star restaurant in the country was, and they all gave me the same name, the biggest name in food at that time, the first-ever real rock star celebrity chef. Marco Pierre White.

CHAPTER SEVEN

By the winter of 1994 when I, a seventeen-year-old dropout with a junk habit and five quid in his pocket, decided I was going to work for him, Marco Pierre White was already a legend. He was as famous for his behaviour as he was for his food.

Like many others, I had bought and been captivated by his book, *White Heat*, with its monochrome photographs of this supercool chef with his long, unruly, rock star hair. Marco was rarely photographed without a cigarette hanging out of his mouth, and never without a brooding expression on a face lined and gaunt with exhaustion which, it was widely believed, came from a relentless passion for perfect food.

He had a reputation for being very intense, both with his staff and his customers. He was famous for personally throwing punters out of his restaurants if they didn't seem to appreciate his food enough. In 1994, he was the first British chef to get three Michelin stars and at thirty-two, the youngest. A legendarily talented chef, who also had this mystique as wild and unpredictable. All that appealed to me.

I decided I would turn up at Marco Pierre White's restaurant in Hyde Park in London, knock on the door and ask him for a job. That was the whole plan. Simple.

So I put my knives and my chef jacket in a plastic Tesco supermarket bag and snuck onto the overnight train to London. I spent the night moving from carriage to carriage to avoid ticket inspectors and arrived at Victoria Station cold and tired, and rapidly running out of ends to lose.

I knew only one person in London, a lad called Andy Baker I'd met in Ayr who I used to bounce around Glasgow with. He'd taken up a plumbing apprenticeship down in London.

I called and told him I was coming down to London to see about a job, and asked if I could crash at his place.

'Yeah, yeah,' he said. 'You can stay at mine no worries, come on down.'

Andy wouldn't be home from work for a while, so I went straight to Knightsbridge and the Hyde Park Hotel where Marco Pierre White had set up his restaurant. The plan seemed really solid – until I was standing outside the Hyde Park Hotel, this fancy-as-fuck Victorian pile, and the ground-floor restaurant itself with the Marco Pierre White brass plaque and the menu in the window.

I read through the menu, thinking to myself I could probably handle everything on it, but was floored by the price – £85 for the set menu, not much less than a week's wages. Spending that kind of money on a meal seemed outrageously expensive to me.

The restaurant had its own entrance so I knocked on the grand double doors. No response. After a while I started to get uneasy, because I was standing there hammering on these doors, trying to see through the window, and customers going in and out of the hotel entrance nearby were looking at me funny.

I didn't want to walk in through the hotel entrance since I was wearing the scruffy clothes I'd caught the train down in and holding my supermarket bag. I started to think that this had been a bad idea, and was about to give up and limp off back to Chester, when all of a sudden the doors swung open and there, filling the entire doorframe, was Marco.

I'd never seen him in person, only his grungy photos, where he looked like some gaunt guitar dude, so I wasn't expecting him to be so big. He was just a tank of a man, a big fucking unit of a chef. The abrupt shock of having the celebrity chef swing open the door of his own restaurant, coupled with his physical presence, discombobulated me a bit.

'Can I help you?' he asked in a very posh voice, which tripped me up further, because you're not used to hearing that refined English accent from a guy who looks like he could break you in half with his bare hands. 'What do you want?'

I was standing there, sort of stammering and tripping over my words, 'I . . . um . . . that is . . . I'm after a job . . .' when he cut me off.

'You'd better come in then,' he said, then turned on his heel and walked back down the corridor.

I dithered for a moment: was I was supposed to follow him or go and see some kind of HR person? Meanwhile Marco was striding off down that corridor, so I scurried after him.

Marco's office was on the small side, more of a cupboard than a room, maybe a few metres deep and one across. Most of the space was taken up by a desk, and the rest was taken up by him. He sat, leaning back in his chair with his hands folded behind his head, relaxed and very much at home.

I felt like a person might if they'd suddenly been dropped into the lion enclosure at the zoo. I was very aware that Marco Pierre White was probably the most talked-about man in the restaurant world at that time; the epitome of British cooking. There was very little about the situation that wasn't intimidating.

'I'm Marco,' he said, extending a hand to shake.

'Shit . . . this is actually happening,' I thought as I took it.

'I'm Jock, it's a p-pleasure to meet you,' was all I could stutter out.

'No,' he said politely, 'it's a pleasure to meet *you*. Please sit down.'

I did so, feeling a little more at ease, then started stammering out my story, eventually managing to spit out what I'd come for: 'I want a job here.'

'Where were you before now?'

'I did my apprenticeship at the Turnberry Hotel.'

'Some good boys come from the Turnberry,' he said, and rattled off some names, just sort of letting me know he knew everything. 'Where else?'

'I've just come from the Arkle. I did a year there.'

'Oh yeah, that's good. That's a good kitchen.' He nodded, registering that I'd worked in a Michelin star place, and I started to relax a bit. Then he asked, 'Why did you leave?'

My heart sank. It was one of those moments when I had to make a choice. Do I tell the truth? If I told him I got sacked, chances were he wasn't going to give me the time of day. On the other hand, if I got caught lying, that would be even worse. I could see my life branching off in two very different directions depending on how it went – getting this job was pretty much the only way I saw to go forward. If I fucked this up, I didn't know what I was going to do.

'I got sacked,' I said at last, and he just nodded, then leaned in and said quietly, 'What do you think your mother thinks of that?'

I blinked. That was not what I expected. 'What?'

'Do you think your mother is proud of you?'

I didn't know what to say, and felt as though I'd start crying if I tried to speak. I was already carrying around a great deal of shame about how many times I'd embarrassed my mother over the years, and somehow Marco knew that. He was staring at me with piercing intensity. 'I guess she wouldn't be very proud about it, no.'

'Tell me what happened.'

So I told him the whole story of how I ended up running the kitchen and losing my temper at the waitstaff, leading to my termination. I didn't hold back.

Marco listened to the whole thing without changing his expression, and then said, 'If I rang the executive chef, what sort of reference do you think he'd give you?'

'Probably not the best, I imagine.'

At this point, I understood I wasn't getting the job, but I'm glad I told the truth, because Marco was already picking up the phone and asking to be put through to Paul Reed. The operator patched him through to the Chester Grosvenor.

'This is Marco from the Restaurant Marco Pierre White, Knightsbridge, London. Am I speaking to Paul Reed, the executive chef?'

'Fuck off it is!' I could hear Paul's voice over the phone. 'What are you talking about?'

He couldn't believe Marco was calling, thought it was a prank and hung up on him. Marco rang back again: 'Don't hang up the phone, it's Marco Pierre White from the Marco Pierre White in London, and I'm ringing about a reference for Jock Zonfrillo.'

That got Paul's attention. He set off on a diatribe: Jock's scum, he's a drug addict, drug dealer, shit cook, couldn't hold down his section – all of the worst things I could imagine a chef saying about me, and I was so close to the phone I could hear every word.

The whole time Marco was just staring at me unblinking while I was holding back tears, thinking that I might as well pick up my Tesco bag of knives and fuck off back to Chester, because apart from being brutally embarrassing it was clear my plan of working for Marco was just not happening.

I didn't even have money for train fare: how I was even going to get back to Chester? So I was sitting there worrying about that while my former employer gave his doctoral dissertation on what a bastard I am. After about five minutes, Paul finally stopped talking.

'Are you finished?' Marco asked calmly.

'Yeah, I don't need to say anything else.'

'I think you've said quite enough, thank you for your comments.' Then he hung up and looked at me for what seemed like an endless stretch of time.

'How do you think your mother would feel about that? Do you think she'd be proud?'

'Yes, well, I don't think she'd be very happy,' I said.

'What do *you* think of it?'

'I'm fucking angry about it,' I said. 'But I'm not worried about it. I'm here about a job.'

There was another pause then, and I was just squirming. This was my first taste of something I came to know well about Marco, which is that being the size of a lorry is the least intimidating thing about him. He has a knack for sizing up a person and homing in on exactly what makes them vulnerable. It's like a superpower, this ability he has to hit you where you're most exposed.

'I'll give you a chance,' Marco said. 'Get in the kitchen.'

I trialled that afternoon, did the service that night and at the end of the shift Marco told me I could start next week. I walked out of the restaurant pretty much melting with relief.

Things were looking up for me. I had a job at what was universally considered to be the best restaurant in London and I had a place to crash, so I took the Tube up to Earls Court where Andy Baker lived and tried to find his place. It took me ages. Glasgow was busy, but nothing in comparison to this sprawling fucking metropolis. I got out of the Tube and there were people coming from all directions and I had no map or any idea where to go.

Eventually I found the address Andy had given me, which was a plumber's shop with flats above. It was one in the morning by then, and I spent twenty minutes banging on the door not knowing if I was in the right place before Andy opened it and invited me inside.

He took me into the shop, then down into the basement, and what was clearly the storage area for the shop – pipes and washers and taps and shit all over the place – and Andy had rolled out a sleeping bag in the middle of the floor.

'Are you supposed to be here?' I asked him.

'Yeah, don't worry about it, it's part of the job.' He waved his hand airily, and I could see he was wrecked from smoking too much pot. I didn't believe him, but where else did I have to go? Andy rolled out a spare sleeping bag for me and I climbed in. The next day was Sunday and I wasn't due to start work until Monday, so we went out and got pissed then came back to crash under the plumber's.

I crashed out, pissed, on the floor, and woke up to a ruckus. Andy's boss had come into work early, just after 5 am, and he found his apprentice and some other lad clearly living in the basement of his shop. He was yelling and screaming at Andy. I didn't know what was going on, but it became obvious that Andy wasn't meant to be there, and I certainly wasn't, so I was out on my ear.

Now I had nowhere to stay in addition to no money, and a new job I was meant to start in a couple of hours. All I had was my chef's jacket, the clothes I'd been sleeping in, and my knives, but I figured I could sort out where I'd sleep when the time came. I had a job to get to.

CHAPTER EIGHT

On my first day I was very much in awe of the fact that I was working for Marco Pierre White, this godlike chef whose food was all anyone in the field of gastronomy talked about. I thought it was fucking amazing, and so did everyone else in the kitchen – a cult of personality had attached itself to Marco, and so everything in the kitchen was in orbit around his reputation. The understanding was that we should be grateful to be able to work there, and we were. All these incredibly talented chefs running around the place, but all very focused and driven to do their small part to keep the machine running.

It quickly became apparent that the difference between a one-star and a three-star kitchen was huge. You'd start at seven in the morning and you'd be there until one in the morning. All day, every day. The job would have been advertised as a split shift – and sometimes you got maybe a half-hour break – but a lot of the time you'd just work through depending on how busy it was and how much you had to do. It was sort of understood, especially on my first day, that you didn't want to take a break because you wanted to keep on top of what was going on. It was super-regimented, with every minute of every day accounted for.

Everyone was gunning for perfection, in every way, all the time, and that vibe permeated the place from the guy washing the dishes to the guy with his name etched in brass on the front door. It was infectious, that energy: everyone had this vibe that everything worked to the fucking minute, so if you fucked up, you were wasting everybody's time.

When I walked in, I was given an apron and two tea towels by the *saucier*, a chef called Jimmy, and told those were the only two towels I'd be allowed to use the entire day. The reasoning was that if a chef was messy enough to need more than that to keep on top of their work, they had no fucking business being in that kitchen.

The kitchen spilled over onto two levels. Upstairs was the service kitchen on the same level as the restaurant dining area. There you found the pass, the meat section, the fish section, the pastry over in the corner and the veg section down the other side. Downstairs you had the pastry prep kitchen, the veggie prep kitchen and then the *garde manger*.

I was put on the *garde manger* section, where my job was to pick herbs. We had clip-top jars holding all the picked herbs for all the different dishes, which I'd take upstairs to Marco who'd use them while assembling the dishes. My other job was to prepare tomatoes for concasse – I'd blanch, peel, deseed and dice them perfectly so they were silky smooth and ready for service.

It was a bit of a gear shift for me, coming from a one-star kitchen where I was basically running the place, to being told I was picking herbs and dicing tomatoes, which is usually what apprentices did.

'No worries,' I thought, 'there's no way they'll have me on tomatoes all day. How could you spend all day on that?'

But sure enough, that's what I did. That was the process of a three-star place where everything had to be absolutely fucking perfect.

Each morning twelve trays of beautiful plum tomatoes came in. Then the chef de partie would pick through them, discarding any fruit that weren't perfectly ripe, coloured or shaped, and end up with four to six trays. The discards went straight into staff food or the bin. This seemed like madness to me, the waste at that level of cooking, and it still does.

Then the chef de partie showed me the *exact* way they were to be prepared, blanched in this way, peeled that way, put in a specific tray to dry, then taken out again to make the dice.

Then there were three different dishes that required three different sizes of diced tomato: a one-centimetre square, a two-centimetre square and a brunoise tomato dice, which is the extremely fiddly technique where you julienne a perfect slice of tomato petal, turn it, and cut a cube of precisely 2.5 millimetres.

Then someone would come along and inspect it and if they found one little piece of tomato that wasn't completely to spec they would lose their shit. The chef who was demonstrating this on the first day was deadly serious, and when I started joking about, saying surely Marco wasn't so uptight, the guy looked stricken.

'God fucking help you if Marco comes to check them and they're not fucking perfect.' I thought he was exaggerating, but sure enough, that's what Marco did. If he saw one element on a prep tray that was less than the platonic ideal of a tomato brunoise he would pick up the whole thing and launch it against the wall.

That was his process. Everything was either perfect or he wasn't having it in his kitchen. A limp chive tip could send him to violence. He had a dish that incorporated a chervil garnish. So you'd send him a jar of these beautiful, picture-perfect chervil sprigs and he'd scatter a handful on the bench to choose the perfect one or two, then sweep the rest back into the jar. If he saw one sprig that was less than perfect – it sounds daft, but they had to have a lovely little bend in the stalk, perfectly shaped little leaves, and terminate in a perfectly formed leaf – he would throw the entire jar in the bin, regardless of how many good ones were in there.

So the station I was on was a high-pressure yet hugely monotonous job. I understood they'd put me on it as a test, to see if I'd crack. It was a trial of perseverance and character, so I vowed I'd do it for as long as it took.

Besides, I had bigger problems than the concasse. I didn't have anywhere to stay that night. On my break I rang Andy at the plumber's shop and asked him what was going on, and he told me he'd been kicked out of the basement and was homeless too. 'I'm on a mate's sofa tonight. I can't help you.'

After the restaurant closed I walked around Hyde Park trying to work out what to do. In the end, I went back to the restaurant staff entrance and got back in by punching the passcode into the keypad. There were corridors linking Marco's kitchen and the Hotel Hyde Park kitchen, and in that underground area there were facilities for the staff.

There was a little changing room reserved for Marco's staff, with a shower room, and a line of lockers and coat hooks.

I stood in the doorway and realised I didn't have anywhere else to go. It was sleep in there or in the park. So I curled up on a pile of linen bags right at the back of the row of lockers under the coat hooks, getting up bright and early before anyone arrived and pretending I'd just been bright-eyed and bushy-tailed to start the new job.

On my break I went and tried to get a room at a hostel for young hospitality workers, but they just shrugged. 'We'll put you on the waiting list, but it'll be a while before you can get in.'

That was pretty much my only chance of finding some-where to sleep in London. I had no money to get a flat, and the advance I was about to ask for would be spent on gear, because my dependence meant I was cooking up heroin at a good clip.

So that night I again slept in the changing room. I'd get up before the restaurant opened, walk around the park until I could go back into work, and pretend I'd just come from home. I ended up doing that for a week, then a month, then another.

The weeks passed and I was still in the kitchen, still on the concasse. I was blitzing through it, no worries, then I came in one day and they'd turned up the difficulty. One of the specials featured tomato concasse prominently, which effec-tively meant double the workload. That meant someone further up the chain was trying to ruin my day: I was being set up to fail.

So I was standing there, with my knives and my two tea towels, staring at a thousand plum tomatoes. The way they wanted them, as extra-large dice, I knew I was going to get one, maybe two perfect cubes out of each tomato petal, and then I could either throw half that tomato in the bin or I could pick through it and try to salvage what I could. That would be so time-consuming there'd be no way to get the prep done.

'Right, I'm going to do this my way,' I thought. I'd been staring at tomatoes so fucking long I could take them apart in my sleep, so I took a minute and had a close look at one of them and figured out a better way to do it.

I cut the top and tail off, then lined them all up on a board and got a long, thin paring knife to core them. Placing the now-hollow tomatoes neatly lined up on the board, I then ran a carving knife down the middle of each row, leaving me with perfect rectangles instead of petals of tomato.

I now had a system that was far fucking better. It was faster and made for a much more exact dice. I did this for two days before our *saucier*, Jimmy, came downstairs to check on me.

By 9 am I'd finished the concasse and herbs, and had moved on to other jobs. Jimmy had expected me to be on tomato right up until service so when he saw me working on a bucket of crabs he was all over it.

'What the fuck are you doing?' he said. 'You've got all that concasse to do.'

'I've done it.'

Jimmy was furious, and accused me of trying to pass off yesterday's concasse as fresh. He couldn't get it through his head that anyone could get that much work done so fast.

The next morning, while I was still doing the concasse, Jimmy came downstairs, saw me doing my new trick with the paring knife and lost his fucking mind.

'You're not supposed to do it that way!' he hollered. 'Who told you to do that?'

He ran upstairs, gleeful little shit, to tell Marco what I was doing. Sure enough, seconds later I got hauled upstairs and Marco was already furious.

'What the fuck are you doing to my tomatoes?' he wanted to know, and I was trying to explain, and sort of tripping over my words and in the end he just dragged me downstairs and told me to show him what I was doing.

I showed him, with Jimmy standing there gloating, and when I was done Marco picked up a diced tomato and turned to Jimmy and said, 'He's obviously got a much better brain than you have,' and that was that.

After that, Jimmy must have known he looked like a dick for grassing me out instead of just recognising a better system than the one the brigade had been using.

I might not have made a friend in Jimmy in the sauce section, but it was a turning point for me in the kitchen.

My sous chef, Richard Turner – a hard-as-nails ex-SAS paratrooper who'd done his time in several super-hot kitchens in the UK and was well-liked and respected as a chef – had a good laugh about the whole thing.

'Don't worry about things,' he said. 'Just keep doing what you're doing. You're doing a good job and Marco can see that.'

After that I started to get closer to the real action in the kitchen, out of the prep section and into foie gras parfait, crabs, lobsters – the sort of food Michelin kitchens are all about.

I was also really pleased that Marco was the kind of chef who would take on an idea that was clearly better than their established technique, which is a leap of logic that's just too fucking far for some chefs at that level. It proved to me that I was right to push back sometimes if I knew my way was better, faster and cleaner, and I felt like I'd finally found a home in the kitchen of Marco Pierre White.

It was always in the back of my mind that I'd been sacked from my last job. I was now working at arguably the best restaurant in the country, maybe the world. I needed to be able to focus on my work. I needed to be the best. Everything else could wait.

Meanwhile, the rest of my life was a mess. I was still living in the changing room at work, because I just couldn't get the money together for a flat. I got paid at the end of the month, so by the time payday came around I was a month in debt to heroin suppliers around London and was back at square one.

I sent a message back to Bob asking him to empty out my rented room in Chester, and at night I would shoot up, bed down behind the lockers, and wait for a room to free up in the hospitality workers' hostel. Three months passed that way.

One night I'd just put my head down and suddenly all the lights came on and someone came into the changing room and walked over to grab their jacket from right above where I was huddled with a blanket over me. They left without a word, but I knew that I was sprung. I thought that the next morning I was getting the sack, for sure. There was no good reason for me to be curled up on the floor of the fucking changing room at three in the morning.

Sure enough, at ten the next morning Marco called me into his office, where he looked me over.

'Where are you staying?' he said.

'I'm actually . . . well, I'm sleeping in the changing room.'

He just sort of looked at me in disbelief. 'What the fuck do you mean, you're sleeping in the changing room?'

I started trying to explain that I had no money and nowhere to stay, but I was getting very worked up because I thought I was done, no question. So there was this big outpouring of emotion because I was exhausted and strung out, and after a bit of that Marco nodded and motioned for me to quit talking.

He didn't fire me. Instead, he picked up the phone, put in a call to the hostel and asked them to fast-track me on the waiting list and find a bed for me. In the meantime, he put me in touch with a couple of boys from Canteen, the other restaurant he owned, and arranged for me to sleep on their sofa until I could get my shit together. He even advanced me some cash to tide me over.

He would have been well within his rights to throw me out on my ear, but for some reason he sort of took me under his wing. Perhaps he'd seen some potential in me and wanted the talent I could bring to his kitchen, but maybe part of it was that he recognised something about himself in me, messy as I was. He had this famous backstory about coming to London as a commis with nothing but £7 and a box of books. Which was pretty much the stage where I was, but with a healthy junk habit instead of the books.

Whatever it was, he gave me – yet another – last chance and sorted me out with a place to live, and I was very grateful. At least, until I'd been there a couple of days.

The house he'd billeted me at was in Stockwell, which has a huge Afro-Caribbean community, and was pretty eye-opening for a Glasgow boy, where being half-Italian was considered a bit too exotic. I remember getting on the bus and sitting down and realising I was the only white guy on it.

You'd walk down the high street and there'd be chilli, garlic and lime wafting from these Jamaican restaurants and Portuguese football bars crammed in next to old-fashioned workers' cafes where you could get a chip buttie. I thought it was fucking amazing.

Emmett, the guy whose couch I was crashing on, wasn't a fan of the culinary wonders of the cultural melting pot, because he was a Nazi. He was in the National Front, the far-right political party notorious for being racist and in particular anti-black.

On the Sunday I was staying with Emmett and his flat-mates, they invited me out to watch a football game – he was a big Chelsea fan as well as a fascist, and I hadn't quite figured out the second part yet, so I went with them. You don't really have a choice when you're crashing on someone's couch: if they want to hang out, you're obliged, so I was up late every night drinking and smoking pot with them until they wanted to sleep.

Afterwards, we were walking home from the Tube station when we passed the Swan Pub, a pub in Stockwell popular with African guys. As we walked by, Emmett casually bent down, picked up a brick from the side of the road and threw it through the window. Then he ran up and stuck his head inside and started screaming this full-on white power diatribe through the broken glass.

I had no idea what was going on, so legged it down the road, and then all these African guys started piling out of the pub and chasing us through the streets of Stockwell. So that was a bit of an eye-opener as well.

It was not good. I already didn't feel great about crashing on Emmett's couch. You don't want to feel like you're imposing on someone, especially when they're a fucking Nazi. My tolerance for racism or suppression of culture was zero and the situation I found myself in was horrific.

I stayed there a couple of weeks until a spot in the hostel opened up, then I was out of there. I shared a room with another young lad who was cooking at the Ritz Carlton, and I started to work out life in London.

CHAPTER NINE

All I knew of Marco before I arrived was that he was *the* guy, the rock star chef with this white heat attached to his reputation. So for me if I were going to work anywhere, it would be for him. Learning from the greats was how he made his name, and pretty much through sheer force of will he changed the way the world thought about fine dining.

Marco came up through the kitchens of Le Gavroche, and Pierre Koffmann at La Tante Claire, Raymond Blanc at Le Manoir aux Quat'Saisons and Nico Ladenis at Chez Nico before opening his own place and starting to rack up the Michelin stars.

He made no secret of the fact that he'd work in a kitchen until he'd mastered their signature dishes, then he'd nick off to the next place and do it better than the inventor. That's what made him Marco. He was up-front with it all. He had the famous 'Pig's Trotter à la Pierre Koffmann' proudly on the menu.

'It's not my dish,' he said, 'but when I cook it, it's better.'

Which was a bit cheeky, but at the same time, his *was* better.

Marco took established ideas about food, put his spin on them, and made them both more exciting than they'd ever been and much more difficult to cook. He pioneered so many things and set the standard for haute cuisine to this day.

There was the chicken liver foie gras parfait, which I think is one of the most plagiarised dishes in the world. He was using a Thermomix before anybody knew what that was, and what he did to chicken liver was sheer beauty. So smooth, so rich, like a chicken liver crème brûlée, and a flavour like nothing else on earth. When he put it on the menu it was this resounding statement of mastery, and it's still echoing. You can see some version of that dish on literally thousands of menus today. I think you always will.

Or look at his pressed leek terrine, which took something as simple as a leek and turned it into the most extraordinary dish.

To create this stunning terrine, the leeks had to be exactly the right size, cooked in a certain way, then pressed with an exact amount of weight for a precise amount of time.

We added a water vinaigrette, so when you served it with extra virgin olive oil it split all over the plate in a gorgeous pattern.

When I first learned to cook the dish it took my breath away, but at the same time, in the back of my mind was the thought, 'How much effort do you want to put into a fucking leek?'

Every leek had to be precisely the right size, shape and colour. You'd go through a box of leeks to sort out the contenders and end up rejecting half of them, which would probably end up in the bin. So the flip side of that pursuit of perfection was a grotesque amount of waste. It was inevitable, unless you had some kind of sister restaurant using the rejects and offcuts. I look back at some of the food we used to cook and can't believe the extremes we went to chasing an idea of perfection.

Take the potato fondant: a halved and squared off potato browned in butter, cooked in a little stock and roasted until crisp. Marco couldn't just serve it shaped like everyone else. One of his had to be shaped like a banana, which was very hard to cook because it was all in different widths, but brought all these deep layers of texture and caramel tones to the thing. Visually beautiful but also the tastiest potato you'd ever meet.

And those were simple dishes. There was a mille-feuille tomato with crab that was just this epic journey to prepare.

You took Cornish mud crabs, cooked them to order, picked the meat, seasoned it perfectly, layered it with beefsteak tomatoes that had been made into tiles, a chiffonade of iceberg lettuce, a brunoise of Granny Smith apple and some avocado, all set in intricate layers, stacked one on top of another.

It was so delicate you had to cut it with one of those electric carving knives that grandparents bust out for the Sunday roast, but you'd trim it into this perfect diamond.

Then you'd plate it up with a tomato coulis and these emerald green dots of chlorophyll mayo around it. Absolutely stunning dish; insanely expensive to produce. It took a small army to get it on the pass every time someone ordered it.

A salmon ballotine: two fillets layered with gelatine, paprika and seasoning, coated in mustard and finely chopped herbs wrapped in cling film then a tea towel, tied with string and finally poached in salted milk. Why? Because the buoyancy meant the ballotine floated in the middle of the pot, neither floating to the top nor sitting at the bottom, and gave the fish a perfect cook. I mean really: who thinks to float a fish in salted milk?

It was about perfection, and nothing was ever anything *but* perfect. The soufflé had to have perfectly straight sides or the chef would throw it at your head.

It was all cooked to order, and customers paid an extortionate amount of money. But frankly, you'd sit down and have a meal that would stand up today as some of the greatest food you'd ever eat. It was luxury; pure luxury. You hear people talk about the heyday of fine dining – and I'm suspicious of nostalgia and people who think things were better back in the day – but food just isn't like that any more. Never will be again. It was a time and a place.

In his day, Marco was an incredible leader of a kitchen, although one that was run on fear and intimidation. He had this physical presence that was larger than life, this way of commanding attention without saying a word. You'd be in the kitchen working away at your section and he'd look up from his bench and somehow you'd know that he was looking at you, and what he wanted. It was uncanny; it was as if he could sense that your chiffonade wasn't quite right from across the room, and he was letting you know with a look. He was such a commanding presence that you knew what he was going to say without a word, which in real terms was a very good way of bringing the team together. He led us to the top of our game and kept us there, hour after hour, service after service.

When he came in and was working next to you, it was inspiring. He'd plate up a dish and the food fell off his fingers in such a beautiful way. He had all his training, and his drive and over the top intensity and all of that, but behind it all was just this raw talent.

Middle Eastern cooks talk about certain chefs with *nafas*, which translates roughly as 'breath' or 'spirit'. It's that thing some chefs have: an energy where what they cook is just magnitudes better than someone else making the same dish, with the same ingredients, in the same kitchen.

There was a pastry chef at Turnberry who had an unbelievable natural talent for pastry; incredible ability to manipulate chocolate and piping and all the rest of it. He was very skilled at that sort of craftsmanship – but every decent chef is very skilled. The difference was that he had a mastery, the way he handled himself at work, whatever he was doing. Rolling out pastry, tempering chocolate; whatever it was, he made it look effortless.

I'd encountered a few chefs like that: just regular guys on a section of the restaurant who were simply much better than they had to be. They might be flipping burgers or peeling a bag of spuds or making granola, but watching them up close, I could see that there was something going on that was deeper than just skill and training. I knew that I wasn't there yet, but I was sure how to get there.

Years later, I saw a video by Ira Glass, the famous radio journalist, about 'the gap' – that time when you get into a creative field because you have good taste, but for the first couple of years your work isn't all that good. And you know that your work isn't good enough, because you have the good instincts to tell quality from shite, and those instincts tell you your work isn't good enough.

That's fine; that's part of becoming a better professional but the problem is, at the beginning of your career, nobody tells you about that gap. So for years you can tell that what you're making isn't as good as you want it to be, that it falls short in some way, but you don't know how to rise to that level yet. It can be really disappointing and disheartening.

Everyone who does interesting and creative work, no matter what the field, goes through this. It takes a huge amount of work, years of grinding away at it, to close that gap so that your talent matches your ambition. It's normal, it takes a while, and you just have to fight your way through it. The only way to get there is to keep working at it: trying, failing, then trying again and again, and getting better in the smallest increments.

That's a huge part of every chef's career, but nobody ever bothers to tell you about it, which I find very odd. Back in the day, hospitality did have this weird masochistic thing about it, which was that you got really good eventually, but very few people helped you along the way. The attitude – which was absolute bullshit – was that if it wasn't as hard as possible for you, you hadn't earned it. It actually suited me – my entire life I've always taken the most difficult path from A to B – but I've seen some really gifted chefs lose heart and give up. What I can assure you is that talent left unacknowledged turns into resentment and fucking dies, and while I was lucky enough to find amazing mentors who guided me forward, there was still a period of frustration when I knew I wasn't living up to my potential.

There was this stretch of my career when I would see these guys in action and I knew that they were brilliant, and I could tell *that's where talent lies*, but I was a million miles away from it and had no idea how to get there.

But when I met Marco, I'd never seen anything like it. He had *extreme* talent. That was part of the presence he had that filled up the room, and allowed him to manipulate and power a kitchen of some of the biggest egos that ever picked up a chef's knife.

The most intimidating thing about him wasn't even his physical presence, but this aura about him of total culinary mastery. The fact that anything he said about food could be backed up in a moment. You didn't argue with him about anything he said, because he'd be right, without exception. The guy could make a sandwich and it would just take your breath away. He couldn't not make a perfect sandwich. It's just not in him.

That drive for perfection was integral to who he was, and who he was is what made his kitchen great. In that way, he was an extreme version of many of the head chefs I'd encountered before. Mark Bull at Turnberry was exactly the same: ferociously competitive and everything had to be fucking perfect. Davie Auchie, the two French guys; all the chefs I've worked for, they're all single-minded, highly competitive, very creative. Every one of them was out to prove to the world that they were the One.

As far as London was concerned, Marco *was* the One. Back in the day, being a chef wasn't a glamorous proposition, even the most famous weren't household names and didn't get profiled in the weekend papers, but Marco changed all that. The press could not stop wanking over him. It's hard to convey just how famous he was at the time. There's no equivalent in today's world. He was the first person you could call a celebrity chef, long before that was a concept. Now there's thousands of them, but back then, it was just Marco. Through sheer force of personality, he basically invented an entirely new type of celebrity.

It didn't hurt that there was a constant stream of other celebrities lining up to eat at Marco's. I met so many famous people while I was working there: Tom Cruise and Nicole Kidman, Oliver Reed. Every day there'd be at least three celebrities coming through and having a look in the kitchen. I'd be leaning over a counter trying to get a piece of fish plated up then turn around and Dustin Hoffman would be standing there watching me. It was a bit of a statement, a real status symbol, to say you'd visited at Marco Pierre White and eaten a Marco Pierre White menu.

One of the dishes that drew in the rich and famous – *the* most Marco Pierre White dish on the menu – was the foie gras terrine. A legendary dish. In my opinion, it's one of the most perfect dishes that has ever or will ever exist in all of history. If you are into foie gras, that is. Let's leave aside for the moment the cruelty of force-feeding a bird so you can take its engorged liver.

Baby Jock with big sister, Carla.

Jock, Carla and their dad, Christmas 1977.

Birthday parties were a big deal
in the Zonfrillo family.

With their Scottish Grampa on Carla's first day of school, August 1979. Jock was three years old.

Jock aged about four with his dad.

The Zonfrillo family in 1961. *Back row, left to right:* Jock's Uncle Leo, Uncle Tony, Nonno, and his sixteen-year-old dad. *Front row, left to right:* Aunt May, cousin Marina and Nonna.

Jock's Scottish forebears, 1952. Jock's Grampa is in the back row, second from right.

Jock's dad's first barber shop, Levano's, Central Arcade, Ayr.

Jock's dad with his
brother, Uncle Leo.

Jock and Carla with their beloved Nonno on Jock's first day of school.

Jock's grandfathers in younger days. *Left:* Nonno; *right:* Grampa.

Jock aged five with his mum.

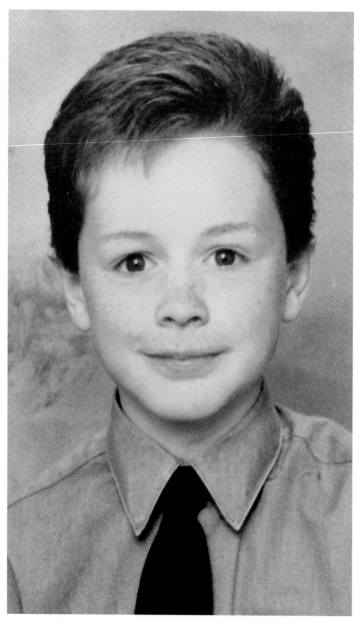

Five-year-old Jock was tagged as 'trouble' as soon as he started school, after accidentally breaking a window.

With Carla, about to set off for his first day of high school and a hazing tradition he'd been dreading for months.

Above and below: Aged twelve on holiday in Budva, Yugoslavia, where Jock experienced street food for the first time.

Twelve-year-old Jock and fellow kitchen staff from his first job at North Park House, where he started off washing dishes.

In full chef whites: 1992, aged fifteen.

Winning
Young
Scottish
Chef of the
Year, aged
sixteen.

Kitchen king

We don our aprons
and take a peek inside
the Turnberry
workplace of an
award-winning young
chef.

Page 7

◆ Young chef of the year, Barry Zonfrillo, who works at Turnberry Hotel. (CG 2442)

Chef scoops prizes

A PROMISING cook at Turnberry Hotel is a kitchen champion after winning the Kyle and Carrick Young Chef of the Year competition.

Barry Zonfrillo beat seven other finalists in the contest at the Kyle and Carrick Food Trades Exhibition at Prestwick Airport. His prize consists of a trophy, a gold medal, a set of knives and a certificate.

The finalists, all aged under 19, prepared chicken, salad and sole dishes in their bid to impress the tastebuds of judge Thomas O'Donnell, who is

head chef of Chapelton House Hotel, Stewarton. Barry's entry was judged to be the most succulent after the 40-minute cooking session.

The restaurants and cafes of Carrick have also been winning prizes, with a total of 12 establishments receiving food hygiene awards.

Seven awards for 1993 went to owners in Girvan and Maybole. They were: John McIlvenney, the Grey Man pub, Maybole; W. R. Leith, Baker, J. A. Stewart, Queens Hotel, Robert Jardine, Tasty Bites;

Koon Wong Lee, Good Luck Carry Out; Kenneth Scobie, Butcher, all Girvan and Tom Pitcher, Glen Tachur Hotel, Barrhill.

Five-year awards went to: Christopher House, Turnberry Hotel; Mr and Mrs J. Allan, Balkenna Tearoom, Turnberry; M. McIlwraith, Bow Window Restaurant, Ballantrae; William R. Kerr, Malin Court Hotel, Maidens; and John Davidson, The Coffee Pot, Girvan.

◆ Comment: Page 4.

Receiving a prestigious
Salon Culinaire Award,
aged seventeen.

Eighteenth birthday.

Working for Marco Pierre White, aged about eighteen.

The first adventure in Australia, 1995.

About to get married, aged nineteen. Edinburgh.

Heading up the restaurant at Hotel Tresanton, Cornwall, 1998. Jock may've been an addict, but he still had to look the part in crisply ironed whites.

The last few months of the heroin addiction, 1999.

Right and below: In Australia in 2000: a new millennium and a new, drug-free Jock.

The texture, the taste; this perfectly moulded, rich, sophisticated but so simple dish. It's the very height of what terrine
can be, an already decadent food elevated to something you'd
expect to see at the fall of Rome. It comes out so glossy with
fat it looks like it's carved from marble. Then it's served with
this vibrant sauternes jelly piped around it. A thing of beauty.

It was a wildly expensive endeavour, because on top of
the hours required to make terrine it involved cooking about
sixteen birds' worth of foie gras and yielded less than a dozen
slices. One slice cost about £30 to make; we actually lost
money on it when we served it as part of the menu, but it was
that sort of thing that made us the best kitchen in the UK.

One Saturday morning I came in early because I wanted
to make the terrine. I'd been out all night Friday, so I was
loaded. No sleep, loads of pills, some grass to balance that
out, the normal baseline of junk, some Charlie to keep me
upright – and a terrine to make.

The dish was the epitome of simple elegance. You'd take a
lobe of foie gras and use the back of a spoon to gently separate
the lobe so you could take the veins out. Then season that
with cognac, *sel rose*, white pepper, put it back together again,
lay sixteen lobes on a tray and roast them in the oven. Then
remove, dry, and layer in the terrine mould. All the fat renders
out, which is perhaps 80 per cent of the volume of the thing,
but what little protein there is sets into a block which you'd
later trim up, plate, garnish and serve.

So, an incredibly intricate, delicate prep job, and I was
very drunk and high, and concentrating as hard as I could
on getting it right, when something scurried by me in the
kitchen.

This was London. There were rats everywhere, and even in the best kitchens in London it was not unusual to see a rat the size of a football running about a basement kitchen. I turned around to get a look at it, but it was gone, so I turned back to focus on the terrine.

So I was at the bench, facing a wall, and really trying to keep it together because I was a little bit bent, and if I ruined this terrine that's a loss of hundreds of pounds, and then I heard it coming back. Just in the edge of my peripheral vision I saw the rat, this big shaggy fucking rodent, scurrying happily along behind me. I didn't move, just kept working on the terrine with my little spoon, because I knew he'd be coming back this way again and this time I'd be ready for it. The little fucker ran right behind me, and I turned around and put the boot into it as hard as I could.

Then I heard the scream. This piercing, blood-curdling scream from the middle of nowhere, which was very unnerving because there was nobody else in the kitchen. So I screamed. Then the rat screamed again. Then I got a better look at it while it scooted off into the pastry section and I realised it was very shaggy for a rat. Never seen one like it, so I ran after it into the pastry kitchen, thinking I was going to have to kill this rat – because I was only functioning on a fairly basic level and besides, I had a terrine to make – and I was lifting my boot to stomp it at which point the rat ran out at me and I realised it wasn't a rat at all, it was a dog. A fucking Chihuahua, and it was barking at me.

The dog skittered past me to the door, where all of a sudden this woman had appeared. She was in a baseball cap and a bomber jacket and she was hysterical, screaming at me to leave the dog alone. Then she picked the dog up and ran off.

'Well, that was weird,' I thought, and went back to the terrine. 'Did that really happen or was it all in my head? I'm pretty sure it really happened.'

This was around nine in the morning. Around two o'clock, I got called into Marco's office and he was pissed off.

'What happened this morning?'

'What do you mean?' I get a bit worried for a second that he's got a problem with the terrine. 'I made the terrine. I cut a slice off, it's perfect. What's the matter?'

'Not that. Did you kick someone's dog this morning?'

'Well yeah, but I thought there was a rat in the kitchen, so I turned around and kicked it. Who lets their dog in the kitchen?'

'Madonna,' Marco said. 'Madonna lets her dog into the kitchen. Yeah, that was Madonna.'

So I'd kicked Madonna's dog, and Marco was very, very angry about it. In the end he had to send chefs up to her hotel penthouse to cook a private dinner for her and her backup dancers. I was spewing because I didn't get to go, because obviously I wasn't very welcome.

I maintain a Chihuahua has no business being in a kitchen at 9 am when hardworking chefs are going to be in there coming down off some serious drugs, but Marco took Madonna's side because they were mates. He knew everybody. Marco had such status that anyone who was famous came to town to eat at our restaurant. As far as hip, high-end dining was concerned, our little kitchen at the Hyde Park Hotel was the centre of the world.

CHAPTER TEN

Everyone was trying to get at Marco's food: tycoons, actors, musicians, royals. One day Marco came in and announced that we'd been hired to cook at a function for Prince Charles at the Prix de l'Arc de Triomphe, the famous French race that takes place at the Longchamp racecourse in Paris.

Marco was cooking the best French food in Britain, no question, but he'd never been to France. He used to bang on about it all the time – the irony of the fact that he was without peer in the field yet he'd never been to Paris.

Six guys from the kitchen were selected to go, and I was one of them. I was pretty excited because I'd never been to Paris either and here was a chance to get out of the kitchen.

We got all our gear together, loaded the van and drove to France via the Channel Tunnel, which had just opened. Marco was supposed to come in the van with us, which I was excited about because I thought maybe we'd get some face time and perhaps also get up to no good, but he changed his mind, telling us to go ahead without him and he'd meet us later.

When we got to the racecourse, there was a field kitchen set up under a marquee. Marco wasn't there yet, so we unloaded all the gear, produce and prep, and waited for Marco so we could get started. We waited, and we waited. No Marco. This was before mobile phones, so we didn't know what had happened but eventually we realised we were on our own.

There was another famous Michelin star chef taking part, a Frenchman who was there with all his guys, and they were giving us the evils while we were pottering about working on our fish. The rival chef came over to us and started in on us in this heavy cartoon-French accent: 'Where is zis Marco Pierre White? Is his head so fucking big he cannot fit through ze door?'

Without Marco there they saw an opportunity to stitch us up and embarrass him. The menu for the event was our signature foie gras terrine, a sea bass dish and a lemon tart for dessert. The sea bass needed to be seared in a pan then finished in the oven; a simple enough dish in a normal environment but this was Marco's recipe, so it was precise down to the second. This many seconds of searing, this many in the oven, then finish and serve the fish the second it's out with accompaniment, garnish and sauce.

As soon as the French crew realised that we couldn't do our service without ovens they immediately filled them all up so we couldn't use them. They were just taking covered pans out and putting them back in and arcing up every time we went to use one of them. All we could do was sear the fish, put it in the hot boxes we used to heat plates for service, and hope it would slow-cook. Which is what we were doing when Marco finally arrived.

He'd decided to drive over with Jean-Christophe Novelli, a famous French chef working in London. Jean-Christophe was driving Marco's car because Marco had a Range Rover, but no licence. Marco also didn't have his passport – couldn't find it before he left – so he'd taken his wife's passport with a little photo of his face sellotaped over her picture.

As you'd expect, they got turned away at the Channel Tunnel. From there they drove to Dover where the boat to France leaves from, and Marco hid in the boot under a pile of jackets and wellies. He's nearly two metres tall, this guy; not a petite person, and they smuggled him into France like a bag of hash. He arrived five minutes after service started, and lost his mind.

Now he was looking at 200 portions of beautiful sea bass that had been browned on one side but were now just sitting in a hot box growing stale. He couldn't handle it, started screaming, throwing shit around, turning tables over. All the French guys who'd been having a lend of us a minute earlier shit themselves because this fucking giant was bodily destroying the kitchen in a blind rage.

Then Marco disappeared, just sort of vanished into thin air, and we were left freaking out. It was a disaster, no doubt about it, but we all just put our heads down and started chopping faster to get the service done. The French chefs had been intimidated by Marco's little rampage, so they backed off and let us use the ovens. We finished the service, served Prince Charles a lovely three-course meal, and then got absolutely fuck-eyed.

On the drive back to England we treated ourselves to all the drugs and drinks in the world. We stopped at McDonald's on the way for dinner and there we were, these elite Michelin star chefs, all stoned and drunk, eating cheeseburgers. Then one of us, Chopper, took a bite and winced.

'These burgers are shit,' he announced, and threw the burger at me. I threw one back, and then it turned into a bit of a burger fight. The poor staff at McDonald's called the cops on us, so we piled back into the van and got out of there.

As the three Michelin star place we were *the* height of perfection. We were considered to be the epitome of kitchen excellence, and were held to extremely high standards.

We were in this environment where we were fuelled by adrenaline and pride in producing the absolute pinnacle of haute cuisine, but at the same time stressed out of our minds. The flip side of the pursuit of ultimate culinary elegance and perfection was some properly degenerate behaviour. At the end of service, you would be so wired from the thrill of performing at that level that the easiest way to wind down was to go out and party to excess – to the point that you just fall over.

Some days we'd race through our prep so we could fuck off to the pub for an hour or two of beers and chat before service. It was a touch of normal life away from the highly particular and dysfunctional reality of Marco's kitchen, and we all craved a little bit of normality. One afternoon we got absolutely rat-faced and fell asleep in the park in the full sun. We all got massively sunburned and came into work in a fair amount of pain. We had to sneak in, feeling sorry for ourselves, and pretend we'd been downstairs all along. We were already the colour of crayfish and as we worked the rest of the night we just turned redder and redder as the sunburn got worse.

Marco was pretty exasperated, as obviously we'd not got ourselves sunburned in the prep kitchen, but he was surprisingly understanding of that kind of thing – as long as you kept up the standard of work.

Again, it was this paradox of parallel lives: you're pursuing excellence in the kitchen and you're harnessing all that training and drive and passion to create this absolutely fucking wonderful food, but whenever you're not pursuing that culinary perfection, you're trying to erase yourself from the face of the planet.

One time I was so trashed at work I started to gob off to Richard, the SAS paratrooper-turned-sous chef. He'd made a lobster salad, and told me to take it upstairs to the pass.

'No way I'm taking that up,' I looked at the lobster salad, then at Richard, then at the salad. 'It looks like shit. If I take it upstairs I'll never live it down.'

Richard, who was literally trained to jump out of planes and kill people for a living, was not used to being talked back at, so he looked a little surprised. He reminded me he was my boss and that I was going to take it to the pass. I insisted I wasn't, so he made a counteroffer: 'If you don't take it upstairs,' he said, 'I'm going to knock you the fuck out.'

'Go ahead,' I said, 'I'm not taking it up.' And he did. Knocked me out cold with one punch, then took the salad up to the pass. It went out to the restaurant, and I went to hospital. He hit me so hard I didn't even remember it until he reminded me about it years later. Apart from that, we got along great. A wonderful guy – liked a bit of a party, and a close mate to this day, some twenty-five years later.

Everyone in the restaurant got a salary, and on top of that you got the tronc. These were the pooled tips that went through some weird filter that no one really under-stood except that it meant an envelope of cash on top of your expected wages.

The salary, about £350 a week, was reasonable for the times, and then on payday you'd get this wad of cash which seemed to have all the consequence of Monopoly money. We had no real use for it except to invest it in a marvellous weekend. Which usually meant hanging out with the guys from the kitchen and doing all of the drugs.

You learned to take pride in mixing up a cocktail that suited you. You might plan a night out based on a gram of Charlie, four pills and at least an eighth of weed. At home you'd always have your works and enough heroin to see you through a couple of weeks in case of financial emergencies. Sometimes you'd do pills and speed, or pills and Charlie, or you'd have some nice skunk from Amsterdam and smooth that out with a few pills.

The weekend I turned eighteen, we went out on the Friday night. We'd arranged to go clubbing, but I decided to warm up by drinking a bottle of Jack Daniel's – looking back, I can't believe I would insult myself by drinking fucking Jack Daniel's whiskey – and got trolleyed. I went for a walk with the bottle and ended up being shaken awake in Trafalgar Square by two coppers.

They took me back to the hospitality hostel I was living in, but I didn't have a key so just sort of slumped against the doorway and went to sleep. I figured when the guys on breakfast shift left, I'd be able to go in and get some sleep before the Saturday service. Sure enough, I woke up just kind of sliding off the doorstep because someone inside was heaving against the door, trying to open it, but impeded by my dead-weight slumped against it.

I got inside the hostel where all my mates were getting ready to leave for breakfast shifts in their restaurants. They took one look at me and started taking the piss, because I had to be at work pretty soon, and I was clearly in a bad way. It's worth mentioning that I don't get hangovers, never have (don't hate me, I sympathise with those who do . . . it looks awful), so without a good tempering hangover I turned up to work still drunk, but now coked and junked up in a vague attempt to straighten myself out.

I turned up to my shift completely shit-faced, and Richard Turner took one look at me and kicked me back down the stairs before Marco saw me. He knew that Marco would go ballistic if he saw the state of me. Inevitably, Marco noticed I was missing and started yelling for me, 'Where the fuck is Jock? Tell that lazy fucker to get in here!'

So I had to go up and face him and he just gave me this look that let me know that I'd disappointed him. If Marco was yelling at you, it meant you'd fucked up. If he was too angry to yell at you, that was even worse. I slunk back to my station with my tail firmly between my legs.

It was Saturday, also payday, so everyone else in the kitchen was in a good mood, ready for a big night out that night, and I was wondering if I could curl up in the corner and get a bit of kip before we inevitably got started.

We got through the day, service finished and we got out around midnight, then went straight from the kitchen to the Ministry of Sound and started dropping pills. There were five of us, all cashed up, and we were sort of pushing each other to take it up a level. I remember taking so many drugs; strangers were walking past me and putting pills in my mouth.

At 3 am we left Ministry to go on to some other clubs. Richard had to go by the restaurant because he had gravlax on the menu and needed to turn the salmon over. While we were there someone had the idea that we should grab some booze, so we walked out with a bottle of *very* expensive cognac.

From there we went to Strawberry Sundae at Cloud 9, a day club where they would let you enter in pretty much any state of disrepair, but not with a bottle of cognac.

'You're going to have to finish that,' the bouncer said, to which we said, 'Okay'.

We all took turns having a swig, and when it got to me there was maybe two-thirds of the bottle left. I took this huge pull, and my throat was burning. This is a 40 per cent strength alcohol in a handcrafted decanter designed to be carefully sipped after a meal then linger on the palate for the rest of the evening – not intended to be sculled under the judgemental eye of the bouncer of a day club.

I took a breather and the bouncer snorted. 'I knew you couldn't finish that.'

I was already intoxicated beyond belief, sort of weaving on the spot, so of course I said, 'Fuck you', and downed the rest of the bottle. I handed him the empty bottle and he sort of grunted, half impressed and half disgusted, but he let us into the club. We hadn't been in there more than two minutes before a mate walked past me and dropped two pills in my mouth.

I lasted maybe five minutes after that before I literally hit a wall. Just smacked right into it and then blacked out for a bit. When I came to, I was sitting down at the side of the club. One of my mates came over and bent down to check on me.

'Are you all right, Jock?' He looked a bit worried, and I would have reassured him but I'd lost the ability to speak some time back, and just sort of ground my jaw at him.

'Come with me,' he said, all business. 'You're just on your way down. We'll do some Charlie and that'll pick you back up again.' So we went to the toilets and did a whole heap of Charlie, which definitely made me feel better.

We got out of there around lunchtime Sunday. By then there were only three of us, and when we emptied our pockets, we only had £50 left. We'd gone out with at least £300 each, and we'd spent the whole lot on drugs. A stupendous amount of money. But the sun was out, and we had enough for a case of beers and we decided to go and sit in the park. I got chatting to the girl in the bottle shop and asked her what time she finished work.

'I'm done in an hour,' she said.

'We're going to go sit in the park, you should come have a beer.'

'Perfect,' she said. 'I'll bring some pot over.'

So she joined us, and we were sitting around having a time of it, and eventually my two mates fell asleep in the sun.

The girl took out her lipstick and started drawing shit on their faces. When they woke up and each saw that the other one had squiggles and love hearts and dicks drawn all over their faces, they both kept it quiet, thinking it was only the other guy. And I didn't say anything, because at the time it seemed like the funniest thing I'd ever seen.

In the end, they went home with the shit drawn all over their faces, and I had to walk home because I'd spent all my money and couldn't even afford the Tube. So I went home, had a shower, then we all went out again to a mate's buck's do, and straight from there to work on Monday morning, where it was just another eighteen-hour day in a three-star.

On the Monday none of us could really remember the whole weekend, we had to piece it together with the fragments each of us could remember. But that was a pretty standard weekend.

I kept up that pace for six months, living in the hostel until Lucy, my girlfriend from Chester, came down to join me and we got a flat together. She was a pastry chef, so I helped her get a job at Criterion, another of Marco's restaurants. After we moved in together, I calmed down a little. But not that much.

It was a small kitchen, and all of us went pretty hard, except for Marco. He didn't party with us, not in that way. His thing was fishing, and if he invited you out to go fishing it was a big fucking deal.

He might have been bollocking you all through service, really just reaming you, stripping you of all your dignity because you'd given him an imperfect bit of chervil or whatever, but then service would end and he'd come up and put his arm around you and say, 'We're going fishing tonight.' He never drove, so you were always expected to be the driver. You'd have to drive to the middle of nowhere, in the middle of the night. Then you'd spend the next eight hours on the banks of some river with the fishing rod in the water, and every time you got a bite, you'd hope it wasn't bigger than the last fish Marco pulled in.

The same traits that made him a transcendent chef made him pathologically competitive. If I caught a bigger fish than he did I knew I was in for hell until he found a way to get that credit back. He needed to win at all costs. If it meant staying up all night, then that's what happened.

If this was Friday night after service, it meant you weren't sleeping. You'd get back to London at maybe ten in the morning, drop Marco off, go home, have a shower, and then you'd have to be back at work by twelve at the latest, work all afternoon, and then go out after that.

It was understood that a fishing trip with Marco was a great reward. One of the more manipulative mind games he played with his staff was the way he played favourites. Every once in a while at the end of service, Marco, who might have been screaming at you all night long, would suddenly pull you off your station and take you out to dinner with one of his celebrity mates.

It was very public; very ostentatious. The entire staff would see one of the chefs tapped on the shoulder to go out to experience Marco's world, so they'd be off drinking wine and eating caviar with Björk while we were back in the kitchen scrubbing grease traps. The mind games and manipulation were relentless, and the fishing trips were an extension of that.

Nevertheless, I jumped at every chance I had to go on those fishing trips. Any opportunity to get some one-on-one time with someone like that was valuable to me – *proximité* in action. I had a huge amount of respect for the guy, both as a chef and as a person, and just hanging out and talking with him I learned as much about cooking as I had working double shifts in other kitchens, and I worked in a few of them back then.

CHAPTER ELEVEN

After service, when the kitchens had been hosed down and the chefs from the Michelin star places around town tumbled out onto the street still wired, they'd go to a bar called Down Mexico Way.

The food was standard Mexican: very tasty, very simple, the sort of thing that chefs like to eat after work. When your palate has been fried by tasting a thousand fucking sauces, you don't crave a plate of tomato foam with basil jelly or whatever nonsense is in vogue. You want a bucket of fried chicken so greasy the container falls apart.

What chefs eat in their downtime would horrify your average food snob. Generally, the better the chef, the more basic the dinner. It wasn't unusual for Marco to unwind by eating a jar of peanut butter with his fingers in the car on his way to the fishing spot. It was fucking gross, man. I craved sweets, especially the cheap stuff: your basic dairy chocolate, lollies, those bags of nasty artificially flavoured gummy animals. There's a particular Scottish confectionery called Tunnock's Caramel Log, categorically the best biscuit in the world, the only exception being a teacake also made by Tunnock's. To this day, I'll go a long way out of my way for a Tunnock's.

That, or Italian comfort food – pasta, bread and salami straight out of the fridge; lasagne still napalm-hot from the oven. That was what I made a beeline for, if I was hungry after work – which wasn't that often, because with all the substances I was going through I rarely had an appetite. I wasn't the only one. To tell you the truth, chefs went to Down Mexico Way for the drinks more than the food.

At Down Mexico Way, the gang from Marco's kitchen would go upstairs where there'd be a table waiting for us, and at all the other tables would be the crews from all the other three-star London restaurants.

Imagine some of the biggest talents and biggest egos in one of the best culinary cities in the world, all winding down with some very stiff drinks after a 100-hour working week.

The vibe was very prison mess hall: you kept to your own table and your own pack, and gave each other the evils. Now and again there'd be a bit of a ruckus, a bit of a brawl that necessitated taking it outside.

But occasionally you'd get to talking to a chef from another kitchen, because even if we were bitter rivals, we all fucking loved what we did, and we had that in common. It was through Marco and the crew that I first met Heston Blumenthal, and we became pretty good mates.

Around that time, I also met and befriended a rising chef, a lovely bloke who'd just opened his new restaurant. To fund it he'd used pretty much every pound he had and tapped out every line of credit.

As it happened, I knew of a restaurant a lot of mates worked in, where a fine-dining shingle was joined to a luxury hotel kitchen by a basement corridor. The idea was that staff could scamper from one kitchen to the other, but it also meant that at night you could wander from the restaurant kitchen to the hotel kitchen and have a poke around after lights out, something I did when I had the chance. I'm Scottish; I love free stuff.

It was a luxury hotel kitchen in a luxury hotel in London, so as you can imagine it was pretty flash. Huge, well-staffed, well-stocked, well-equipped. A little too well-equipped. All the pots and pans in the world. So one night, a group of us went in there and liberated a few items: planetary mixer, gastro trays, spoons, whisks, pots, pans, chinois, fucking potato ricers. You name it, we nicked it. We filled a three-ton truck with gleaming kitchen equipment and drove it to our mate's new restaurant.

Years later, I was in England and went to see that chef, and we talked about old times.

'Do you remember when we took all that shit?' I asked him, and his face turned white.

'You know, I haven't even thought about that until today. I didn't think anybody remembered.'

I sure remembered. It was a proper caper, Grand Theft Kitchen. I guess the moral of the story is that when it comes down to it, a good chef knows when another chef has good intentions, and will go out of their way to help them.

As the months went by, I got the chance to know people from other top-tier kitchens, and every once in a while I'd get the chance to do a *stage* with them. A *stage* (pronounced staahj) is a sort of internship where you go to another kitchen and work for free, just for the experience, and to see what's going on in a different kitchen. Like a tiny little apprenticeship that lasts anything from a few days to a couple of months.

It's a long tradition, fairly noble as far as modern kitchens go, and one of those bat-shit contradictions that somehow hold the world of fine dining together. On one hand you're so competitive with your rivals that you'd happily throw down with them outside the Mexican bar, but I've never met a real chef who wouldn't put aside any kind of animosity to share some really exciting recipe they'd found. *Stages* are a bit of pureness and goodwill in an industry that thrives on competition and aggression.

Marco's was the exception. Marco's kitchen hated it when you did a *stage* at someone else's place. It meant Marco was losing you to a competitor, and because Marco's was the best kitchen in London, whatever secrets you brought back with you probably weren't worth it.

I did *stages* at a few places, including Le Gavroche, La Tante Claire and Chez Nico. I was particularly interested in the famous kitchens that Marco had come up through. He told me all these stories about those kitchens, how fucking hard they were, and I wanted to see for myself. Turned out, he wasn't exaggerating.

La Tante Claire was hard. And weird. Pierre Koffmann, who was Marco's first mentor, was the main guy there. He'd stand at this butcher block at the head of the kitchen and do the butchery while watching over the rest of the kitchen.

He didn't like any music or chitchat in the kitchen, so it was just dead silent; no sound except Koffmann getting stuck into a side of beef with his knives. If you ever had to ask a question then everyone in the room could hear and all heads would turn to you. So if I wanted to check something with the other chefs I'd sort of mutter it in case Pierre overheard and came for me.

It was a tough environment.

Nico Ladenis – an autodidact genius chef, the only self-taught chef to ever win three stars – was just as intense, but in a very different way. It was more like being targeted by a sniper. If you messed up somehow, he'd just sort of sense it and you'd look up to find him staring at you – this very intense, super-focused, uneasy energy. It was a very unnerving kitchen to work in.

Every three-star place had a version of that. Marco's had a sort of fear and the sheer intimidation he could turn on you; he could up the adrenaline levels in the room by raising his voice. But after a while I started to miss that.

Marco's was always a relief to come back to. At least you knew the crew: you knew everybody and you knew who was trying to stitch you up. In that way it was home for me. A family.

To work in the other three-star kitchens was shocking because you knew that there was nowhere to hide and no one you could confide in. It really challenged you. But it also opened my eyes to the fact that I didn't want to work in any of those other kitchens. Or any three-star kitchens. In fact, through my experiences across the board at those places I began to realise that my ambition of one day having my own three-star kitchen had faded.

Like most guys who worked with Marco, I used to fantasise that one day I was going to open my own restaurant; that I'd be the youngest chef to ever hold three stars.

But then once I actually worked in a few three-stars, I realised that wasn't what I wanted to do. Marco was passionate and driven in his pursuits, and so was I, but he was at the nose of the fish, and I was down in the guts seeing the carnage and the wastage that's the fallout from a restaurant like that. When I got some perspective, when I could get out of the tribalism of my own kitchen and all my mates, a lot of the stuff that happened in three-stars didn't really make sense to me.

Say you've got lobster on an à la carte menu: you might prep a dozen lobsters and sell six. The rest are going in the staff food or the bin. I get that the customer is paying for perfection and must have the best lobster, something that was swimming around pretty much right up until it's on the plate, but it's still maddening. When they're not sold you're throwing away a perfectly good lobster that will still be edible for another four days. The waste we churned through was fucking crazy.

After a year or so of seeing that sort of hubris when it came to waste, my idea of what excellence was started to evolve. Sure, at a Michelin place you're seeing excellence on the plate, in the service and wine and all the rest. But when you're buying ten cases of produce and throwing half of them away because they are not precisely the aesthetic ideal you're going for, that's *not* excellent. It didn't feel excellent to waste all that food. Little by little, I started to feel a bit jaded with the whole Michelin ideal. I'm glad to say I know of three-star restaurants today that are the complete opposite, but back in the day it's just how it was.

At the same time, the rest of my life wasn't going so well. My relationship with my girlfriend, Lucy, was a bit shit. It had already been a bit rocky in Chester before I moved to London, and six months of hoo-ha and carry on with the drugs and the booze hadn't helped. It wasn't the most functional relationship at this point, and communication was poor. We didn't really share our inner lives with each other as much as we might have. She didn't, for example, know I was a heroin addict.

Although I had a serious habit, I could keep it from my loved ones pretty easily. My arms were free of track marks, because I rarely shot into them. There are plenty of veins elsewhere in the body – miles of them. There are bigger veins behind your knees, toes, in your knob; what I'm saying is, you've got options.

It might sound like more self-delusion or some kind of daft, misguided fucking pride – which it most assuredly is not – but I was very good at being a junkie. Even if I didn't think of myself as one.

You get to a point of dependency on junk where it changes your entire mindset, so although I was aware that I had a dependence on heroin, I never really thought of myself as an addict. As a junkie, you learn to rationalise almost anything – we are capable of incredible feats of self-delusion.

As far as addicts go, I was very high-functioning. I could dial my level of fix up or down depending on the situation and how tuned-in to reality I needed to be. Through a combination of instinct and experience I could tell how much I needed in the morning to fire me up, and exactly how much to take so I'd be able to sleep at night and still open my eyes in the morning.

Once in a while I'd come across a batch that was really cut-up piss-poor quality, or unusually pure, and the maths would be off. There were a couple of days when I'd go into the restaurant toilets to shoot up and realise that I'd overdone it. I'd be crouched over in the toilets feeling like I'd gone over the edge a bit and that maybe this was it, until I pulled it together, vomited, then went back to service.

You're on a path where junk is the baseline and lets you operate. Without it you can't get up in the morning, brush your teeth, hold a conversation with someone. You certainly can't go to work and hold down a section for eighteen hours.

But I couldn't hold down the habit, the intensity of the Michelin restaurant *and* the failing relationship, so something had to give. Towards the end of 1995 I decided I needed a bit of a break from London. Bob and I had been idly talking about packing it in and going for a working holiday in Australia. I didn't know that much about it, but it looked pretty nice on the brochures, *Home and Away* and *Neighbours*. We decided we were going to do it, so we went down to Australia House to apply for visas.

'You're lucky boys,' the woman at the desk said as she stamped our passports. 'These are the last two visas for the year.'

So Bob and I were pretty happy. Lucy, not so much. I went home to tell her that I was moving across the world for a year and she didn't take it too well. Smashed our coffee table, glass everywhere, broken plates flying about; it was a bit of a scene.

At least she took it better than Marco. I was dreading having to tell him. If there was one thing Marco hated, it was anyone leaving, especially if he liked you. If you'd been there for any amount of time, if he'd invested in pulling you up to his level of cooking, then he expected eternal loyalty. I get it; I took a spot that thousands of other ambitious chefs would have killed for, but still, I didn't really expect the backlash that occurred.

I remember telling him in the office that I wanted to leave and go to Australia for a year, and he spun right off the handle. He was really very angry, even for Marco. In those days there were no HR processes or exit interviews or handover periods. You just told Marco you were leaving and he stood up and roared at you for a while then told you to fuck off, and you left immediately. So that was the end of that. It was a bit heart-breaking, to be honest, but I couldn't expect anything else.

Those twelve months of my life were probably the most intense I'll ever experience. I was dependent on heroin, yes, but it was also a crossroads in my career. Truthfully, I didn't know what I'd do after working for Marco. He was an incredible mentor. His kitchen was the first time in my career that I wasn't discriminated against for my accent or my age or my rough edges.

He was generous, humble, loyal, kind; these may not be the first things people think or say about Marco, but behind the brash public persona, they are his defining traits.

There was no better place for a young chef to be in the 90s than on his team. You just need to look at the guys who came up through Marco's kitchens: Michael Lambie, Donovan Cooke, Stephen Terry, Shannon Bennett, Curtis Stone, Gordon Ramsay, Spencer Patrick, Charlie Rushton. Marco was infinitely generous throughout his career with chefs he trained and continued that generosity long after they had left him, so to leave his fold was really one of the most difficult choices I'd ever made.

At the same time, it wasn't sustainable. The list of super-star chefs forged in such kitchens is long, but there's an even longer list of casualties: people who burned out and never set foot in a kitchen again. In some ways kitchens such as Marco's were last-of-their-kind, dinosaurian kitchens run on aggression, and there are many who carry lasting psycho-logical issues from such environments. I've been one of the lucky ones.

The whole experience was a double-edged sword really. To me, to be part of that team, that kitchen at its peak, was a fucking honour. It was really important that despite all the turmoil in the rest of my life I was able to still function and operate at the top of my game as a chef. I owe that to Marco.

Luckily for me – or perhaps not, as it turned out – during that year I learned to operate at a very high fucking level while on drugs. Whether I was drinking, or using gear, or pills or dope, whatever: no matter how fucked I was, I could still operate at a level where I could hold down a section at a three-star restaurant. Nothing I did again would ever be as hard as that.

What Marco taught me changed me forever. It reinforced an unshakable need to hold myself to a certain standard. This is the level you can cook at. It doesn't matter if you're making a sandwich or cooking à la carte or breaking down the rules of cooking: if you've set yourself a standard you never fucking let it go. You never drop your standard, no matter what happens. And my standard was the best kitchen and best chef in the country.

CHAPTER TWELVE

The problem was, now I'd been let go I was unemployed and still had rent to pay. The winter of 1995 was a bitter one, and I didn't fancy living on the streets. I didn't have a huge amount of money. To get the visa to Australia I'd had to prove I had a return ticket, so I'd spent all my cash on the return airfare. But until we left I needed to live somewhere, buy gear and so on, so I had to find some work to fill the gap between quitting Marco's and getting on the plane.

I started asking around for some casual work in the industry and got a job at Quaglino's, the legendary brasserie in St James's. It had been around for nearly a century, one of those London institutions that had stood the test of time and gone through various owners. At the time it was owned by designer/restaurateur Sir Terence Conran, so it had been fitted out as the most beautifully designed space with a grand staircase spiralling down in the middle of the dining area so all the diners could see who was coming to eat there. Back in the old days, it was very much an old-fashioned people-watching place; people would rock up in top hats and tails to eat. I got a full-time job there, working forty hours a week, which after a year in a Michelin kitchen felt like being on holiday. I was getting a full-time wage for just forty hours? It seemed laughable.

But then I discovered how much food that place served. We'd average 800 covers in a service, which was a gear-change for me, coming out of a three-star that might do only thirty covers a service. And now I was on the rotis-serie section, literally strapped in with a seatbelt so I didn't collapse, and I wasn't moving for six hours. I'd never seen anything like it in my life.

It was a bit of an attitude adjustment for me, because I was used to doing a finite number of dishes in a service, but doing them perfectly. This place was a little bit rougher around the edges. It didn't matter if your fish and chips went to the pass with a fingerprint on the plate, because you had another 300 serves of fish to get out there before the night was over.

Then someone told me there was work going with David Cavalier, who was Marco's nemesis. Back in the day there was Harveys, which was Marco's first restaurant, and there was Cavaliers. Both were the buzzy two-star restaurants that were gunning to get three, but when the Michelin inspectors came around they awarded Harveys three stars and left Cavaliers with a paltry two.

David Cavalier knew he was a very talented chef, and he doubtless envied Marco, whose whole world changed when he became a three-star chef, while David's didn't. That rivalry was still apparently simmering when I found I needed a job.

Now David was opening a new restaurant called Chapter One in South Bromley and he was looking for guys who'd cooked in Michelin star restaurants. I gave him a call and he told me to come down any time I wasn't working at Quag's and he'd give me casual shifts, cash in hand. I could work my full-time job at Quag's and moonlight at the proper fine-dining place with David.

That sounded perfect, so I took the train to South Bromley in Kent. David picked me up from the station in his sports car and I cheered up immediately. That was more my speed, literally.

David turned out to be very much my kind of chef: highly perfectionist; hugely creative. The food was very different from Marco's, so I was learning quite a lot. The chefs were a real motley crowd – all these dropouts from really good restaurants, all with very different styles, so together we were cooking some pretty amazing food.

The restaurant was owned by an Italian family who we didn't really know much about. But we did know that, apart from the restaurant, they'd splashed on staff accommodation, buying a house in a really posh little pocket of South Bromley.

I'd stay overnight at the staff house if I had two shifts in a row and just hang out with the lads from the restaurant. One of the boys had a car, so we'd finish work, do a shop at Sainsbury's, then back to the staff accommodation where we'd heat up frozen pizzas, smoke some pot and tan a couple of cases of beer. That was our little ritual – pizza, pot, beer. The beers would alternate between San Miguel and Red Stripe, and we used the different-coloured cans to build a decorative wall of beer cans on one side of the living room. It was a gross, messy lads' house.

We were up late every night. We were all highly ambitious and it was one of those kitchens where everybody was really trying to make it the best we possibly could. Part of that was trying to find my feet again after having fallen out with Marco, so I was really striving to do good work.

But that meant we came home at two in the morning absolutely fired up from service. We were doing all the beers, all the drugs, screeching up the driveway in the middle of the night honking the horn and yelling. There were a couple of Polish guys, an English guy, an Irish guy, and me with a skinful of booze and my Glasgow accent fully fired up. All these accents, and we're in this super-posh miniature English ethno-state.

By now it was early 1996, and at that time there was all sorts of IRA shit going on in London. A terrorist bomb had recently gone off on a double-decker bus, with eight casualties. So London was on a knife-edge of tension, and we were rowdy lads who weren't really thinking about it.

One of us, the English bloke, had brought an air rifle and a few 9 mm pellet pistols from home. The pellets were harmless, but the pistols and air gun looked just like real firearms.

The wall of beer cans had got too tall to safely continue its construction, so one night we started putting the empty cans and bottles out on the front lawn and shooting at them with the air rifle from the window. So now on top of all the ruckus and yelling and music playing full blast in the middle of the night, we had an Irish guy yelling out the window and shooting bottles. You can imagine that in a posh fucking cul-de-sac the neighbours didn't appreciate that too much.

We were watching the video of *In the Name of the Father*, that harrowing movie about the Irish political prisoners known as the Guildford Four, when the power went out. We'd run out of 50 pences to feed the meter. Now it was dark and freezing, so we all went to bed. The place was a mess. Broken glass everywhere, weed and Charlie all over the table, plus my works. I was so smashed that I couldn't even get up off the sofa to go to bed, so I just passed out where I was.

I woke up to banging on the door. The front door opened onto a small porch, behind a wall of frosted glass, where you could hang up your coat before coming inside. I sat up, still all messed-up, and it took me a second to realise what was going on.

The noise that had woken me was someone kicking in the front door. I could see the silhouettes of two men through the frosted glass. It was the middle of the night, the power was out and these strangers had kicked in the door: I thought we were getting burgled.

I jumped up and barrelled towards them. My plan was to kick through the frosted glass door and start swinging. But as I got within a metre of the door it exploded inward, and all of a sudden there was broken glass raining down on me, and flashlights going everywhere, and this guy had an assault rifle pointed at me and he was screaming, 'Don't fucking move! Hands in the air! Now!'

There were fifteen cops in full tactical gear with assault rifles all pointed at me. They got me up against the wall, and one of them had his gun pointing right at my face, with the flashlight right in my eyes, screaming at me to tell him what I'm hiding under my coat.

'What's in your jacket? What the fuck have you got in your jacket?'

I was shitting myself, no idea what he was on about, and I looked down. I'd fallen asleep on the couch wearing a fleece jacket, a really cheap one with a stiff zip which had caught and was making this weird bulge down near my belt, sort of like you'd have if you were hiding a gun there.

I went to unzip my jacket and show him I didn't have a gun hidden there, and the guy with the assault rifle just smacked me one – bam! – and told me not to move.

I froze. Meanwhile everything around me was just ruckus. Cops were swarming all over the house, coming in every door, spilling down the stairs. They started dragging all my mates out from where they were sleeping upstairs and off into the night. The two Polish guys were in their boxer shorts, nothing else, and I saw them getting dragged out by these burly coppers. The cops were screaming, I could hear helicopters outside hovering over the cul-de-sac. It was full on.

Once everyone was taken away, they got me off the wall, put my hands behind my back and put the zip ties on me. The cop with the gun in my face had calmed down a little bit and he said: 'Where's the explosives? Where are all the guns?'

'What are you talking about?' I asked, very confused. I was still high from the night before and I thought the cops were here about the drugs. 'This is all a bit much isn't it? It's just a bit of drugs.'

'We're not here for the fucking drugs, son,' one of the coppers, a Scottish guy, growled, and then I got turned around and dragged outside with a copper on each arm.

Outside there were police everywhere: attack dogs, squad cars, flashing lights, a helicopter overhead with a search-light, snipers on my roof with their rifles trained on me.

I got slammed against the garage door and held there while a meat van reversed up the driveway so they could throw me into the back.

Then I was alone in the van and all I could think of was the scene from *In the Name of the Father* when Daniel Day-Lewis gets wrongly imprisoned for-fucking-ever and all I'd heard from the coppers was talk of guns and explosives . . . and the penny was starting to drop.

After a while, a plainclothes cop climbed into the back of the van and asked me my name.

'Jock,' I said.

'Fuck off. Your name's not Jock.'

'Oh yeah,' I said, 'my name's Barry. Barry Zonfrillo.'

'Italian?'

'Yeah.'

'Right.' The guy nodded. He asked me where I lived. I gave him my address in Shepherd's Bush, which was miles away from where we were in South Bromley. Then of course he wanted to know what I'm doing there in the middle of the night if I don't live there and I started trying to explain myself.

'So where are the guns?' the cop kept asking, and I kept telling him that I didn't know anything about guns.

'Mate, what are you talking about? Fucking guns?' I protested. 'I'm a chef!'

The cop nods again, and repeats my story back to me.

'So, you're an Italian chef, but you're actually Scottish, and you live in Shepherd's Bush and work at Quaglino's, but for some reason you sleep in South Bromley. Am I getting all that right?'

He kept probing, asking me who my Irish mate was, what the story was with the Polish guys, and it was one of those situations where everything I said made me sound guilty of something, so I realised I was going to have to come clean.

'Look, I am a cook. I'm full-time at Quaglino's and when I'm not there, I come here to work cash in hand.'

The cop nodded, then went back to asking me where the guns are.

'We're not here on spec, mate,' he said. 'We know about the guns.'

'What are you talking about?' I started arguing, and then it dawned on me that he was talking about the air rifle and pistols.

So I explained about them, which they would have found anyway because they'd raided the house, and beyond that I shut up. The other guys would have done the same, I thought, but who knew, because we were all in five different vans in this cul-de-sac. Then we were driven to five different police stations all across London where we were interviewed separately.

I was taken and processed, which included a strip search. They told me to bend over, spread my arse cheeks and cough, and I was like, 'What the fuck are you hoping to find in there?'

After hours of interviews they suddenly just let us go with no explanation. 'What was that all about?' I asked one of the coppers.

'One of your neighbours complained that they thought there were terrorists living in the house.'

He went on to explain that any reports of terrorist activity got taken seriously because of all the recent IRA activity. So when a report was made a couple of times from different people in the neighbourhood, the whole tactical exercise got set up. They'd spent hundreds of thousands of pounds to do this swoop on what they thought was an IRA safe house.

I couldn't stop laughing when I heard that. The cop didn't like that.

'Mate, it's not funny. It's pretty serious.'

Anyway, it was this full-on counterterrorism operation over a bunch of lads making a nuisance of themselves in the middle of the night, and by the time we got it sorted out it was nearly midday and I was starting to fret, because we should have been in the kitchen by now. We had the coppers who were driving us home drop us off at Chapter One, but by then David Cavalier had already cancelled lunch. The local paper came out straight afterwards with a front page story on 'The South Bromley Five' who had been wrongly accused of terrorism, with a photo of all five of us outside the restaurant. It was the first time I'd been in the newspaper since winning a cooking competition as a young lad.

It was hilarious – in retrospect. At the time David did not find it very funny at all. He was livid. We told him the whole story, and that only made him angrier. He told us it was our own fault for acting up in a posh neighbourhood and that we only had ourselves to blame.

So we went into the kitchen to get started on the dinner prep. The last time we'd seen each other we were being frogmarched out of the house in zip ties in the middle of the night, so we had a lot to discuss. We had a bit of a laugh, did prep, did service, then sent one of the guys to get pizza and beers and we went back to the house.

The place was trashed. The door was hanging off its hinges, all the furniture was smashed. We fixed it up as best we could, taped some cardboard up over the door to keep the wind out, and went to bed. It had been a rough day. We'd all been woken abruptly, interrogated for hours on end by cops as suspected terrorists, and then worked a full dinner service.

The next day we went to work then came home to find we'd been burgled. If you can call it that – a burglar comes in through the window, I guess, but these guys just took the cardboard down and walked right in. They'd taken some valuables, some drugs, just petty theft, but we called the cops to report it. We had to call twice before they would believe us. When the cop came to take our report, it was one of the cops who'd been there the night before for the raid, and he thought we were stitching him up.

So, anyway, all signs pointed to it being a good time for me to get out of Dodge. I saved up as much cash as I could for those two months, then thanked David for taking me on, the lads for not grassing me up as a terrorist and my parents for understanding that I wouldn't see them for a year while I went off and saw the world. Then I took a cab with Bob to the airport.

I watched from the window of the plane as we climbed through the dreary, grey cloud that loomed over London all through winter, until the plane burst through the clouds into a brilliant blue sky. Such a beautiful sight. I stared out that window fairly vibrating with excitement until the drinks trolley came around, which was also a beautiful sight.

What awaited me in Australia I had no clue. I didn't really know anything about the place beyond a glance at a postcard, but I was nineteen years old, had my best mate by my side, a cold drink in my hand and was on my way to literally the other side of the planet on an adventure. Whatever that involved, I was sure I could handle it. What could go wrong?

CHAPTER THIRTEEN

Bob and I were in fairly shabby repair as we split up into different queues to go through Customs in Sydney. Poor Bob was still recovering from the bends after an ill-advised scuba dive which had left him curled up on the bottom of the boat vomiting, and bleeding from the ears.

Stopping off in Bali for a few days' holiday, we'd blagged our way onto a dive by telling the operators we were scallop divers and that *of course* we were trained and understood the risks and knew about the dangers, like how surfacing too fast gave you compression sickness, or what to do if a shark came over to check you out.

Every diver I spoke to in the aftermath was gobsmacked, and told me frankly we were lucky to be alive. Not only had I survived unscathed, but I'd had a great time, and taken away a lifelong love of diving.

I had, however, also taken away from our Bali sojourn the worst sunburn I'd ever had, compliments of going surfing with a 'London tan' and no sunscreen. It had only worsened on the flight, and by touchdown in Sydney my face was covered in nasty oozing blisters. The severe burning on the backs of my knees meant I could hardly walk. On top of that there was a touch of jet lag, and on top of *that* the first signs of junk-sickness were niggling away at me. Little pangs of nausea were starting to roll over me, and my nose was running so badly I had to keep wiping it with the back of my hand.

The woman at the customs desk had a good look at me, then very gingerly took my passport and flipped through to find my working visa. She asked me where I was staying.

'Not sure, yet.' This was around 10 pm.

'I need the address of where you'll be staying.'

'It's fine: we'll get a hotel or something.'

'Hasn't your work organised accommodation?'

'Haven't got a job yet, but I'm going to work for Stephanie Alexander. I used to work for Marco Pierre White.'

'So you don't have a job,' the customs officer said now, very slowly, 'but now you're going to go find Stephanie Alexander who's going to give you a job?'

'Yeah, you got it.'

'How are you planning to get there?'

'I'll take a taxi.'

That made her blink. 'Sir, I don't think you can afford a taxi from here to Stephanie Alexander's restaurant. It's in Melbourne.'

'I'm pretty sure I can afford a taxi,' I scoffed. I'd never actually looked at a map of Australia that closely, so didn't understand the geographical reality of the vast distances involved. I was from the UK, where for the most part you can get from your home to the next major city on a pushbike.

'Sir, Melbourne is nearly 1000 kilometres away, you're not going to be able to get there tonight, you'll definitely need to find a place to stay in Sydney.'

'Right,' I said. Time for a change of plan. I remembered Bob mentioning a place called Kings Cross, which was where all the backpacker hostels were located, so I took a stab at it, surmising there would be a 'Kings Cross Hotel' there somewhere and told her she could find me there. She wasn't convinced, but stamped us through, and our Australian adventure began.

We took a taxi to Kings Cross, got a room in a hostel dorm lined with bunks, dumped our backpacks on some spare bunks, and went out for beer.

Much later, we came back pretty sauced, and found some other traveller asleep in Bob's bunk. He'd thrown Bob's backpack on the ground, and all his worldly goods were now scattered across the floor.

We were pretty pissed off by this, and shook the guy awake, who instantly jumped up ready to fight. It became apparent that this guy was very drunk, very angry and very Scottish. As you'd expect, a brawl ensued, the three of us absolutely going to town in this little dormitory, and Bob and I got thrown out.

It was three in the morning now, we were drunk and had taken a few good knocks from our Scottish friend, and had to find another place to stay. We ended up getting a room in a gnarly Kings Cross hotel that was clearly meant for sex workers and their clients. Like, sticky carpet, blue lights in the toilets so it's hard to shoot up; the whole thing.

Heroin was absolutely everywhere in Kings Cross. Completely out in the open. It was like a farmers' market for bad Cambodian brown. You could walk up to one of a hundred people on the street and score. So that was convenient.

In the morning we took stock. Clearly we'd not thought through the Stephanie Alexander thing because we'd landed in the wrong city, and now that the plan was held up to scrutiny obviously it wasn't going to happen.

On the other hand, Sydney was gorgeous. There was the Harbour Bridge, all these amazing beaches, everyone was really tanned and fit, the weather was just violently pleasant. The food situation looked hopeful too, at first glance. The cities I'd lived in weren't exactly drowning in top-notch Asian restaurants, so it was really exciting to walk down the road and see the blinking signs for this amazing diversity of cuisines.

I was absolutely blown away by the quality of Asian food here: Vietnamese, Thai, regional Chinese cuisine. In Scotland or even in London, you weren't exactly spoiled for choice and now I could wander around and find specialists in Sichuan and Yunnan cuisine, food I'd never dreamed existed. It was a whole new world for me.

The cafe scene didn't hurt either. I was pleasantly shocked to find that Sydney had fabulous coffee, and that pretty much every cafe knew how to poach an egg perfectly. And this obsession with avocado and toast, as pilloried as it is now, was and still is a fucking delicious meal. Smashed avo on sourdough, a bit of chilli, lime and a poached egg on top. Maybe a little bacon on the side? I'm a happy man.

Combine that with the relaxed, outdoorsy attitude of Australian cafes. You'd walk in and the waiter would take your order and wouldn't write it down, just wander off and fetch it. Half the time they'd forget and come back to ask you again. By rights, that should have set off my more OCD tendencies, but I loved it. It was a licence to be a bit more loose and free and easy within hospitality. I could walk into any halfway decent cafe and relax over a perfect breakfast with real espresso instead of a sad mug of builder's tea. That was miles ahead of the UK, so Bob and I talked it over, and decided to make a go of it in Sydney.

The first thing we did after locating an inexpensive place to rent in Kensington, about 6 kilometres south-east of the CBD, was to find jobs. The *Michelin Guide* doesn't cover Australia, so in its stead the arbiter of good taste is the *Good Food Guide*, a travel/foodie guide covering all the capital cities, which awards restaurants up to three 'hats' instead of stars. Different symbol, same idea: a three-hat place is the best the country has to offer. So we got our hands on a Sydney guide and looked at our options.

At that time, there were only a handful of three-hat places in Sydney: Rockpool, Claude's, Tetsuya's and Restaurant Forty One. I rang around the first three and each time they told me they didn't take travellers. That was it; the whole policy: they didn't hire anyone who wasn't going to be there for the long haul. So that was a bit of a spanner in the works.

Because Bob hadn't just come from the Michelin tradition, he wasn't hung up on working in a prestige place, so signed up to a temp agency, which farmed out chefs to ordinary restaurants that needed temps. So I got on their books, too, and they sent me to a restaurant somewhere on Sydney's upmarket North Shore.

What that restaurant asked me to do was challenging to me on an emotional level.

Before I came to Australia, I had this vision of what the food culture would be here. I imagined this vast cornucopia of exotic fruits and vegetables, the meat of weird animals and ancient culinary traditions, maybe with a bit of a fusion spin to reflect the cultural melting pot the tourist brochures were always banging on about.

There was none of that. There were pies, lots of pies, and these chain restaurants where you could go in and get a big oval plate that was half spaghetti and half schnitzel. I remember looking down at this plate with dismay, just baffled by what I was seeing: 'What's going on here?'

Even in the UK – which back then was derided around the world for its boring cuisine – you could get a decent pub meal. Maybe some nice crisp bangers with an onion gravy or a hot pot; even a pea and ham soup with a roll would have some dignity.

Now I was being asked to serve salt and pepper calamari. With sweet chilli sauce. What. The. Fuck? I couldn't get my head around it.

My first service was just this endless gauntlet of salt and pepper calamari. Two hundred covers came in, and every one of them salt and pepper calamari. It came frozen in a plastic bag, you tipped it straight in the deep fryer, piled it on a plate with a sad little side salad and dribbled some bottled dressing over it.

After coming out of three-star kitchens, I was appalled. It's not that it was inedible, or that it was beneath me, but I was used to this really intricate, amazing food that was at once technically brilliant and deeply loved by the chefs cooking it. What they were asking me to cook wasn't that: it was a hate crime.

I called the agency and told them I just couldn't do it, that I needed to be in a proper restaurant.

'This is just a trial period,' they said. 'Once we see you can do it, we'll move you somewhere else.'

'I understand that, but I would rather not cook at all than do this.'

A couple of days later, they rang back, very excited, 'We're going to send you to the Opera House!'

'Awesome,' I said. 'Brilliant.' I'd heard that there was a really good restaurant at the Opera House, so I was pumped. The paperwork they sent over said I'd be employed in the Green Room. The green room, of course, is the room where they park the talent – the famous actors and singers and whatnot who perform – when they aren't on stage, but I didn't know that. I was still a good decade from being allowed anywhere near a television studio, so I looked at the paperwork and thought, 'Green Room: that sounds like a properly fancy restaurant. Fabulous.'

I got on the train to Circular Quay, copped that million dollar view of the harbour from the train as it came out of the tunnel – nothing quite so spectacular in all of Sydney as seeing that for the first time – jogged down the water-front and barrelled into the Opera House, like: 'I've arrived, where do I go?'

I was taken to this proper kitchen: huge, well-equipped, and I'm thinking, 'Awesome!'

The head chef was as tough as nails, and she was all over everything: very loud, very aggressive, very efficient. Cool: I liked everything about that; it felt as if there was a grown-up in charge.

But I quickly realised I'd ended up in what was effectively the staff restaurant that served the back-of-house. It wasn't for any of the posh public restaurants and didn't serve the public at all.

Chef gave me the prep list. The first item on it just said, 'goat curry, 80 kilograms'. I thought surely that was a typo, what would anyone do with 80 kilos of goat curry? So I double-checked.

'Yep,' she said, 'here's the recipe, just go ahead and get started.'

I knew how to follow a recipe, obviously; I could handle a curry, so I took it and started getting my station prepped.

Then I looked more closely around the kitchen, with escalating anxiety at the general level of cleanliness. The further I got into prep, the more I kept noticing: smears on the benches, grime around taps, cobwebs in the corner, dirty light switches.

There was a huge double-wide bratt pan on the stove for the curry, and once I finally had all the meat and vegetables diced and ready to go I opened the lid, and recoiled in horror: it hadn't been properly cleaned after the last use.

I put the lid down, then went to the head chef and told her, 'All the prep for the curry is done, it just needs to go in the cooker, but I need to go. Sorry, I need to get out of here. I can't cook in a kitchen that's not clean, at the very minimum.' She was furious, chewed my head off, was still yelling as I went out the door and the lift doors closed on me.

I was in a bit of a mood now and must have looked downcast on the lift ride down to the street and certain unemployment, when a cleaner got in.

'Hey mate,' he goes, 'are you new here? Haven't seen you round before.'

'I was a new cook, but I'm leaving today. I just quit.'

'What's the matter?'

'The kitchen's pretty gross.'

'Did you see a rat or something?'

'No, just really gross.'

He laughed. 'You want to see something *really* gross?'

The cleaner took me down to the lowest level, to a trapdoor to a sub-basement. He opened it, and it was just blackness down there, so he took a torch and shone it down into the hole, and I just gasped, 'Oh my fucking god!'

Down in the basement were rats. Hundreds and hundreds of these gigantic – Madonna's-dog-sized – rats, just thrashing about in a few inches of water. They were screaming and scrabbling and jumping all over the place. I could not believe what I was looking at. It was a massive, seething, living septic pit of absolute grossness.

'This whole building is on reclaimed land,' the cleaner told me. 'It was sacred land before that, a really important Indigenous place, and look what we've done here.' He explained how the Opera House, Sydney's pièce de résistance, had been built on Tubowgule, a tidal island once reached by walking across shell middens. It had been an important gathering place for the Gadigal people of the Eora Nation for thousands of years before it became the site of the shining landmark.

He closed the trapdoor, and I scarpered, away from the Opera House and – to my mind – out of Australia. I went home to Bob in a real state and told him I was ready to go home. I was here for my career, so if no fine-dining places would take me because I was a traveller, I couldn't stay in Sydney, cooking goat curry while life passed me by.

Bob was more relaxed. He was pretty happy to bounce around cooking pub meals and going surfing.

'Calm down, mate,' he told me. 'Let's go out and get absolutely rat-arsed and think about it.' So that's what we did: went to the Kensington Hotel, had all the drinks, then came home. That's when I decided to make a call.

The one three-hat place I hadn't tried was Forty One, the French fusion place owned by Dietmar Sawyere. For some reason, Dietmar himself picked up the phone, and I went into a whole diatribe. (I was very, very pickled.)

'Hi, I'm Jock, I used to work for Marco. I can't get a job anywhere because it seems Australia thinks travellers are lepers, but I'm fucking good and I've got good experience and if you don't mind me being a traveller I'd love a job with you.'

'Okay,' said Dietmar, 'come in Monday and we'll talk.'

So I did, first thing Monday, sober now, with my jacket and knives, did a trial, got the job, and ended up staying for the whole year.

*

I was very happy at Forty One. After the horrors of temping in Australian hospitality, I cannot convey how good it felt to be working there. It was a very cool, very luxurious restaurant on level 41 of the Chifley Tower, which at the time was the tallest building in Sydney, so it had stunning views across the whole city. Dietmar was literally above every other restaurant, and in pretty much every other sense as well.

He was a Swiss dude: spoke German, French and English. Big reader, great taste, an outstanding chef. He'd worked all over the world before coming to Australia in 1988, opening Forty One in 1994, and he was one of the driving forces behind French-Asian fusion food in the 90s.

From a career perspective, working at Forty One was the first time I'd really been exposed to Asian food. All my training had been in classic French gastronomy and every restaurant I worked at was focused on some iteration of European fine dining. My exposure to food from anywhere across Asia was really limited to eating at Chinese restaurants in the UK, so Australia was a bit of a revelation.

It blew my mind the first time I opened the dry stores cupboard at Forty One: all these ingredients I'd never heard of. Bottles of sauces with Chinese, Japanese, Thai writing on them. No idea what any of them were.

It was like going back to the start of everything and learning all my fundamentals from scratch. All new techniques, all new flavours. I mean, imagine being a chef, having worked in one of the best restaurants in the world and now you're picking up a bottle of fish sauce for the first time. It was a whole new world. I hadn't been so excited about food for ages.

Life was just generally pretty exciting then, and once we had a few pay cheques in our pockets, Bob and I bought a Datsun 300B to cut around the streets of Sydney in and we were set.

Sydney is a stunning place to live, especially when you'd grown up in a city where it's a point of national pride that the weather is reliably miserable.

There was a fairly healthy party scene in Sydney. House music was huge, the clubs were great, pills were relatively affordable, and we had the time of our lives. Bob had an urge to travel, so after a few months working around Sydney and getting some cash together, he took off to see the country. I stayed at Forty One. That was where my career was focused. I was learning all these incredible new techniques and flavours and how to use them with what was already in my arsenal.

Oysters were served with a Vietnamese dipping sauce, and the antipasto plate came with a sushi roll made with couscous. This was long before Ottolenghi reached Australia, so couscous alone seemed staggeringly exotic to me. There were curry sauces inspired by Indonesia, Thai salads and preserves alongside the finest French-style braised lamb I'd ever seen. I was eager to learn everything I could from Dietmar.

I'd also met someone. Kelly was working part-time as a waitress at Forty One while she was at uni. We got talking at work, hit it off and things got pretty serious pretty quickly. We were very into each other, had a lot in common, in that we both loved good food and a stiff drink, and we knew we didn't have time to waste. My visa for Australia was only for a year, so at the back of our minds, we knew there was a clock on it.

One night, six months into the relationship, we'd booked a room at the Hyde Park Hotel where I planned to drop some acid and a pill and ask Kelly to marry me. I went and picked out an engagement ring beforehand – a sapphire surrounded by a ring of diamonds, which was the best I could afford at the time – and once the drugs kicked in I got down on one knee and asked her to marry me. She said yes. We were still teenagers.

The months zipped by, till suddenly we were nearing the end of my one-year working visa. The 457 visa Bob and I were on was notoriously hard to extend. Bob had returned to Sydney with a tan and hundreds of war stories about his travels, and was ready to go back to the UK. I was not, and Dietmar was trying to wrestle a bridging visa for me so I could stay on, but without success.

I'd have to return to the UK so I asked Kelly to come back with me, which would mean giving up her studies and her whole life in Sydney. No small thing to ask of her.

Obviously, I had to do the right thing and ask her father for his blessing to marry Kelly and take her overseas. The problem was that her dad, Steve, was in jail. Back in the day he'd been a drug trafficker in Sydney. The story goes that he'd been trying to get out of the business, and was doing one last huge drug deal when the cops got him. It turned out his partner had been wearing a wire for twelve months, so the police had the whole thing under surveillance.

The partner went into witness protection, and Kelly's dad went to prison.

He was in a maximum-security prison up in Brisbane, so we travelled up there to meet him. It was the first time I'd be meeting him, and I was going to be giving him the news I was marrying his daughter and taking her overseas.

Getting in to see Steve was full on. First we met up with Cheryl, a former member of his crew, and she sort of vetted me before we went to the prison. We passed through multiple scanners, gates and steel doors until finally we were led into an open space with a square of grass and barbecues, bizarrely like an idyllic little outdoor picnic area in the middle of this maximum security prison.

Then I saw a guy waving to us across the yard. He was wearing Levis, a white T-shirt and a pair of sunnies, all this floppy hair and a big smile. He looked like he could have been one of the lads.

For some reason I thought Steve would be weather-beaten and ground down by spending so much time in prison. In my head, I had this image of an old jailbird: maybe a bit angry, maybe a bit withdrawn. This guy just looked like a cool dude without a care in the world.

He gave me a firm handshake and looked me right in the eye. He was perfectly polite, but there was something about him that was just utterly intimidating. I started bricking it, turned to Kelly and whispered to her not to tell him anything until I'd had a chance to break the ice.

We sat down on one of the park benches. Cheryl had brought a picnic lunch, so we sat in the sun unpacking cold meat and cheeses and oysters.

There we were, enjoying fucking oysters *naturale* in a maximum security prison. I mean, clearly Steve knew some people and had managed to work himself out some creature comforts within the prison, but this was just taking the piss.

While I'm pulling oysters out of the bag and setting them up, Kelly starts with, 'Dad, I've got something to tell you.'

And I gave her a look, because this was not going to plan, and I thought it was important that I be the one to ask him, so then she clammed up and went for a walk around the park with Cheryl, leaving me and Steve alone. I was shitting myself, but I pulled it together and began the speech I'd carefully prepared.

'Listen, I know I've only just met you, but I wanted –'

'I know,' he cut me off, 'I noticed the ring on her finger.'

'Yeah, well,' I stumbled a little, the wind very much taken out of my sails, 'I asked her to marry me, and she said yes, and I wanted to ask your permission. We want to go to the UK because my visa runs out soon.'

'As long as you look after each other,' he said, 'I don't care what you do. Just look after each other. But if you fuck her over, I'm going to come down on you like a ton of bricks.' I took the warning seriously, because . . . a dad who's the former head of a crime syndicate? You're going to listen.

Vague death threat aside, all in all, he was really cool about it. He and I weirdly hit it off, just became really close friends pretty quickly. I visited him a couple more times in prison but then we were off to the UK.

Bob, Kelly and I got on a flight back to the UK. Bob went back up to Chester; we tried to make a go of it in London. I started calling up guys I used to work with and asking them who the hot chef was in London these days, and everyone gave me the same name: Gordon Ramsay.

CHAPTER FOURTEEN

ordon was an old protégé of Marco's. Like all of us, he'd come in full of piss and vinegar and Marco had taken that raw talent and aggression and turned it into something he could use – Marco had famously made him break down and cry in the corner during a dinner service – and he had opened his own two Michelin star place, the Aubergine. He gave me a job there and I was to start work in four weeks, but that still meant I wouldn't be bringing any money in for a whole month, and we had next to nothing to survive on until then.

We took a room in a cheap hotel while we looked for proper accommodation. Eventually we found a two-bedroom flat in Kilburn that the landlord told us had been recently vacated by his family. He wanted a month's rent, £1120, plus another £1120 bond in advance. We had very little money, but it was a great apartment so we gave him the full amount and signed a lease.

We were a bit concerned to find there was still a lot of stuff in the flat, clearly the belongings of the previous tenant, but the landlord assured us it was stuff his family was storing there and he'd get it out the next day.

So in we moved with our suitcases. The next day came, and the landlord didn't come to move the shit out. A couple more days passed, in which I was busy at work and Kelly was out looking for a job, until Saturday arrived, when I had the morning off and finally had time to look around.

Checking through the cupboards, I started to realise that something wasn't right. They were full of clothes and personal possessions, paperwork, correspondence: it looked very much like someone else was actually living there. I started to realise we'd been scammed, and this guy had given us the keys to some random family home. So I rang him.

'Mate,' I said, 'we want a refund: this looks as if it probably isn't your house to rent out.'

He just laughed at me: this bellowing laughter down the phone line. I hung up and realised we had to get the fuck out of there before the real owners showed up, so yelled out to Kelly to pack her bag. She was hysterical. It was her first time out of Australia and this was a fairly rough entry to London life.

We walked out of the flat and dragged our suitcases up the road to the landlord's office.

As we reached it I saw him pulling up in his car, a beautiful Mercedes C class convertible. He jumped out and went into the office and up the stairs.

I left Kelly outside with the bags and ran up after him. I could see him up ahead, this big unit lumbering up the stairs, and I called out his name. He ignored me. Then I got to the reception desk. I told the receptionist I was there to see the landlord and smiled politely.

'Sorry, he's not in at the moment,' she said.

'I just saw him go in!' I barked, then bypassed her completely and barrelled straight into his office. He was in there, sitting behind his desk, just kicking back, dead calm.

'Mate, I need that money back,' I told him. 'Money's really tight and it's all I've got right now.'

'I don't know what you're talking about,' he smirked at me. 'I've never seen you before in my life.' Then he leaned back in his chair and let out that bellowing laugh again, and I realised that I'd really been shafted. I'd paid him cash, had left the lease with him, and I had no proof that I could take to a court. There was really nothing I could do.

I left, knowing that I'd been fucked over, and furious – I'd never been so angry or felt so helpless. I emptied my pockets and found ten pounds cash and that was all the money I had left in the world.

With that realisation, the rage started to fade and I began to feel utterly at a loss. What the fuck was I going to do? I'd convinced Kelly to give up her life in Australia and fly to London with me, and the first thing I'd done was get ripped off. Now we had nothing but our suitcases and we were riding some random bus to nowhere in particular, with nowhere to go. Not a very good feeling, not at all.

Eventually we found a phone box and I rang my parents. I related the story to Mum and asked for their help to get a place to stay that night. There was a pause at the other end then Mum said she'd have to discuss it with Dad and she'd call me back at the phone box.

I thought that was a bit rough, to be honest. They were having some kind of weird conversation about me and whether they should help me while I was just hanging out in a phone box on a random London street.

Eventually they called back, then wired some money to my bank account so we could put a deposit on another flat, but it was devastating to realise we'd already sunk ourselves in debt before we'd had a chance to get our bearings.

Kelly got a job as a waitress, and I kept working at the Aubergine.

Gordon ran a hard kitchen. That will not be a shocking revelation to many, given that he is globally famous for yelling at people in kitchens, but I had a miserable time there.

While Marco's kitchen had been psychologically intimidating – there was always the sense of danger in the air, the possibility that despite Marco's soft-spoken, posh demeanour he might arc up and really tear you to strips one of these days – Gordon's was more emotionally gruelling.

At the time, Gordon Ramsay was King Shit of London gastronomy. He'd come out of Marco's kitchen so was from that pedigreed line of outstanding chefs trained in the French tradition. He was an immensely talented chef; no question about his being able to cook. However, I was only getting face time with the people who worked for him. To be honest, I didn't think much of the food. It was fine; it was a two-star place, but to me it seemed like a watered-down version of Marco's food. Marco always said that you won three stars by playing an attacking game, and you kept them by playing a defending game. The vibe in that kitchen was very much a two-star place that desperately wanted its third, but didn't quite have everything in place to get it. Not at that time anyway.

I was also jaded by the whole three-star frenzy. My whole way of thinking about classical French food had changed since I left Marco's. My time with David Cavalier had been really inspiring, and then Dietmar and Restaurant Forty One had introduced me to all these amazing Asian ingredients and techniques. Coming back to a two-star kitchen felt like regressing.

I had grown indifferent to churning out the same French classics at some iteration of the same restaurant. I was also aware of just how wasteful that style of cooking was, and having seen a bit of the world now, I had a bit more of an understanding of how egregious it was to waste all this produce in pursuit of some arbitrary idea of perfection.

On top of all that Aubergine had that aggro, macho, bullshit vibe where people were always getting pushed and shoved and almost coming to blows.

So I didn't love it, but it was a job, and I had a debt to repay to Mum and Dad, so I put my head down and got on with it.

About six weeks later, an envelope came in the mail with Mum's handwriting on it. I thought, 'That's nice, Mum's written me a letter', so I opened it. It was a credit card statement. I called her up and asked her what was going on.

'Well, when you rang us about borrowing some money, we wanted to make sure that there was some way that we got the money back.'

Their solution was to take out a credit card in my name, which I could then pay off. At first, I was incensed by the idea that my parents didn't trust me enough to be straight with me. But I soon calmed down.

'Okay,' I said, 'fair enough, I'm a bit of a mess.' My parents weren't wealthy; this was their solution. Then I hung up and looked more closely at the statement and realised that I was in deep shit. The interest rate on that credit card was obscene. I ran the maths in my head, and realised that there was no possible way for me to pay it off. Even if I made the payments every month, I'd never get ahead of the balance, and while that was going on I wasn't getting out of Gordon's kitchen. No matter what happened, I needed the job. A month passed, two, and then one day towards the end of my third month there, right around the time I should have been moving up in the kitchen, the Canadian chef came in.

The Canadian chef was new, and a lovely bloke. The most Canadian guy you're ever going to meet; nice guy, hardworking, pleasant demeanour. He was going to be on the veg section. So the chef who'd been on that station was showing him the ropes, and it was all going fine, all through lunch service, then dinner service starts, and Gordon came and all of a sudden there was a problem with every single dish coming off the veg section.

Old mate came up to the pass with a *pommes Anna*, Gordon saw it go by and he froze.

'What the fuck is this?' he roared, picking up the dish and slamming it upside down on the pass. 'What are you doing serving this shit in my kitchen?'

The dish smashed, potato and butter going everywhere, and with it went that service to the table. *Pommes Anna* is a delicate dish, you have to make it to order: you mandolin perfect wafers of potato, layer them in butter, turn them as carefully as a sleeping baby while they cook. There's no way to rush it, you're looking at a minimum of eleven minutes to cook another one, which meant that all the dishes for that table would have to be cooked again from scratch.

So the Canadian went back to his section and started cutting more potatoes, and Gordon was right behind him, calling for his *pommes Anna*.

'It's coming!' the poor guy wailed. 'Nine minutes.'

Gordon fucking erupted: 'Nine minutes!'

The chef never finished his *pommes Anna*. He was done for the night, and in that kitchen. Gordon whisked him into the dry stores and the whole kitchen could hear him being absolutely verbally demolished by Gordon Ramsay in full flight. When it was all over, he was shown the back door, literally – his career at this Michelin star-level restaurant was over.

Business as usual. We put our heads down and worked faster and harder, because we didn't want to be next. But all through the service and the rest of the night, I couldn't get the expression on that poor guy's face out of my mind.

We were colleagues. It's not like the Canadian and I were best buddies, but I considered him a mate. But because this was Gordon's world, and because all it took was one bad reference to fuck up your resume, I didn't do anything. You just dealt with it and kept cooking. I felt guilty, and it got worse and worse as the night went on.

I went home, had a shower, put toothpaste on my brush, and just sort of stalled in front of the mirror. I couldn't look myself in the eye. The image of me doing nothing while it all went on. It was dawning on me that standing by and not intervening was nearly as bad as doing it myself. It didn't feel good.

So I got changed again, went back to Aubergine and let myself in with the 2.30 am milk delivery. I spent the rest of the night setting up my section for the day ahead, and then at seven in the morning when the executive chef came in, I quit.

'The section is all set up; everything's ready; you've got three *stages* on today; you'll be fine. But what happened last night, I can't have it.'

And that was it. I went home, feeling even worse than before, because now I had pretty much no prospects. I'd burned my bridges with Marco when I left to go to Australia, and now I'd done the same with Gordon, who was going to take it extra-personally because I was one of Marco's boys, just like him.

Sure enough, when I got home there was a message on my answering machine from Gordon. You can imagine what was on it, lots of effing this and blinding that and 'who do you think you are?' and 'you'll never work in this town again' and so on. Great start to the day.

I got into the shower and stayed in there until the water went cold, just worrying about what I was going to do. I had no prospects, had made some significant enemies, no job, bad debts. How was I going to pay rent? Or look after Kelly? How was I going to score? Already I was about due for another fix.

When I got out of the shower, the little light was blinking on the machine to tell me there was another message. It was Marco.

'I heard what happened. I'll put the kettle on, come down for a cup of tea.'

I was gobsmacked. This was the first I'd heard from him since he'd told me to fuck off and never darken his door again. So I rang him back, and then went down to meet him at the Oak Room, where he'd moved after the Hyde Park Hotel. And it was as simple as that. Marco took me in, delicately poured me a nice cup of tea with his giant mitt, and suddenly I was back in the fold, and Marco had an offer for me.

CHAPTER FIFTEEN

I found myself sitting in front of Marco after a gap of two years, in a different restaurant and a different office, but pretty much in the same desperate state as the day we'd met. I was still broke and strung-out, and he still took up half the room.

In the time since our falling-out he'd only grown in status – still the coolest chef in the world, but he was expanding into new businesses and opening restaurants all over the UK. Ever since the Hyde Park days, Marco had featured a quote from Salvador Dalí printed on his menu: 'At six I wanted to be a chef, at seven Napoleon, and my ambitions have been growing ever since.' Marco's ambitions weren't slowing down and he wanted me to be a part of his growing empire. Whatever anger he may have had for me was gone, and he wanted me to come back and work with him at the Oak Room, which was the new iteration of his flagship restaurant, although with an even more elaborate menu and a far vaster wine list.

We hadn't spoken in nearly two years, and the way we'd left things I'd never expected to hear from him again, but I still had a huge amount of respect for him so I was very touched by the offer. At the same time, I had no desire to go back into three-star Michelin-level service or the waste that involved. By this stage, Marco's brigade were making gravy by roasting thirty-six chickens a day just to press them for the jus before discarding them – simply to accompany a dish of roast chicken.

My idea of what excellence was had evolved after experiencing Dietmar's food, and David Cavalier's before that, so I wasn't sure I would be an asset to the Oak Room. I tried to explain to Marco that I didn't want to get back into the whole Michelin star thing, and much to my surprise, he listened and said he understood.

He made me another offer. He'd just bought Les Saveurs, a one-star restaurant in Mayfair. Marco and his investors snapped it up with a view to installing another chef to gun for some more stars. He wanted me to basically caretake the restaurant until the Michelin inspectors came through in January. In March, once the guide announced their awards, the star was safe for another year, and Marco's investors were mollified, they'd move in the gun chef, and I'd be moved onto something new, something I'd really enjoy.

So I took the offer and went to Les Saveurs, along with Richard Turner, the former SAS trooper who was my sous chef at Marco Pierre One and who'd once hospitalised me with one punch over a lobster salad. That was a happy reunion. A great bloke, and there's no one you'd rather have in your corner, in a kitchen or out of it.

We took over the kitchen, kept the menu exactly as it was, churned out some competent one-star food until the inspectors came through, and that was that.

I was back in the fold. It was comfortable, if not exactly where I wanted to be, and I was straight back on the treadmill of turning out Michelin food at one of the new outposts of Marco's empire. I was back to doing eighteen-hour days and then winding down with booze and dope. Holidays weren't really an option, but once during my time at Les Saveurs I had to go and ask Marco for one.

'I need a day off, Marco.'

'What for?'

'I'm getting married.'

'You can have Monday off,' he said, 'but you're not having a fucking honeymoon.'

One day was enough. The wedding could be on a Monday, which meant I'd finish work on the Saturday, fly up to Edinburgh, get happily-ever-aftered, and be back for prep on Tuesday.

The ceremony was going to be very small, just an exchange of vows at the Edinburgh registry office. It was the spring of 1997, and we'd chosen Edinburgh as a lovely romantic venue, and a place that my family could navigate, and that Kelly's could reach via a flight from Australia. I'd wanted to get married in Glasgow, but Kelly had never felt safe there, so Edinburgh was a compromise that kept the wedding in Scotland.

I could be up and back on a plane to London without drama. It would even give me time for a wee stag's night on the Sunday.

Now, this flawless plan was complicated by the fact that, in the lead-up to the wedding day, I'd been on a stag's night pretty much continuously for two weeks. Just one endless bender, which culminated with me and Bob, my old mate from Chester and my best man, flying up to Scotland.

We got to Edinburgh, no worries, and on the morning of the wedding, Bob and I went for a pint to help with the nerves. This was first thing in the morning, and it really helped settle the butterflies in my stomach. So we had double whiskies then another pint, and a game of pool, and a pint, and so on, until at some point Bob looked at his watch.

'Jock?'

'Yeah?'

'What time are you supposed to be there?'

'Oh fuck.'

By now it was 11.15. The ceremony was at 12.30, in a registry office miles away. We couldn't get a taxi, still needed to get dressed, and were a good half-hour away from our hotel, so we raced back to get our kilts on; just sprinted, which wasn't easy because we were so smashed that walking in a straight line was a bit of a challenge.

At the hotel, we started getting kitted up, but Bob had never worn a kilt in his life, so I had to help him get dressed. As I said, we were quite drunk at this point, so trying to make ourselves presentable was a bit of a procedure. I'm fucking around trying to get his sporran on, he's doubled over laughing and despite it all, we were in a great mood, having a very fine time, but it was clear we were going to be late. We didn't even manage to leave the hotel until fifteen minutes after the ceremony was supposed to start.

We flagged down a taxi and the taxi driver asked us if we were dressed up for a wedding.

'Yeah, I'm getting married today,' I said.

'Don't do it, mate,' the driver caught my eye in the mirror. 'I'll take you straight to the airport and save you some trouble. This is your last chance to get out of it.'

'I'm good, man. Take me to my wedding.'

We arrived at the registry office well after I was already supposed to be married. As the taxi pulled up there was a guy from the registry office waiting out the front, pacing and tearing his hair out. He rushed up to the taxi as it pulled up.

'Are you Jock?' he asked.

'Yeah,' I said. 'How much trouble am I in?'

'On a scale of one to ten? About a hundred.'

Bob and I barrelled in, all drunk and merry and happy to be there, to find a room full of people in tears because they thought I'd left Kelly at the altar.

Her mum and aunt, who'd flown over from Australia, were distraught. My mum and dad were there, not looking too happy either. Kelly was beside herself, make-up all smeared and ruined by tears, but still beautiful in her dress. So that was getting married. It was a pretty bad start to a life together. In retrospect, I would like to have done things differently. It would have been poor form for me to pull that stunt at any time, but Kelly had given up her whole life to join me in the UK. Not my finest moment.

It took some time for everyone in that room to forgive me and my grievous lack of responsibility, but you can rest assured I was back at work first thing Tuesday morning, knives shined and sharp, nothing changed but the ring on my finger. In my mind, I suppose it would have been worse

for me to disappoint Marco than anyone else in the world.
He'd invested in me, and he had big plans for me.

Pharmacy was a high-concept place that was meant to be
something between a posh restaurant and an art installation. It was backed by Matthew Freud, the mega-powerful
PR specialist and grandson of Sigmund, and artist Damien
Hirst. At the time, I didn't know who Damien was, and
Richard had to explain to me that he was the artist who'd
put a shark in a formaldehyde tank and made US $8 million
from it. I'd heard of that, so I was like, cool, got it; that *is*
a big deal.

Freud had already hired a three-star chef, Sonia, a
protégée of Alain Ducasse, and flown her over from France.
Her reputation was good, but Freud's reputation was at stake,
and he had invested a great deal financially, so he brought
in Marco, who had a reputation as a culinary starmaker, to
oversee the project.

In turn, Marco sent in his trusted seconds, Richard and
me. Basically, we weren't going to be handling much of
the high-rank chef stuff, we were there to keep an eye on the
running of the kitchen and step in if it went pear-shaped. It
was all a bit weird, but then it was a weird place.

Sonia as head chef would be upstairs in the restaurant
proper, doing the fine dining thing, and in the meantime,
Richard and I were stationed in the downstairs bar kitchen.
We were cooking high-end versions of British bar food —
beans on toast, boiled eggs with toast soldiers, that sort of
thing. Our menu had a cool retro vibe, which nobody else
was really doing at the time. It was fun, but at the same

time absurd, because we were both pretty good chefs, with immaculate pedigrees, and we were going to be serving Scotch eggs and pickled onions.

When Richard and I first went down to check out the Notting Hill site it was just a gutted shell of a building. That didn't worry me; restaurants have a way of coming together at the last minute. Some of the best restaurants I've ever known have looked like a bomb hit them until the night before the first service.

Getting towards open, it was still looking pretty rough, but Damien Hirst started moving his art in. As part of his investment in the restaurant, he was fitting the place out with his artworks.

Down the line he would take the whole outfit to Sotheby's for auction and make a mint from everyone wanting a little piece of the restaurant, but for now he was just doing the decor, which to my eye involved nailing a lot of medical-themed shit to the walls. There were display cabinets all over the place filled with scalpels, callipers and catheters all in neat rows. The seats on the barstools were shaped like ecstasy tablets, which on the street were stamped with symbols: ohms, strawberries, white doves, playboys, flatlines . . . all the popular brands were there.

Everything in the bar had some little flourish like that, right down to the smallest detail. There was nothing that hadn't been themed. Even the urinal in the men's bathroom featured an installation: a clear wall with condoms and used syringes suspended behind perspex. The whole place, from the door to the restrooms, was this amazing work of art, and I had no idea what the fuck any of it meant.

A few days before we opened, I saw Hirst helping to install his artworks. So I went up to him and said, 'Hey, mate, could you explain what I'm looking at? I don't really understand what's going on here.' He seemed a bit taken aback.

'And who the fuck are you?'

'I'm just a chef. I'm on the toast soldiers,' I explained. 'But I'm interested. Like, what's going on here? What's with all these scalpels?'

He told me he'd explain it to me after it opened.

A few days later Pharmacy opened and was an immediate hit: A-list celebrities everywhere, security at the front door. That kind of place.

That first night, I was in the kitchen doing service and I got a tap on the shoulder. I turned around, and there was Hirst. He said, 'Come on, I'll show you what's going on.'

Together we walked around the outskirts of the bar, which was lined with those glass cabinets that you'd see in old fashioned pharmacies. Inside them were surgical instruments: scalpels, forceps, IVs; all sorts of stuff all neatly arranged.

Hirst knew what every single instrument was for and explained each use to me: they use this tool when operating on a damaged liver; this is for skin grafts if you hit the road after a motor accident. He knew every instrument, every detail, right down to every pill built into the bar stools, and what they were for.

Then we went upstairs to the fine-dining area. Downstairs was a hectic bar – people yelling, music, cocktails being shaken – by none other than legendary British bartender Dick Bradsell – but this room was completely calm. Hirst showed me the wallpaper, which from a distance and with the mood lighting, just looked like an attractive abstract pattern. But close up you could see it was really an intricate pattern of different pills. Then we went downstairs, back to the bar.

'So that's it,' said Hirst. 'That's everything. Do you understand now?'

'No,' I said. 'Not at all.'

'Ah,' he said, and motioned to follow him again.

So then we walked through the middle of the bar where all the private booths were, every one of them occupied by some super-famous person. I passed Madonna and her dancers in one of the booths (scarpering quickly before she could recognise me as the guy who kicked her dog).

This was London, 1997, and this was the kind of bar that famous people could come to and just get loose. Everywhere, celebrities were drinking and doing coke on the tables, and Hirst walked me through the room pointing them out: an actress doing cocaine, a rock star who was high on heroin.

One by one Hirst considered each of them, and predicted the specific medical conditions that all the excessive drugs and alcohol that these people were doing were going to lead to. The drugs and implements they were surrounded by were what would be needed to save their lives down the line. So, for example, the guy from a popular Britpop outfit downing vodka and cocaine was seated next to the medical instruments necessary to repair the cirrhotic liver he would cross paths with later in life.

The whole bar was the work of art, but it wasn't complete until it was full of people, and exactly the right kind of people – wealthy, powerful and debauched – doing exactly the right thing. Without the decadent drug-pigs of London high society the artwork was meaningless. It only became a statement when they turned up in their limos to be part of the new, fashionable, PR-darling restaurant.

'You sick motherfucker,' I said to Hirst, genuinely mind-blown. It was a real moment for me, I couldn't get my head around that level of involvement and engagement and thought. That level of connection between art and food and concept was not something I'd ever been privy to before. I thought it was fucking crazy and I loved it.

What Hirst had done just made me so excited to be working in food, and kind of levered open my mind to the idea that food could be a conceptual statement as well as a culinary one. It just sort of clicked with this sense I'd been developing since I first went hunting and foraging at Turnberry: that cooking could be a way to anchor a sense of a moment in time; that taste, memory and emotion were all facets of the same elemental thing. That's what cooking could be if you really had the talent and the vision. You could tell a story through your food, put a narrative down on the plate along with everything else that made the food work. I didn't realise it then, but the seed of an idea had been planted for what would one day become Orana. That was a long way off as yet, however.

The next assignment Marco put us on was as far away from that side of British life as you could get, both in terms of lifestyle and as the crow flies. It was in Cornwall, on the western tip of mainland Britain.

One of Marco's business partners was Sir Rocco Forte, son of Lord Forte and from a family of legendary hoteliers. His sister Olga Polizzi was a highly respected hotelier with an eye for interior design and a talent for bringing out the potential in places.

Olga had just bought a hotel in St Mawes, a sleepy little fishing village a few hours south-west of London, which she was going to refit into what would be the Hotel Tresanton. The vision was to revamp it into a weekend retreat for well-heeled Londoners, so she needed a restaurant that would act as a drawcard. For that, she needed Marco, and he asked Richard and me to go and build the restaurant from the ground up. He trusted us to make sure it was all primo, because there were some big reputations at stake and nobody involved wanted any bad press.

Kelly and I discussed moving down. We thought we might like the peace and quiet of country life. London could be a bit grim; a bit relentless, and if you're new to town like Kelly was, it could be a hard city to crack. It was so expensive, too. Just paying the rent and our debt was such a grind that we did nothing but work: me in the restaurant, Kelly as a waitress at a pub in Knightsbridge. Six nights of the week I would come home at two in the morning after finishing service, and if we ever had a day off together, we'd be too exhausted to do anything.

One evening we tried to go out to dinner. We got all dressed up, went to a lovely, dimly lit fine-dining place and took our seats at a corner table. The waiter came over to take our drink orders, from Kelly first, but when he turned to me I'd fallen asleep. Not an efficient, ten-second 'just closing my eyes' power nap either, but fully collapsed, head back, mouth open, snoring in the candlelight. Kelly had to keep kicking me under the table so I'd open my eyes. That was as close as we got to a normal life in London. We were in one of the most vibrant, exciting metropolises on the planet and all I wanted was a kip.

So we packed up our life in London and drove down. At the time my car was a Ford Sierra Cosworth, a really fantastic rally car I had de-badged and sprayed burgundy to stop people from stealing it all the time. At the very least, living in a small town where everyone knew everyone meant I could park it on the street without it getting nicked. I loved it, and enjoyed nothing more than getting on a good country road and flooring it, so I had a good feeling as we drove south-west out of London.

When you open a restaurant, there's a bit of a preamble where you've got to decide what style the food is going to be, what sort of menu you're going to create, and where you're going to source the produce from.

If you're in central London or Sydney the world is pretty much your oyster. You can decide on your menu, then just pick up the phone, call a butcher and ask for the best beef they've got. But out in Cornwall we didn't have any of our normal suppliers; no chains of supply. So we had to get out and explore and talk to people, and see what the countryside had to offer.

That was fine – it was an excuse for Richard and me to bomb around Cornwall in my car. I could basically go full Gran Turismo on those empty country roads. I loved fast cars then, and I love them to this day. I've never really grown out of a childhood spent admiring big engines, and that car was an absolute weapon.

We talked to a local fishmonger, and started realising how much of the fish that ends up in London actually is docked in Cornwall. Sea bass, turbot: it all comes off the boats on the Cornish coast, then travels on from there twenty-four hours later. So what we were seeing was even better produce than we'd seen in central London. We got to know a local diver who could get us scallops right out of the ocean. There was talk of poachers who could bring us wild pheasant and partridge from the woodlands.

We were pretty excited about the potential and what we could do using only local produce, but we couldn't locate a local supplier for farmed meat – your beef, pork and lamb. Then one day while pulled over on a back road to check the map, I looked up and noticed a hand-painted sign with an arrow pointing down this lane. It said 'Farm Butchery'.

'Let's go,' we said, and bombed down the tight little country lane just big enough for one car to squeeze through. Through a gate we came to a building that looked exactly like a council house plonked in the middle of a farm. We parked and went in.

Once inside, we pushed through thick Perspex curtains – rather like something out of a slasher movie – and found the most beautiful butcher's counter I've ever seen in my life. It was huge, 10 metres long, and stocked with the most pristine, beautiful meat I've ever laid eyes on.

There was a section just for sausages, and the little cards describing each sausage had these incredible flavour combinations you just didn't see back then: 'Tamworth pork, cider, fennel, hickory smoke.' Fucking poetry.

Richard and I looked at each other because we realised we'd struck gold. We asked to speak to the butcher, and this guy came out to introduce himself.

Ralph Michell was the butcher and owner, working alongside his son Mark and two other people, Varna and Alan, who knew absolutely everything there was to know about the meat.

The provenance of meat – where an animal came from, what it ate, who raised it and who slaughtered it – wasn't really on my radar. There was a bit of that at Turnberry, when we'd hunt wild game, but in the fine-dining world back then it was more about consistency of product from a supplier. Ralph took me to the counter and showed me the difference between similar cuts from different breeds and the marbling of this cow versus that; what each would taste like and why.

The trend was for Black Angus steak at the time (and still is in Australia), but Ralph schooled me that for the cooking I wanted to do, the English Longhorn cow was a better choice because it was a longer animal so the tenderloins, the sirloins, the rib eyes are all more substantial, and that it has more marbling than any other breed on grass. Ralph also showed me exactly what the marbling meant on a Blackface Suffolk sheep, and how it would elevate the meat on a slow cook. And why an Oxford Sandy and Black pig will always be a better-tasting pork than nearly any other.

Not only did he have the knowledge, but all the animals were right there in the fields. You could walk out the door and go and meet them. He was one of those farmers who loved and cared for his animals. When I went around to his house for cup of tea, more often than not there'd be a sickly pig or sheep he'd brought into the house to look after. An amazing guy, such a kind bloke and an expert butcher.

Richard and I kind of fell in love with him and what he stood for. I really connected with that passion for the breeds and feeds of animals, and the difference that made to flavour, texture and marbling. It was intoxicating for me, the door Ralph opened into the world of animal husbandry, and the responsibility that comes with that. If you're going to take an animal's life to feed yourself or your family, then you have a responsibility to respect that sacrifice. You'd better make sure you're treating that meat with all the care in the world. I don't think there's a chef who met the man without coming away inspired to think more carefully about their relationship with the animals they eat.

Bit by bit, the menu fell into place. Everything that had been simmering away at the back of my mind started to come together with the inspiration for what we would do at the restaurant. For years I'd been trying to get closer to capturing those authentic moments in time that I'd experienced in food along the way. I grew obsessed with finding a way to share how it felt to eat that venison smoked on wild wood from back at Turnberry – or if not that, an iteration of that.

In this restaurant, I could give the punters something new, an experience of eating they'd never had anywhere else, and never would again, because it was all about the taste of the fish that had come in off the boat *that* day, eaten while the sea breeze from the ocean it was fished from blows in.

Sure, I used all the high-end culinary technique I'd been trained in, but it was about honouring the taste of the Cornish coast: I could do French food, but it didn't make sense to fetishise *coq au vin* when Burgundy wine and poultry were hundreds of miles away, and the ocean outside my door was full of rich, wild scallops, crabs and sea bass that tasted like nothing else on earth. That was the thread I'd been chasing for years, and now it was all knitting together in the new menu.

Olga Polizzi was all in on the idea. She was a fantastic hotelier, and her daughter Alex Polizzi (also on the team) was an equally talented restaurant manager – so sharp, so talented – and if they thought it would work, it was going to work. Right from the start we trusted each other absolutely, which was important, but we were both hard-headed, absolutely focused and career-driven, so we had a great working relationship. And it did work. I'm so hard-headed in my ideas sometimes that it takes an exceptional manager to check my worst impulses and bring out the best in me, and there were none better than the Polizzis.

After the restaurant opened Richard ended up going back to London, but I stayed behind and took over as head chef. I needed a sous chef, so I called Bob and convinced him to come down and join the team, and everything just sort of fell into place.

I loved what I was doing in terms of being a chef – professionally, it was everything I'd ever wanted – but Kelly was desperately unhappy. She was working front of house, which was just a job for her, really; it wasn't what she'd dreamed of doing with her life. She had a whole life back in Sydney and missed it a great deal, and I had my blinkers on for my career. We were both gliding through life at that point, taking it one day at a time and not really thinking much about the future. Which was fine for me, because I loved what I was doing every day. For Kelly, not so much.

It was a tiny little town, fewer than 500 people, most of them tending towards middle age, and we were barely twenty. There wasn't much to do in terms of a social life except go down to the sailing club to sink pints and play snooker. As the months went by, our snooker game got better and better, and our relationship worse. Every day Kelly got lonelier, and I continued to ignore her to concentrate on my career and the food I could create in my very own restaurant kitchen.

This was an opportunity to source the most incredible food to work with, and I'd never been so lucky. The fish was the freshest I'd ever seen in my life, the scallops were brought to the door twenty minutes after they got pulled out of the water. Every so often you'd get a knock on the back door and it'd be a poacher with wild sea bass or birds or a deer draped over their shoulder.

Because the farm butcher didn't deliver, I could jump in my car and fang it to the butcher shop down those amazing winding country roads in the early hours of the morning when the roads were dead. I loved it, I'd never been so professionally satisfied, seeing what the ocean and the community brought in every day and working out what I could do to make it sing.

Anyone else would have been content in life at that point: I had a lovely little cottage in the country; newly married to a beautiful wife; I was in charge of my own kitchen, where

I was my own boss; I was working every day alongside my best mate in the world and plating up beautiful, thoughtful, honest food that I truly loved.

The hotel and restaurant took off as a culinary getaway from London. Because I'd worked with Marco and David Cavalier and even Gordon, I was on the radar of posh foodies, and they would come down for a weekend and check it out.

That was part of the problem. As word spread and discerning diners started to visit the Hotel Tresanton to see what all the fuss was about, the standards I held myself and my staff to became ever higher.

Looking back, I was in this obsessive-compulsive moment in my career of searching for perfection in everything. From my point of view, from my first position as a head chef, every plate that went on the pass was a reflection of my entire being.

Of course, not everything can be perfect. That's not how life works, and that's certainly not how a kitchen works, but I was so highly strung I'd lost touch with that reality. Pity my poor staff who had to deal with my expectations that were totally skewed and completely unrealistic.

One night, a particularly busy night, we had a food reviewer in – the front-of-house staff had ID'd him when he arrived. He ordered sea bass, and Bob was on fish that night.

I saw the plate go on the pass, and watched it go out before I had a chance to send it back. It was fine, a perfectly good sea bass, but it wasn't *perfect*. It wasn't piled on the plate *exactly* as I wanted it. There was a *speck* of dressing out of place on the porcelain. And it was going out to a *food reviewer*.

I couldn't see it as anything less than a betrayal from Bob. My best mate was my right-hand man but he wasn't meeting my expectations.

'There's no gentle way of telling you this, but actually you're shit,' I said to him. 'Your cooking isn't that great, and it's not good enough for my kitchen.'

That was the gentlest thing I said to Bob that night. There was nothing kind or understanding in the way I spoke to him. Essentially, I gave him his marching orders, told him to fuck off back to London. I sacked him, and cut him out of my life. We didn't speak again for years, and in my mind I was in the right. I don't even remember if we got the review, but on the day it was more critical to me that some reviewer enjoyed my cooking than it was to do the bare minimum to save the relationship with my best friend.

It was vitally important to me that every diner had the best meal of their life, every night, night after night. Otherwise, what was the point of anything? I think I honestly cared more about respecting the produce than the feelings of my loved ones or any relationship in my life.

One of the menu items were these Cornish brown crabs, which we got straight out of the ocean. Huge, succulent crabs with these beautiful fat claws on them, just as good as Australian mud crabs. We'd cook them in sea water, a very old-school technique which cooked this gorgeous salty brine flavour into the crab meat, rendering them perfectly seasoned.

One day we were down the beach collecting buckets of sea water, and I saw this guy strolling down the beach towards us, a weird-looking cat. He was wearing a navy-blue linen safari suit, with a hat. In a town where no one wore suits, he stuck out like a sore thumb. Obviously he was down from London. As he got a little closer, I saw he was working some worry beads in the fingers of one hand. Then he stopped.

'What are you doing?' he asked me, in a real posh voice.

'I'm getting sea water to take to the restaurant. To cook crabs.'

'To cook crabs?'

'I work up in the Hotel Tresanton.' I pointed up the beach to the hotel, and the guy looked up, nodded, and went on his way. I realised that he looked familiar and as he walked off, it came to me: he was the notorious food critic Adrian Gill. I'd seen his photo next to his by-line.

Adrian Gill was easily one of the best food writers in Britain, an astonishing writer, scathing yet hilarious. Renowned for tearing new arseholes, if he reviewed you, he had a way of articulating everything that was wrong about your cooking in a way that was funny but at the same time made you wince. You didn't want to be at the receiving end of it. He could absolutely make or break a chef and a restaurant.

I raced back up to the restaurant where Kelly was on the reception.

'Is anyone booked in under the name Adrian Gill?' I asked. 'I wouldn't be surprised if we get reviewed tonight.'

He'd booked in under a false name, of course, but someone on the back shift had taken his credit card and noticed it was different from the reservation. So that was confirmation: it was 100 per cent him.

All of a sudden everyone was at battle stations. Being reviewed by Gill was a big deal. I got straight onto Alex, half freaking out.

'Adrian Gill's eating here tonight,' I said. 'It's happening!'

She was right on it, and we got into this whole life-or-death decision about what we were going to feed him.

One of the fishermen had just brought in some sea bass, a really fashionable, prestigious, high-class fish to have on your menu. And it was good, but it wasn't absolutely spanking.

At the same time, the fishmonger had brought in some grey mullet, which was a poor man's fish. It's what you bought if you couldn't afford anything else. I'd made a special of it, which was a way of showcasing and elevating what most chefs saw as a bottom-shelf fish to something really special. That's what I was all about at that point, really celebrating the flavour of what the fishermen had caught right at our doorstep.

I told Alex and Olga I was going to serve him the mullet, and they were furious.

'You're going to fuck this up,' Alex told me, head in her hands, but I'd made my mind up, and Adrian got the mullet.

Then there was an anxious wait for his review to come out in the paper, and when it did, it was good. Four out of five stars, which would have been great for a regular reviewer, but was basically a ringing endorsement from Gill. If Gill reviewed you and you got away without your ego and dignity torn to ribbons, that was a win.

The fact that I'd disowned my best friend in the world over a fish fillet, or that my wife was miserable, didn't seem as important as that validation from arguably one of the world's finest food critics. It made me so happy. What's a little misery compared to that?

CHAPTER SIXTEEN

Two years passed like that. My reputation as a chef got better and better, and Kelly got more and more homesick. It wasn't the greatest marriage at this point. I don't know that we could have expected much else. We were too young and stupid to get married. We got engaged when I was tripping, which is maybe not the most auspicious start to a happily-ever-after. In some ways it was a relationship built on chemicals.

We were partying too much in our little cottage in Cornwall, with nowhere else to go. And I still had a full-on heroin addiction.

The situation was becoming untenable. It wasn't that simple to hide a raging heroin addiction from everyone in your life. My employer didn't know. Kelly didn't know. It wasn't exactly easy to score the industrial-level quantities of heroin I needed to stave off withdrawal, so I had to keep finding money that Kelly wouldn't miss and excuses to drive up to Cardiff or London to score. At this point in my life I was 23 and had a nine-year heroin habit. More than a third of my life had been spent as a junkie, and I was running out of veins I could use and keep hiding my track marks.

Looking back, Kelly and I were barely treading water and needed a lifeline. It came as a phone call. Late in 1999, Dietmar Sawyere, the owner and executive chef of Restaurant Forty One, got in touch. He'd been following my career all the way from Sydney, and had an offer for me. Forty One was struggling a bit, and had recently lost a hat, and he wanted me to come to Sydney and take up the position as head chef.

It seemed like the right time. Kelly was desperate to go home, and I was junk-sick and saw an opportunity to get a clean break.

I was sick of being a junkie and the lying, the running around – the fucking frantic hamster wheel of drug addiction. There was this thing that had priority over every other part of my life, and I hated it. I knew it had to stop. I could not keep living the way I was, hiding my works, shooting up in the toilets, feeling physically shit and constantly guilty. It was crippling, the fucking guilt. The relentless shame.

So Dietmar's offer seemed perfect. As head chef I'd have the freedom to create my own menu that really made the most of the incredible produce Sydney had to offer. With everything I'd learned these past years, and the abundance of Australian and Asian ingredients, I could do something different, something meaningful.

More importantly, I saw my chance to make a clean break; to leave behind all my bad habits and the bad circles I'd picked them up in. This was the moment to kick the habit, and I wouldn't have this addiction hanging over me constantly. I would get my life back. A fresh start: it would be as simple as that. So we decided to move back to Sydney.

We bought tickets to fly out on New Year's Eve 1999. This was right in the middle of the millennial bug panic, when everyone was convinced that computers were going to freak out when the date turned over to 2000. People thought that planes would drop out of the sky, so we were able to get flights to Sydney for next to nothing.

All that was left to do was find our passports, pack up the house, say goodbye to our life in country Cornwall. And there was the small issue of my heroin dependency. I'd tried to kick it a few times, but it seemed impossible. I was lucky to go eight hours from shot to shot without withdrawal symptoms starting in on me.

First there was this nagging sort of craving at the back of the mind, like 'Hmm, a wee bit of gear wouldn't go amiss.' Then that thought process moves to the front of your mind, and then it's all you can think about. This low-level hum of anxiety starts turning up in volume and then there's this one intrusive thought that just keeps hammering away at you, which is that you absolutely need a fix. Right fucking now. This second.

That anxiety gets worse and worse, you start yawning involuntarily, itching, then sweating, then you start to get properly sick. Between the diarrhoea and the vomiting, you're going to dehydrate, and good luck holding down any water. Heroin feels great, yes, but the junk-sickness is what really makes heroin addictive. You need it to get up in the morning, through a day's work, to sit quietly in the evening and watch the telly with your wife. If you don't get the drug, the sickness will find you soon enough.

Then the pain, so bad it even cuts through the nausea, which feels like someone is grabbing every bone in your body and wringing it from the joint. There's nothing you can do about it but thrash around and hope you'll pass out from exhaustion for a few minutes, because you're not going to get any sleep for the next three days.

Even if you can get through all that, you don't come out the other side bright-eyed and bushy-tailed. You're exhausted; just utterly spent, physically and emotionally. The two weeks on the other side of cold turkey are a deep-dive into the blackest, most miserable depression you can imagine while your brain tries to rewire itself. Then even if you can get through that, whatever underlying factors drove you to pick up a habit in the first place are still there, waiting for you, undiminished by the years. Junk-sickness: not a very nice time at all.

I did my last shot of heroin on New Year's Eve in the toilets at Heathrow Airport. Like I'd done a thousand times before, I tied my belt around my arm, used a lighter to heat the gear on the back of a spoon until it melted into a solution, picked some lint off my jumper to serve as a filter for the solution, found a vein, watched the little eddy of blood swirl up from my body into the syringe, and squeezed down the plunger to take the shot. I remember thinking, 'This is the last-ever time. This is the last shot.' I would never take drugs again. When the plane landed in Sydney I'd be free of all that.

I threw my works out in the airport bathroom, and walked out to where Kelly was waiting.

Fair to say, it was a lot harder than I thought it would be. I got on that flight pretty pickled to begin with, and Kelly and I drank through the night to ring in the new millennium. The New Year ticked over somewhere over the Pacific. The world didn't end, but by the time the plane touched down in Sydney I felt like I was going to die.

We'd arranged to stay at Kelly's mum's place in Daceyville until we got on our feet, and I turned up on her door just absolutely wretched with junk-sickness. I told them I thought I'd picked something up on the plane, and just had to pretend I had the worst flu ever. It was horrific. For ten days I was vomiting and screaming and shitting all over the place before the fever finally broke.

In the 80s and 90s, shooting heroin was the unofficial national pastime of Scotland. I don't know whether Glasgow or Edinburgh was worse, but Edinburgh ended up being the AIDS capital of the world at one point because of heroin users sharing works.

Back then, we all shared needles. HIV and AIDS just weren't on our radar. We didn't know shit from clay, and needles were hard to come by, so we didn't think twice about sharing our works with some total stranger. How the fuck I'm still alive and healthy today is a fucking mystery. Between shooting myself full of needles and people trying to stab me, it's a miracle that I got through more or less unscathed. Part of it was coming from the suburbs and not the city – I've had so many mates who grew up in tenements and never found a way to escape. Boys my age died all the time from overdoses, you heard about it on the regular, but you didn't think too much about it. You were aware of it, but it didn't stop any of us from shooting up. You just thought it would never happen to you.

I had an escape route, I suppose. There's a difference between bouncing around Glasgow as a tourist and growing up there and not being able to escape the gravity of the place. Because I was from the next town over, because I had career in mind and a restaurant job, I was able to go into Glasgow, have a great time, be a scallywag, take my drugs, catch my scars, and walk away. In a sense, I was so, so very lucky. I'd known many people who weren't.

Now it was all over. At the end of the sickness, I could walk out into a beautiful day in the sun-kissed country of Australia and leave all that shit behind me.

I was clean, and when the sun started to go down that day I wouldn't start to shiver with the sickness and have to scurry off to tend to my habit in some rank public toilet. When that realisation struck me, the sheer happiness of the moment overwhelmed me: the fact that I was free. If you've never been a junkie, that thought might seem a bit odd, but for me, it felt pretty amazing.

I was married to a wonderful woman and she was ecstatic to be home; we'd started talking about having a baby; I was the head chef of a hatted restaurant. A new lease on life, after nearly a decade of rank debauchery, and I had left greasy, grey Britain – and the man I'd been there – behind. It didn't get much better than that.

CHAPTER SEVENTEEN

We moved into a really posh gated apartment block in Clovelly, a coastal suburb in Sydney's pricey Eastern Suburbs, where Kelly's uncle had a flat with a spare room that we could stay in until we could get on our feet. The neighbours were proper stuck-up types, and they hated me – for a bunch of reasons, but mostly because of the car.

We bought the first cheap car we saw to get around in, a little Suzuki toy racer – zippy with a very loud exhaust on it. Every time I drove into the apartment's driveway, the exhaust rattled the windows on the floors above. It was obscenely noisy. On top of that, I didn't have a parking spot so I would park in the visitor's space or the car-washing bay, which also annoyed everyone. Every morning I would wake up and find an escalatingly vicious note on the window. So that was a source of tension, and I was keeping an eye out for a solution.

Then I was out for breakfast one morning and saw an advert in the paper from a dealership offering a $40,000 trade-in on any vehicle against a brand-new Range Rover. $40,000 was way more money than I'd paid for my shitty

Suzuki, the dealership was two minutes up the road, so I was like, perfect! I'm on my way.

The guy in the dealership saw me coming a mile away and took me to the showroom floor to show me all these amazing cars I could choose from. I chose a black Range Rover Vogue, a really nice luxury SUV – because how could I not with that trade-in? Of course, the trade-in was a scam, you don't actually get any value, they just add 40 grand to the price of the car they give you, and you don't walk away with anything nicer than a whopping great car lease against your name – but that only dawns on you after the fact.

So I went out for breakfast, came home with a Range Rover and parked it in the car-washing bay. The next morning was a Sunday, and it was looking to be a lovely day.

'Let's go to the beach,' Kelly suggested. Great idea, a perfect day for it. We gathered our towels and sunblock and strolled down to the car park, where Kelly found our Suzuki gone and a Range Rover in its place.

She went ballistic. At this stage we were talking about trying to get our own place and start a family and money was tight, and I'd signed up on a 120 grand lease for a car. She tore strips off me, absolutely verbally demolished me with great ferocity and volume in the car park in full view of our noise-sensitive neighbours and their rattling windows.

But it solved the problem. The neighbours didn't complain about me parking in the car-washing bay any more because the car was the price of a small house and they were snobs.

Snobs were everywhere that year. Sydney was hosting the 2000 Olympics, and the optimism of the new millennium and the promise of tourist dollars had swept the city and supercharged the hospitality industry. Investors were putting million-dollar fit-outs into restaurants and fine-dining places were popping up like mushrooms as cash rained down on Sydney.

Janni Kyritsis had a restaurant in an MG showroom where you ate while looking at luxury cars – and if one took your fancy, you could order it off the menu. With that kind of money kicking around, pretty much overnight Sydney became a food capital of the world in a way it hadn't really been before, and established places like Forty One were raking it in.

There was a great deal of public interest in the 'Mod Oz' movement, which according to food critics was at the fore-front of 'international food' – in other words, French food with a few Asian flavours or some local produce. Some of it was pretty lazy – barramundi on bok choi or maybe a miso beurre blanc – but some places were doing some really inter-esting work. Forty One, where I was now head chef, was one of them.

We leaned hard into that international haute-cuisine thing, with dishes like a caramelised duck with a quesadilla of foie gras and braised spinach, or barramundi with summer truffle and chanterelles that had to be airfreighted from France. Delicious, amazing ingredients perfectly executed, but an incredible amount of work to plate up.

It was an eighteen-hour day, plus whatever else needed doing. I was cooking my arse off; properly tired from burning the candle from every direction. If I wasn't prepping for service or in the middle of service, I was trying to source produce and ingredients for the next service.

The Olympics had smashed food-supply infrastructure and made it really difficult to get deliveries. Suppliers were tapped out as fast as they could bring in produce and the roads were choked from all the tourist traffic. We were getting our veg delivery from a supplier with a warehouse in Alexandria, but one day when I called up to order, they told me they wouldn't be able to deliver until 10 the next morning.

That was way too late; we'd never be able to get the next day's prep done in time, so after service that day I drove the Range Rover down to the supplier to pick up what we'd need for the morning. Their warehouse was a vast food-storage facility with ramps going up to a huge platform where fridges were stacked to the roof with pallets of vegies.

I loaded up the car, had a cup of tea and a chinwag with our produce guy, then got behind the wheel. By now it was two in the morning, I was knackered and almost falling asleep.

I started the car, and looked over the ramp leading up to the platform I was on. There was a truck coming up the ramp, which in my exhaustion I somehow thought was coming up from a basement, so I gunned the car towards what I thought was a down-ramp. Of course, they didn't have a down-ramp. I drove the Range Rover right over the edge of a two-storey drop.

The car teetered, the front wheels way out in space, the whole car caught on the edge of the concrete platform by its transmission system. To get me out of there the warehouse guys had to stack up a bunch of pallets to build a sort of scaffold for me to drive down. In the process I absolutely fucked the underneath of the car. When I later sold it, the guy looked beneath the car and asked me if I'd taken if off-road, the bottom of it was so damaged.

'It must be my wife,' I shrugged. 'Don't know anything about it.'

Of course, it wasn't fair to blame that on Kelly, but there were definitely occasions when our marriage made my life harder . . .

I was making pretty good money at Forty One, but with the hospitality industry in overdrive I saw an opportunity to make a little more. I started a business importing and selling equipment to fit-out commercial kitchens: pots, pans, knives, blenders, dishwashers; stuff from all over the world. It was a lot of work, but nothing I couldn't handle. I fitted it in after I finished at the restaurant or on my days off.

Except . . . Remember my father-in-law, Steve, the well-known former Sydney drug trafficker? Lovely bloke, we were the best of mates, but the fact remained that he'd been caught and imprisoned in Queensland, and the New South Wales Drug Squad (NSWDS) were desperate to get him on something. They'd invested a lot of time, money and police egos in trying to bring him down, then the Queensland Drug Squad had jumped in and eaten their lunch.

Cut to me bringing in a shipment of twenty high-end blenders from Germany, then getting a call from Customs telling me to come down to the port and discuss the shipping requirements.

No worries. I gathered up all my paperwork, trundled down to the Customs office and was shown into this little interview room with three or four people sitting in the corners. Behind a desk, a guy in dark glasses with a moustache opened a folder and started laying out photographs for me to look at.

'Do you know this man?' he said. 'What about this woman? Are you acquainted with any of these people?'

'Mate, what's this about?'

'You've got this shipment of kitchen equipment coming in from Europe. We just want to know if, in the process of purchasing these blenders, you've spoken to any of these people.'

'No. Never seen them before.'

'So,' he leaned back in his chair now like he'd just won some kind of chess move, 'you don't mind if we open up the blenders and have a look inside?'

We all got up and went into the warehouse, where they had set up twenty benches, one for each of the blenders. In hindsight, it was like the most nightmarish *Master-Chef* kitchen challenge you could imagine, only instead of passionate amateur chefs with hopes and dreams, it was pricks with badges and guns.

They started dismantling those blenders one by one, and I had to sit there watching as these huge NSWDS guys took apart my beautiful, intricate German-engineered blenders, and screws and nuts and bolts were rolling everywhere.

They didn't find whatever they were looking for, obviously. So they shrugged, said, 'Thanks very much', then they all just walked out, leaving me with my poor dead blenders. I had to shove them all back in their boxes, take them home and basically teach myself engineering to figure out how to put them back together so I could sell them and get my money back.

Years later, I went to support Steve in court for some old charge they wanted him to testify on, and I was sitting on the benches, listening to the lawyers bang on, and I saw a familiar face sitting on the police side of court. Droopy moustache, dark glasses – it took me a minute to recognise him as the guy who'd ruined my blenders. He saw me staring and just gave me the slightest nod. That motherfucker: full points for confidence.

Despite little bumps in the road like that, the business took off, and it started bringing in a fair amount of money. I used that money to expand into selling wine when I saw an opportunity through Forty One. Although Dietmar had been the executive chef for some time, he'd never been an equity owner, so when the owners announced they planned to sell the business, Dietmar bought it. That came with a wine cellar worth 1.5 million dollars that had accrued over many years of the restaurant running – some really rare vintages and sought-after drops.

Dietmar didn't have a spare million to invest in vintage wines, so he was going to sell the inventory of wine whole-sale. I asked him to give me first dibs on buying the stock, and then started firing off emails to wine merchants all over the country. To each I offered really rare bottles of Grange Hermitage and other prestige wines if they would also buy some of the less desirable stock. It was a bit of a gamble, because I was turning over far more money than I actually had, but I managed to clear the lot, and made a ridiculous amount of dosh.

I invested that in the stock market, which was shooting up, and ended up creating enough wealth for us to live very comfortably, all while pulling in my wage as a head chef.

The Olympics came and went, and journalists and food critics from all over the world descended on Sydney and flew off again, banging on about the new Australian cuisine that I was supposedly a part of.

I didn't get it; couldn't see what was so Australian about what we were doing. None of the heavy-hitters were doing anything I could identify as being part of an authentic, national food culture. Claude's was classically French, Tetsuya's was Japanese, Neil Perry was sort of pan-Asian, and Forty One was French with a little bit of Japanese finesse, maybe. Amazing, delicious food, yes, but was it *Australian*?

The longer I cooked, and the more I heard about how exciting Mod Oz cuisine was, the more confused I felt. What was going on? It felt really odd, as a chef, to land in a country where there was no culinary tradition waiting for me to reach out to, touch, and taste.

The more I thought about it, the weirder it seemed. By 2001, I was increasingly aware that there were all sorts of incredible Indigenous ingredients in Australia that chefs just weren't paying any attention to, and I couldn't understand why. Look at the finger lime alone – a citrus with all these gradations of sweet and sour that basically has the texture of caviar – are you fucking kidding me? Do you know what a decent chef could do with that?

I knew that there'd been an era where 'bush tucker' had been seized on as a sort of national identity in the 80s and 90s, where for a hot minute Australia was excited by damper and witchetty grubs, but that now everyone seemed really burned and embarrassed by. It was weird: whenever I brought it up with other chefs they got really angry. Not as angry as the critics and the punters though.

Mention native Australian ingredients and people would suddenly have a severe case of facial neuralgia – curling their lips and scrunching up their face like I'd just said something obscene.

I started experimenting with a few native ingredients in new dishes for the menu – dried lemon myrtle leaves, frozen quandong – and people lost their minds. In a bad way: with very few exceptions, the feedback from diners who were presented with an ingredient they hadn't seen before, and were informed it was native, was uniform: 'This is shit'.

In the aftermath of being bagged out for that I started talking to those around me, trying to figure out what happened during the bush tucker era that left such a sour taste in everyone's mouth. What I found was this widespread belief that Indigenous ingredients weren't very tasty, or interesting, or versatile – which didn't track with my experience, limited as it was.

Back then, the only way I could get my hands on Indigenous ingredients was to phone a speciality supplier, and I'd get a frozen packet of fruit, or some dehydrated bush tomato, and the way chefs were using it was as a garnish or flourish – a little bit of powdered Tasmanian pepper on top of a soup, maybe.

Everything was a European dish with Indigenous ingredients sprinkled on top, which was going at it the wrong way around.

Take vichyssoise – a soup of leek and potato that takes two simple ingredients and creates this beautiful, silky blend that's far more than the sum of its parts. If I'd never seen a leek before and you gave me a dehydrated bag of leek powder to finish a potato soup with, it would be a very different proposition to vichyssoise. Of course a punter would be underwhelmed by that. The leek is an integral part of the recipe: it's the harmony of the leek and the potato that pulls in the rest of the flavours and makes it such an elegant dish. It's built from the ground up and if you're not thinking that way about the new ingredients you encounter as a chef, then you'll never have a true understanding of how to incorporate them into a dish.

One day I was in the kitchen at Forty One when it struck me that I should find an Indigenous Australian chef to talk to about how they used ingredients and then I might be able to work out how they could be presented in a modern way. That's when it occurred to me that I'd never actually met an Indigenous chef. Worse, I realised that I'd lived in Australia for over two years now, and had never really spoken to an Indigenous person. That struck me as really weird, and it seemed even weirder that everyone else just took that as the norm. I wouldn't even know who to talk to if I wanted to find out what was going on with Indigenous food.

I'd been in Australia for a couple of years now and I hadn't seen much of Sydney beyond the view from Forty One. I felt so embarrassed. When I really thought about it, the only time I encountered any Indigenous people was when I walked past the buskers who played didgeridoos and clapping sticks down on the waterfront at Circular Quay. So I thought I'd start there.

I walked out of the kitchen and down to the waterfront, approached the first didgeridoo-player I saw and introduced myself: 'I'm Jock, I'm a chef. Would it be okay if you told me about where you're from, a bit about yourself and what you ate growing up, what your mum and dad cooked when you were a kid? About your culture?'

'Yeah, man,' he said, 'sit down.'

His name was Jimmy, and what he told me sitting there by the water changed my whole life; just completely rewired the way I looked at the world. I ended up sitting with him for four hours, and could have sat there all day and night.

He started telling me about this particular feast that happened only during a particular time of the year, when the lilies bloomed on the beach. Once the petals started to droop, that was a signal from nature that the flat fish were fat and ready to eat.

Then, when the tide was just right, his mob would walk out into the water to a certain point – he showed me on his shin – and wait. After twenty minutes or so, the flat fish would emerge in great numbers and could be speared. If everything was done right, if all the signs were observed and the steps taken on the right day, at the right time, then the sea would serve up this feast, and they'd take back twelve to fifteen fish for the whole community.

It took me a minute to work out that 'flat fish' was his term for stingray, but I couldn't work out what he meant by 'fat'. So I asked him how he cooked it, and he told me there were a couple of ways to cook a stingray, and in his family there was always a big hoo-ha about whose recipe was better.

'Well, what's your favourite?' I asked. Then Jimmy smiled, and started talking about building the fire up and letting it burn down until the coals are white-hot. He mimed how they'd bend the stingray back and kiss the stretched belly to the coals, and the skin, because it was engorged and stretched, burst the second it hit the coals and the fat could be easily removed.

So I was thinking about how that would work, and it struck me that when he said 'fat' he might be talking about the stingray's liver. When fish get towards the end of the breeding season, when feed is at its peak, the liver gets engorged, a little like foie gras. That's normally at the end of summer, which would track with the petals drooping on the lilies.

Jimmy went on to explain how the liver burst out, and was put aside, then the rest of the fish was smoked over the coals. Then the meat was picked, seasoned with sea water and set aside on leaves. While the fish rested, the liver was seared for thirty seconds on either side, then mashed and mixed through the meat to make fishballs.

At that point my mind just exploded. He was basically describing a sort of brandade – the emulsion of cod and olive oil that is a very old-school Mediterranean dish – but on steroids. Once I clocked what he was telling me about, I got more and more excited. He was telling me, basically, that his community was so in tune with their land that the flowers told them when wild stingray foie gras could be harvested from the ocean, and on top of that there was a traditional recipe using techniques I'd had to go to college to learn.

As he was describing it, I could practically taste it: the smoke from the leaves, the richness of the liver and the slight gaminess of the fish meat ... my mouth was watering thinking about those fish balls.

All the time he was talking I was realising that my hunch that there was something going on here that Australian chefs were ignoring was just the tip of the iceberg. I was hoping for some trace of overlooked food culture, but what Jimmy was describing wasn't just a food culture, it was a *cuisine*.

That's the moment I knew for certain that Indigenous Australian food was not just worth investigating, but that there was something that needed to be acknowledged. I sat with Jimmy for hours, enthralled, and he told me all about his mother's country in Western Australia, and his father's in Arnhem Land in the Northern Territory. He told about all these plants and herbs and seasonings he had no name for in English, and which I was starting to realise were all out there – had been all along – but Australian chefs were just wilfully blind to them.

Everything Jimmy said that day gave me the feeling that there was something amazing here. The food he described excited me more than any three-star restaurant I'd been in for years. It was such an amazing moment for me. I went back to work absolutely fired up about the culinary traditions that Indigenous communities were safeguarding. I was shaking with anticipation; I'd never been so excited about anything. My mood turned around in an instant, and all at once I was so excited to be living and working in Australia.

It didn't seem to me that life could get much better than that. Then, right on cue, it did.

In 2000 Kelly had told me she was pregnant, which seemed totally surreal to me until the day our daughter was born in April 2001. Everything changed for me at that moment; the understanding that you walk into a hospital as two and leave as three.

It changes your whole world view, casts you back to your own childhood and your relationship with your parents, and stuff starts to fall into perspective. It was a revelation.

Things became real. The moment you hear your baby cry for the first time, life is more real than it has ever been. I was responsible for another life, or supposedly responsible, and it had to happen now, not gradually, not on a curve. It was real, *now*.

Looking into your child's eyes for the first time fundamentally changes who you are. You feel your entire being unravel and re-form around the fact that you are now the parent and protector of this tiny, perfect life. It's phenomenal. There's nothing in the world that comes even close to that moment. I just burst into tears, it was such a beautiful space of time – five minutes? half an hour? – when the nurse gave me Ava to hold while Kelly was taken back to the ward, and I just stared into her eyes, this brand-new baby girl. The craziest moment of my life, in the best possible way. If I'm honest, it was at that moment that I realised what love actually was. 'Oh right,' I realised, holding my daughter, 'she's so much more important to my world than I am.'

I was so, so happy. Of course, it's one of the happiest days of any man's life when he welcomes his child into the world, but this was also something I'd wanted my whole life. Ever since I was a little boy myself, I'd wanted to have a family, big as it could be; to raise my kids, and their kids, and sit around the family table eating and yelling. It's weird, but when I was a little kid, my dream was that one day I'd be this Italian *nonno,* just like my own, with this huge family serving *cacio e pepe* to a million grandchildren. With Ava, that dream was coming true. Or so I thought. Life had other plans, of course.

CHAPTER EIGHTEEN

A year later, in June 2002, everything came crashing down. Funnily enough, I'd jumped out of a plane that morning. A mate and I got up in the wee hours to take his new Porsche for a spin to Picton in south-western Sydney and go skydiving. It was a beautiful day. I remember feeling elated as I fell; everything seemed just glorious in the light of a new day. By the time I got home at about 9 am, Ava had already been up and gone down for another sleep, so the house was quiet. I seized the moment and curled up on the sofa for a kip.

When I woke up, Kelly was staring at me with this absolutely furious expression on her face.

'What's the matter with you?'

'Nothing,' she said, walking off. Then she doubled back from the kitchen and stood in front of me. 'Actually, I don't love you. I haven't loved you for four years and I don't want to be married any more.'

I was blindsided. I didn't see it coming at all. If I'd been paying attention, I'd have known it was on the cards. The signs were all there but I wasn't home to see them.

There was rarely a time that I wasn't at work, be it in the restaurant kitchen or running my various businesses. That meant that there was almost never a time when I was at home giving Kelly the support she needed.

With hindsight, my workaholism in those years was just another symptom of a deeper psychological problem. What I told myself was healthy and honourable – working hard to put food on the table – was just another form of compulsive behaviour. I'd swapped smack out for ambition, perfectionism, the drive to be the best chef holding a knife in all Sydney – which in the end was just another drug, and just as detrimental to forming healthy relationships. In a way, my sobriety hastened the death of our marriage. The years spent getting high didn't help.

It's clear to me now that I was a pretty shit husband; there's no denying that fact. Although I was sober, I was still in the very early stages of recovery, and the truth is my memory is so mashed by my years of substance abuse that there are huge, important events in my life I just have no memory of. I cannot recall what my first conversation with Kelly was about, or even what she studied at uni. It's something I regret deeply, but so much of my life, and so many relationships, were squandered in a drug haze. And in the wake of all that, now I was losing my wife.

Things hadn't been right between us for some time. In some ways, we'd been on the rocks since May of the previous year, when I'd come out for breakfast one morning, kissed baby Ava on the head, where Kelly was sitting on the couch watching the telly, then sat down, opened the paper, and discovered that I'd lost all our money.

Early in 2001, I'd grown my share portfolio into a healthy seven-figure sum, and had decided to go all-in on a sure-fire stock, One.Tel. A company invested in by millionaire dynasties the Packers and the Murdochs, among other business luminaries, the prevailing wisdom was that it couldn't fail. The share price was skyrocketing and my plan was to jump in and jump out, making a quick profit, then put it all back into blue chips.

Now the paper was telling me One.Tel was collapsing, and the television blaring from the other room was carrying the story as well. I called my stockbroker, who was at his wits' end. I was the millionth call he'd had that morning, obviously, and he gave it to me straight. I'd be lucky to get back twenty-six cents to the dollar.

I sat there stunned while my coffee grew cold, unable to process it. How does that happen? How do you just lose seven figures overnight? I cannot describe how dismal it felt. What do you do? Do you cry? Do you get angry and smash shit? I didn't know what to do. All I knew was in that moment we went from being a fairly comfortable, upper-middle-class family to broke.

I told Kelly that I'd lost all our money, and I needed her to stop using her credit cards. From now on, we were on a strict budget. Of course, that all only made me work harder and harder in both the kitchen and the business to try and recoup the loss, which only meant I drifted further from Kelly over the next year.

Just a couple of months earlier, when we'd gone on holiday to Thailand, it was obvious things weren't right between us, but I thought that if a relationship is on the rocks then you could always fix it. It had never occurred to me that Kelly would leave, and now here it was.

I tried to talk to her about it – maybe I could change my workload or we could go to counselling? Whatever it took. But it was all too late: she'd made up her mind. We were done.

I was crushed. Ava was just fourteen months old at this point, and now I didn't know how I was going to have a relationship with her. In a second, this image I had of how my life was going to be – that I'd end up as this Italian *nonno* putting down a plate of steaming pasta for the family – went up in smoke. But more than anything, I was worried about what it meant for Ava to have separated parents.

I was so desperate I called my dad for advice: 'I don't know what to do. What do you do when this happens? What if I never get to see my daughter again? What do I *do*?' Dad changed the subject. It wasn't done in our family to discuss that sort of thing, and I was no closer to knowing the way forward.

One of the guys at Forty One had already been through separation and custody battles and all of that grim shit, and he was very rational about it.

'You've got to get yourself a lawyer, Jock,' he told me matter-of-factly. 'You've just got to do it.' It was all very overwhelming, but I couldn't see a way forward. A couple of days later I moved out. I left pretty much everything behind except for a pair of jeans and a shirt.

I needed somewhere to live, and found a room in a share house in inner-city Waterloo, right behind the Cauliflower Hotel, which was a really rough part of town back then.

I moved in with a couple: Phil, who was an ex-soldier, and his partner, Andy. It was a bit of a learning curve for all of us – they were just so different from me. They were very flamboyant dudes; really stylish guys who were serious about interior design. It was a beautiful home, and Phil and Andy helped cushion what was really a pretty rough landing.

On the other hand, I was still me, and I'd moved in with the same restlessness I carried everywhere. I became obsessive with setting my room up, and one day I found the perfect office desk to run my business from. Then I absolutely *had* to have a particular chair to match the desk and couldn't find one anywhere. I searched high and low like a madman, and finally found one that was close to what I wanted, but too tall. Easy: I'd just saw a bit off the legs. So off I went and found a circular saw, and was just firing it up when Phil came home. He came running upstairs.

'What are you doing?' he cried.

'I'm just going to take this saw,' I yelled over the noise, 'and open up the doorframe *here* and *here* to make the room a bit more spacious.'

It was a joke, of course, but Phil thought I was serious and turned pale and backed away, so I had to chase him down the hall, power saw in hand, to calm him down and assure him I wasn't crazy.

They hadn't had easy lives themselves, and were sympathetic to the shift that was happening in mine. They were so accepting of the ups and downs and all the weird shit I got up to, and my coming in late at night or in the early morning.

Those first months after separation were so hard. I'd pick Ava up from her mum's place in the car, and she would just cry for a solid hour because she didn't want to leave her mum and I was fast becoming a stranger to her. Every time I had her for the day it would start like that, and it's hard to come back from that to have a good day, let alone build a relationship and an entirely new life.

It took a lot of trial and error to learn how to be a single dad, and how to rearrange my world to fit a baby girl into it. For a while, I'd take her into work with me and she'd hang out in the kitchen eating lobster caviar with a spoon right out of the jar.

Andy and Phil were amazing with Ava. They'd drop everything to help cheer her up, and they could make her smile when she'd been distraught moments before.

It was a weird, tough time. I was trying to realise a new relationship with my daughter in the new post-separation world where I wasn't waking up and seeing her every day. We had our time on the weekend, and that was it. It was pretty miserable, all things considered.

I'd had tough times before, but I'd always been able to throw myself into my work. Now from a career perspective, I wasn't really happy at Forty One because it wasn't what I imagined that I was going to come back to Australia to do. It was more of the same: high stakes; high prestige; grotesque amounts of waste.

The rest of the time I was alone. I could go out to clubs, but clubs are pretty miserable when you're heartbroken. There was a lot of drinking. At that time alcohol was really my poison of choice. Without heroin in my life I hit it pretty hard as a kind of stocking filler to make up for what had been taken out of my repertoire of substance abuse. I poured a fair bit of booze into that hole that had opened up in the middle of my life, with limited success. The only thing that really kept me going through that time was work, which has always been the thing I've fallen back on when everything else was falling apart around me. My work is what kept me from jumping back on the horse with heroin, but it was only a bandaid solution, which came with its own set of problems.

I was having what I would one day recognise as a total psychological breakdown, but it never occurred to me to seek treatment or help. Instead, I did what I'd always done, which was work harder and harder, while my behaviour grew more and more erratic.

A few months after the separation, I was having a terrible day at work. Dietmar was away in Auckland, I was in the kitchen, and we were slammed. Service hadn't started yet, but we had 180 diners booked for lunch and the same again for dinner, and we were short-staffed. We had just eight people on the roster, a couple of whom were inexperienced, to do prep, two services, and close. A stupid amount of work for too few people, and everyone was pretty stressed-out. When we were in that sort of situation I'd always try to get people laughing and lift the morale a bit before the rush.

I come from a long line of jokers. Back in my dad's shop they'd spend the first couple of weeks of an apprentice barber's career just pranking the poor lad. The classic prank was to tell him the steriliser was broken, so he had to take a bucket across the road to the hairdressers to get some steam. So he'd dash across the road with two big buckets, fill them with steam, and of course by the time he got back they would be empty, so he'd have to go back again. The hairdresser did the same thing to their apprentices, so there was a steady exchange of kids running back and forth across the road with steaming buckets all year round. In a very real sense, taking the piss is as integral a part of being Scottish as the tartan.

That culture of stitching up other staff had been the same in pretty much every kitchen I've ever worked in. Three-star places meant a relentless stream of pranks and stitch-ups. If you were working with a salamander, used for quick-grilling dishes, you were easy prey. If you let your guard down for a second someone would throw a piece of brioche in there, and you wouldn't know anything was wrong until the smoke started pouring out and the head chef was tearing your head off for ruining a brioche. If you could get a bit of a rise out of someone, have a bit of a laugh, it helped get through the day.

At Forty One there was a running joke with the younger staff where they'd sneak up on me in the dry stores and try to give me a heart attack. I'd come in a couple hours before anyone else when it was quiet so I could take inventory and try and plan out the day. The dry stores were kind of dark and spooky that early, so when the younger guys came in they'd find me with my head buried in the dry stores and they'd leap on me screaming. Then I'd jump three feet and brain myself on a shelving unit.

On this particular morning, we had an apprentice on pastry who was moving super slowly. He needed to get cracking or he wasn't going to be ready for service, and everyone else in the kitchen was falling behind trying to coach him through. 'Mate,' I told him, 'you're going to have to hurry up. Do you need help?'

We were going to have a lunch rush and without pastry ready the whole service would be chaos.

Shit was going wrong all over the place. The hot boxes we used to warm the plates for service had broken down so we'd set up sterno cans, little portable stoves that burned clear gel and made a flame just hot enough to keep the hot box warm. We'd put four of these in a hot box and it meant we still had hot plates for service.

I was going past the hot box, and noticed this apprentice was moving like a glacier. He was so slow, he was dressed sort of sloppy, his pants were hanging off him like a plumber, and I had an idea to stitch him up, have a laugh, and get him moving.

The sterno cans hadn't been fired up yet, so I thought I'd get a teaspoon of the flammable gel from the sterno can and slap it on his arse. I thought it would be funny as a practical joke: he'd think he was set to ignite, he'd shit himself and drop his pants, we'd have a laugh, morale would pick up, then we'd push on for lunch.

So that's what I did. I slapped the gel on his arse with the spoon. He just sort of blinked at me.

'What are you doing?' he said. 'Did you just touch my arse?'

No reaction beyond that, no laugh, so I shrugged and went back to the main section where the boys were already starting to set the pass up.

I went to pick up the sterno can in the hot box and burned my finger. That's when I realised that the boys had already lit the gel, but under the kitchen lighting I couldn't see the flame burning. Which meant the gel I'd put on the apprentice . . . was already lit.

I turned around and looked through the pass into the pastry section where the apprentice was crying out and patting at his arse.

I realised I'd actually set this poor kid's arse on fire, vaulted over the pastry section and whipped his trousers down to put out the flames. His bum was fine; if he'd not patted at the gel he would have been unscathed, but he had a bit of a burn on his hand, across two fingers. It didn't look too bad so I got it under the sink, washed it, dressed it, and put a glove on it.

'Are you all right mate?' I asked him, 'Everything cool?'

'Yeah, yeah,' he said, 'I'm fine, no dramas.'

We all went back to work. The apprentice picked up the pace. I returned to the main section, but I didn't feel great about it. As far as practical jokes went, it was a stupid idea on my behalf, and it went seriously pear-shaped. So as the day went on I kept checking in on the apprentice, helping him get through service, and after lunch I took the glove off to have a look under the bandages. By now he had a blister bubbling up, and I didn't love the look of it.

'You've got to burst that blister,' I told him. 'Just go home, don't worry about service tonight.' So he went home, and somehow we managed without him.

The next day he called in sick, and not long after that, the training company he was conducting his apprenticeship with called in for a report. We told them he'd burned his hand, and was off for the day.

The company then called him to check on his wellbeing. His mum, who he lived with, answered the phone. They indicated they were looking into an accident at work, and his mum told them she didn't know anything about it, and he was out for a surf right then. She'd get him to call back when he was done surfing. The company relayed this to Forty One.

That's the last I heard about it, until the apprentice filed a worker's compensation claim, and it turned into a massive problem for everyone.

The claim named Dietmar as the owner of the restaurant, and asked for serious money for psychological damages, as apparently the apprentice could no longer work.

It alleged that I acted like a Nazi in the kitchen; that I even had swastika tattoos under my shirt. (But that was patently untrue, as anyone could see. My tattoos are in fucking good taste, thank you very much.)

I thought that was a bit rough. I felt terrible for him, and I'd been kicking myself over it. Playing a prank on my staff was nothing unusual for me. But something going that wrong and having serious consequences was out of the ordinary, and out of order. At this point, it turned into a nightmare.

I handed in my notice to Dietmar, because it was no good dragging the restaurant down with me. My name was going to be hauled through the mud, and I didn't want that mud to come off on Dietmar.

'This is all likely to end up in the newspapers,' I said, 'so I think I should leave rather than have you sack me.'

'I think that's probably for the best,' he said, and I packed up my knives and left.

Once the dust had settled, I had a meeting with the apprentice, his mother, the training company, and the restaurant to work it out.

'I'm very sorry,' I said. 'I was playing a joke and it went badly. I accept full responsibility.'

The apprentice's mother demanded that I be sacked, so I told her I'd already left. However, the compensation demand against Dietmar wasn't dropped.

It got to the point that I had to get a lawyer to advise me. He told me that I'd done the right thing by resigning, but warned me it could get ugly down the line. In the meantime, Fair Work went through their internal processes of investigating the claim and making their deliberation. Ultimately, they found that the incident was an accident, the burns suffered not terribly serious, and compensation was not awarded.

What I did was egregious, immature, dangerous, and I am thankful every day that I didn't hurt him as seriously as could easily have happened.

I'd lost my job, as I probably deserved to, and the apprentice got to see me twist in the wind for my sins. I have many, many regrets in my life, but my conduct on that day is right up there in terms of sheer guilt, but once the compensation claim was thrown out, I figured it was done.

After that all blew up I was a bit lost in Sydney. No wife; no career; a daughter I barely saw. I felt I was sailing with no compass and decided to go back to the UK and see Mum and Dad. I planned to take Ava with me to see her grandparents and booked seats right in the front of the economy section for a little more space. At the time, in 2003, she was just sixteen months old, but I couldn't see any problem with the idea.

'It'll be fine,' I airily assured anyone who told me I was crazy. Kelly wasn't wild about being without her daughter, but understood that I was seriously in need of help, and wanted our daughter to have a relationship with all her grandparents.

It was fine. Ava was amazing, just an absolutely angelic child on her best behaviour the whole grim long-haul flight to the UK – until we touched down in London, when the poor little girl turned around and vomited all over me.

It was horrific, we couldn't move until the plane had unloaded, so I just had to sit there marinating in that cheesy, acrid stink of toddler vomit. But that was the only hiccup in the entire trip.

Mum and Dad doted on Ava. Introducing my daughter to her grandparents was such a special moment. I remember watching my mum holding Ava and just being overwhelmed with love. It was this very strong moment of clarity; the realisation that, as hard as it was, I really loved being a dad. In some ways, that was the moment I really started to feel like a father. The day she was born was magical, but it was on that trip to Scotland that I felt I started to grow up and into the role of being Ava's dad.

Seeing how much my parents loved my child was a dramatic reframing of how I understood my own relationship with them. I could see in the way they looked at her that they'd once held me and loved me in exactly the same way as I loved Ava. It was an extraordinary moment for all of us.

For that whole month I got along really well with my
parents, saw some old mates and began to repair my shat-
tered confidence. Slowly, over the month of the trip, I started
to feel I had some control over my life again, and the gloom
lifted a little. I returned to Australia determined to make
things work – and got arrested at the airport.

CHAPTER NINETEEN

The police were waiting for me when I stepped off the plane. I had to call Kelly to come to the airport to collect Ava, then I was taken down to the police station in the Rocks and charged with aggravated bodily harm (ABH) against the apprentice.

After Fair Work had ruled against damages, he'd launched a criminal case against me for ABH, as a first step in personally suing me for restitution.

So now it was formal. It was a criminal charge, and I was sitting there being interviewed by the cops. I was well out of my depth, but my lawyer came down, posted bail, got me out of custody and talked to the police about the charges.

While he spoke to them I sat in the station, struggling to get my head around how I ended up in this situation. One minute I was a dad with a beautiful wife, the head chef of one of the best restaurants on this side of the planet; the next I was single, broke and being led away in cuffs. How did I set out to do a practical joke and end up getting arrested in front of my daughter?

I'd made some bad decisions before, but there'd never been a point where my immature fucking around had had such dramatic and permanent consequences.

After a while, the lawyer came in and told me that the apprentice had been unsuccessful with any kind of compensation claim against the restaurant, but that he'd lodged a case against me personally for ABH and accompanying psychological damages.

I couldn't believe what I was hearing.

'They're looking to get compensation from you.'

My lawyer set out just how serious things had become. Because I was on the hook for the burning incident, if they successfully sued for psychological damages, I might be liable to pay the apprentice's potential earnings as a chef across a lifetime, which could amount to millions. According to the lawyers, the case might not be resolved for some time, so I braced for the long haul. It would end up dragging on longer than I could have imagined, year after year.

For several years after the prank went wrong, I didn't look for another job as a chef; I didn't want to be in the kitchen. I had this thing in my head that if I was in Australia then I should be cooking Australian food, but I didn't know what that was.

It's not salt and pepper calamari, as delicious as that is – when not cooked from frozen in rancid oil – and as much as I like eating it. But there's nothing about a plate of it that tells me about Australia.

Remembering that marvellous stingray dish Jimmy the busker had described, I believed there needed to be a narrative of Australian cuisine that included Indigenous culture, but I had no idea where to look for it. It didn't have to be me cooking it, but restaurants didn't want to do it because they didn't make any money, and punters and chefs alike seemed to have been burned by the 'bush tucker' era of the 1980s.

Fine. If I couldn't pursue my passion, I was quite happy to not be in the kitchen. It felt good to leave it behind. When the head chef of a hatted restaurant leaves, especially under a cloud, there's plenty of speculation about where you'll go and what big move you'll make next. My move was to simply drop off the radar.

Without a kitchen to run, I continued the business importing and selling kitchen equipment: pots, pans, knives, blenders – all the stuff that kitchens needed. It wasn't my passion in life, but it was a way to provide for my daughter and wife, even though we were separated, and it was a relief to do something that the hospitality industry appreciated instead of slamming my head against a wall trying to get people to change their thinking about Australian cuisine.

During that period I was reading everything I could get my hands on about Indigenous food and culture, which wasn't much. The more I learned about the history of settlement, the angrier I got.

As I educated myself about the unfair treatment of Indigenous people – the stolen land, the stolen generations – I grew incensed to the point of physical illness. I felt sick about the lack of acknowledgement; the sheer wilful blindness to what was done wrong in this country from day one of settlement. I got stuck on the idea that if the first European settlers had approached the nations they found here with even a skerrick of respect and curiosity about the culture; if the incredibly sophisticated, thriving cultures on this land had been acknowledged, and I mean truly, it would have been very different.

It made me feel so helpless, the dispossession that had happened and was still happening, and that I could not believe the entire country had just decided to ignore. How did you get people to pay attention to a culture they had decided to disrespect? The more I stewed on it, the more I kept coming back to food.

I had this idea that food was the great leveller. Maybe food could be that broker – it brings everyone to the same table, and you can begin to have a conversation through food with someone who you don't share a language with.

I've known stone-cold bigots in the UK who have sat down for a curry and started a journey on which they slowly learn to open their minds just a little bit. Chicken tikka masala has done as much to dismantle systemic racism in some cities as any government education program.

Obviously, my thought process at that point was very naive – there were so many political and historical catastrophes to wade through before food would make any tangible difference – but to me, at that moment, it seemed really easy. If every Australian could have that conversation I'd had with Jimmy, I didn't see how they could ignore the value of it.

I imagined a cuisine that was cooked and shared in a way that wasn't tokenistic. If chefs would take the time to

With eight-month-old Ava at Restaurant Forty One, 2001.

Hanging out with Ava aged nine months and, below, in 2002 aged eighteen months.

Sofia aged ten, November 2015. Basket Range, South Australia.

Making pasta with
Sofia in 2016.

Filming *Nomad Chef* in East Arnhem Land, Northern Territory.
COURTESY DISCOVERY CHANNEL

With celebrated artist and academic Patricia Marrfurra McTaggart OAM, Nauiyu Community, Daly River, Northern Territory. PER-ANDERS JÖRGENSEN

On country with close friend and mentor Bruno Dann. Nyul Nyul country, the Kimberley, Western Australia. LUKE EBLEN

Cooking fish for the community during the building of the Winawarl Community packing shed, Nyul Nyul country, May 2019. LUKE EBLEN

Chefs from around the world explored Indigenous foods during the Margaret River Gourmet Escape, 2012. Wardandi country, Western Australia. *From left:* Alvin Leung, André Chiang, Alex Atala, René Redzepi, Peter Gilmore, Daniel Giusti, Josh Whiteland, Jock Zonfrillo, Justin North, Sat Bains, David Moyle. *Front:* David Chang and Matt Wilkinson.

With the late Adrian Gill (standing) and Marco Pierre White, Margaret River, Western Australia, 2015.

From left: Jock with Marco Pierre White, Richard Turner and Spencer Patrick. They all worked together at Restaurant Marco Pierre White in the 90s. Margaret River, Western Australia, 2015.

Jock and Lauren were married on New Year's Day 2017 in a beach ceremony on Mnemba Island in the Zanzibar Archipelago, Tanzania.

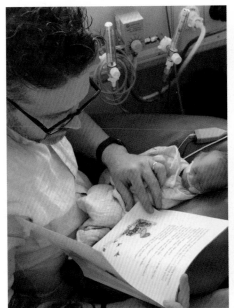

Left: With son, Alfie, at three weeks old, still in the NICU and with oxygen and feeding tubes attached to his tiny body after his premature birth. It was touch and go for a long, stressful time. *Right:* Alfie's first day at home after five weeks in hospital. He still needed the feeding tube.

Left and right: Alfie quickly overcame his perilous start to life to grow into a healthy and active little boy.

At Restaurant Orana, 2018: A laidback baby, Alfie even came to work with Jock. Pictured here between general manager Greta Wohlstadt and head chef Sam Christopher.

Alfie's first haircut was performed by his barber grandad on a visit to Scotland, July 2018.

Restaurant Orana won *Gourmet Traveller's* Australian Restaurant of the Year in 2018, the first restaurant to steal the crown out from under the noses of Sydney and Melbourne in nearly two decades. Jock is with Greta Wohlstadt (left) and wife Lauren Zonfrillo.

Saturday 21 March 2020 was the last service before all hospitality venues in Australia were forced to close due to COVID-19. Ex-managers returned to be part of what was an emotional last service.

Left to right: Jock, Ava, Sofia and Lauren, Thailand, April 2017.

Ava and Jock at her Year 12 Father and Daughter Graduation Night in Sydney, 2018.

With baby Isla, Jock's third daughter, and Lauren in 2021 when they visited him on the *MasterChef* set.

Isla with her dad. She was born during the COVID-19 pandemic, 2020.

Alfie adores his little sister.

Above and below: With fellow *MasterChef Australia* judges Melissa Leong and Andy Allen. KELLY GARDNER

In deep discussion with contestant Reece Hignell during the 2020 season of *MasterChef Australia*. KELLY GARDNER

Andy Allen and Jock joke with contestant Emelia Jackson, who went on to win *MasterChef Australia* in 2020. KELLY GARDNER

Jock on the set of *MasterChef Australia*. KELLY GARDNER

listen to the stories and acknowledge the people who were custodians of those stories and those ingredients. If they understood why those ingredients and medicine were used, and took the time to present it as part of the gastronomy of the day so others could understand. If I could achieve that as a chef, that might be a stepping stone for people to see something beautiful and begin to understand and acknowledge Indigenous culture.

But it was clear to me I wasn't going to learn anything in Sydney, and the only way I was going to start to understand any of that myself was to go out and start visiting communities. So that's what I did. One day I just got in my car and looked at the map. I'd been told that the biggest communities were in Arnhem Land, but looking at the map I realised how far away that was, right at the top of Australia. I decided to start in the very centre of Australia, which would mean Anangu Pitjantjatjara Yankunytjatjara, or APY, lands. So that's what I did.

Some 2500 kilometres later I drove into South Australia, about 40 kilometres south of the border with the Northern Territory, and the middle of the Amata community. I just drove right in and got out of the car and tried to buy petrol. If I'd known what I was doing I would have understood I was breaking about a million laws and basic articles of protocol, and the reception I got reflected that. After a bit of fumbling about some elders came up to me and quizzed me on what I was doing there. Looking back now, I'm horrified at the levels of ignorance I charged in there with.

I sort of bumbled my way through an explanation: I was a chef; I was interested in Aboriginal food. They listened, had a quiet word among themselves, then they turned to me and told me to fuck off, pretty much.

'You don't belong here,' one of the elders told me. 'We don't want you here. Go home.'

So I drove back to Sydney, feeling very ordinary – suspecting I'd done something really disrespectful by just going out there unannounced.

I stopped at a petrol station in Yunyarinyi before I drove back. I was walking out after paying and there was this young mother, probably not even twenty yet, a rusty can of petrol strapped to her head with a piece of string, and a baby in her arms.

How does a person look at what's been done to the oldest surviving culture on earth, and not feel the most incredible sense of theft?

Australians will fly across the world to visit the pyramids as this ancient testament to civilisation, but what the fuck are the pyramids compared to First Nations Australia? What is 4500 years of history compared to the millennia upon millennia of the culture that prospered on this land? It's nothing. Why would you go to a museum to see a 4000-year-old mummy when you can see a boomerang that's tens of thousands of years old, and the first aerodynamic object that any civilisation ever conceived of? A culture does not invent a boomerang – a fearsome, awesome technological achievement – by accident. What has been here forever is so old, and so rich, and it flourished on a vast, dry continent.

On my first visits to communities, that sense of loss was crushing. The impact of settlement and the damage done was a constant reminder that things weren't done properly, and now communities were dealing with these horrific consequences that nobody wanted to talk about, bring to light or have an open conversation about.

I made another six trips out to the same community before anyone would talk to me. On the seventh trip, the elders who had told me to leave time after time sort of softened, and invited me to come and have a cup of tea.

We sat in a circle in the red dust outside someone's home. I was handed a cup of tea, and my hand was shaking so much I nearly spilled it. Literally quaking with fear, because I didn't know anyone or how things worked there, and I'd never felt so much like a fish out of water. At the same time, I was so thankful and excited to be there, and I pulled out a notebook with all these questions I had.

'Put that away!' someone snapped, and I got educated pretty promptly that this was not somewhere you come and take notes or photos or walk away with knowledge that the community has not agreed to share with you. 'If you want us to share knowledge with you, you sit down and open your ears.'

'Okay.' I put away my notebook. 'I'm listening.'

They began to share stories about what they called 'country', and the conversation turned to food as more people arrived from all over the place. In maybe twenty minutes I met so many people, and they were just so welcoming and lovely.

I was just starting to feel at ease when the cops turned up.

A police four-wheel drive pulled up out the front of the house, and these two white cops jumped out. They asked what I was doing there, I explained, and they asked for my permit.

'What permit?' I said, 'What are you talking about, permit? These guys invited me here for tea. I don't need a fucking permit.'

I looked around at the elders, but they'd clammed up. Since the cops arrived they hadn't said a word; just stared off, not even looking at them. Just absolute silence.

'Mate,' the cops squared up to me. 'If you don't have a permit, you can't be here. Get in your car. We're going to escort you off the land.'

So they escorted me off APY lands, and watched me out of sight. When I couldn't see the cop car in the rear-view any more, I pulled over, got out, sunk to my knees and hammered my fists in the red dirt. I started weeping, and then screamed with rage until my throat gave out. I was so angry – at the cops, at Australia, at my own dumb fucking ignorance.

At that point I realised that there was a much bigger problem for me to overcome than I thought. I got back in the car, for what would feel like the longest drive home I would ever take.

Between where we were as a society and any kind of acknowledgement of Indigenous people there were so many barriers that I was ignorant about: political, social, racial, legal. I had just been thrown off Indigenous land by two white coppers because I didn't have a piece of paper. That would have been fine, but for the fact that the Indigenous people I'd come to visit didn't even seem to know that such a permit existed. It was a white law; a police appara- tus of power. Further, if I'd set off to visit a community in

Arnhem Land where visitors don't need a permit, I never would have been confronted by that kind of white policing of those communities.

I needed to get thrown out to understand that they faced problems that I had never comprehended or appreciated. It was a realisation that I'd never been incarcerated on my own land by a different race, which is a privilege that I had always taken for granted because I was white, and from the UK, and to realise, viscerally, that there are people living in this country who aren't afforded that basic human right, was shattering. That was a long drive home as the realisation sank in that I had a lot further to go than the thousands of kilometres left on the road.

Where did I go from here? I was mired, not only in my ignorance, but in this vast, national lack of understanding.

That run-in with the cops was only the first of many, many realisations of how things were. It just got harder and harder. The more work I put into it the more I started to understand the scale of injustice and inequity in this country, which only made it seem like it was the right thing to do.

I never set out to amass Indigenous knowledge for myself. I went out to understand Indigenous knowledge, cultivate my own appreciation of native food that I could then share with proper permission. Every elder, from every land or community that has welcomed me in and shared their knowledge, has asked me to use my profile to share some of their story in the hope it would spark a public desire to bring acknowledgement of their culture, their people, their traditions.

The obsession with Indigenous food came from there, this weird bugbear in my brain about trying to give back, and food was the only thing I knew. So, the way I saw it I had no choice. I had to keep going out there, time after time, until I understood enough to start to share it with the rest of Australia, and to hopefully start a conversation within white Australia about the change we needed to make.

CHAPTER TWENTY

Life went on. I saw Ava on the weekends and tried to build a new relationship with Kelly as a co-parent, which isn't easy at the best of times, and we both came to this new arrangement with pretty significant baggage.

Nothing at that time was very easy, but I kept on with it, getting through the days with the impending court case throwing its shadow over them. As well as importing kitchen equipment, I did a little consultancy work, but any time anyone approached me to work as a chef I turned them down.

Stepping away from kitchens gave me time to make those trips into communities and spend time with elders and Indigenous men and women who shared my passion.

Over the years, as I met more people, as more communities let me in and shared their knowledge, a world of food far richer than I'd ever dreamed existed opened up to me. The sheer variety of flavours and textures that Indigenous people have been eating for millennia – and that mainstream Australia had ignored for centuries – was breathtaking.

Plants like min min, a little green flower with a crisp, sharp burst of pea sweetness; native passionfruit – exceptionally sweet berries; bush onions so sweet you can dig them up, brush the dirt off and bite straight into them like you're Tony Abbott. At the time, every chef was banging on about Szechuan pepper because New York had just discovered that it makes your mouth tingle, and we've had a better version here in Australia all along called Dorrigo pepper (*Tasmannia stipitata*).

Each trip out to the communities opened my eyes a little wider, and I felt I was actually starting to get a little closer to understanding Indigenous food in this country, and how I might start to work towards building bridges between fine dining and Indigenous communities.

At the same time, life was pretty lonely to be honest, and going outback was the only time I could get away from the weight of living apart from my daughter. I had watched Ava grow from a little baby with chronic reflux into a toddler, then into a fierce little girl. On the rare days I got to spend time with her she had always grown so much and learned so many new things since the last time I'd seen her. It was such a confusing emotion, to be so full of joy and pride for my daughter, yet devastated that I was missing so much of her childhood. Those first years of your child's life are not something you get a second chance at, and I'll never stop feeling regret for missing out, far too often, on those fleeting moments of fatherhood.

When Father's Day or Christmas rolled around and I couldn't see Ava, it didn't feel very good at all. On those days I could either sit at home with a bottle and sink into gloom, or I could get into the car and drive out onto those endless red desert roads and do something useful by learning from my friends in Indigenous communities.

Around 2004 I met Nadia at a friend's barbecue in Sydney. We started dating, fell in love, and got married later the same year. It was a small ceremony in Mittagong with just ten guests. My former father-in law, Steve, was my best man. It might seem odd, but he'd accepted that things just didn't work out between Kelly and me, and we'd stayed great mates.

For a while, life was good. Nadia and I started trying for a baby and before long we fell pregnant. I was stoked. It's an overwhelming joy to learn you'll be a father, and this time I was a little older, a little wiser. I understood that I'd sacrificed too many of those precious first days with Ava to be in the kitchen instead of with my family. This time, I promised myself I wouldn't make those same mistakes.

November 2005 I was at work when I got the call from Nadia, telling me the baby was coming. Today my second child would be born. Nadia's waters had broken and she'd started having contractions, so was ready to enact our birth plan, which involved going to the Royal Prince Alfred (RPA) Hospital in nearby Camperdown.

By chance, I happened to be at RPA installing industrial dishwashing machines in their kitchens when I got that call. Perfect timing, I thought.

'Well, I'm already at the hospital,' I told my wife, 'so just jump in a taxi and I'll meet you here.' It turned out that was *not* the right reply and, long story short, I jumped in a taxi, went to our home in Petersham, a suburb away, and brought her back to the RPA.

My wife went into labour, I was pacing around waiting, and after a few hours one of the nurses came up to me to see if I needed something to eat. She was just telling me she could only offer sandwiches as they couldn't wash any dishes because the guy installing the dishwasher had walked off the job, when she recognised me.

'Oh . . . you're the dishwasher guy.'

'Yes.'

'So that's why it's not done yet!'

'Yeah . . . sorry about that.'

So I had a sandwich and held my wife's hand for a while and soon our daughter, Sofia, was born. Second child, just as extraordinary as the first, but followed by just the sweetest moment of my life, which was when Ava came in to visit her new sister. That is a scene I'll never forget: seeing my two children meet each other for the first time. An absolutely pure, wondrous thing; a perfect moment in time. The dishwasher could wait.

In May 2006 the apprentice's case that had been hanging over my head for so long finally came to a head after many delays.

In court, my lawyers explained that it was a practical joke gone awry and that I took full responsibility. It should never have happened, but there was no malicious intent to deliberately set the poor lad on fire.

Ultimately, the court found this to be the case, and recorded no conviction against me. However, it decided that I should be financially responsible for psychological damages and I was eventually ordered to pay just over $75,000, plus costs.

I didn't have that kind of money so asked my lawyer what I could do and his best advice was to declare bankruptcy. So, eventually, that's what happened. The few assets I had left in the world went to the liquidators, and when the dust settled in 2007, I was not doing well at all.

The years of uncertainty and now the bankruptcy were pretty stressful and probably affected my marriage. For the first few months after Sofia was born I was working way too much, not realising how bad things were getting for my wife until it was too late. In many ways, I'd simply replaced heroin with the insatiable need for success. At this stage of my life I was an irredeemable workaholic, which is just as bad as being an alcoholic or a drug addict in terms of invading your family life. If I'd still been on heroin, at least maybe I would have jumped straight in the taxi, instead of wanting to stay and finish installing the dishwasher. Our marriage was failing and I didn't know how to help it. The more I tried to bridge the growing gap between us, the further apart we seemed to drift.

I now realise that I was not in a good mental space; not at all. In between my failed marriage, the disastrous kitchen prank, bankruptcy and forfeiting my career as a chef, I'd undergone a total psychological breakdown which I really should have been in treatment for. At the time, however, that wasn't something I would have even considered. Therapy was just not on the radar for a bloke like me. I just did that bloody-minded Scottish thing of squaring my shoulders and throwing myself into work, even though I was clearly broken.

So I'd come into the marriage dragging all the baggage from my first failed marriage, and had dumped all of it on poor Nadia.

I remember sitting on the steps of our house, turning to her and asking her what she wanted to do.

'We can do anything. What do you want? Think big. Do you want to leave Sydney? Go to the UK or Europe?' I had a sudden image of us maybe moving to Italy, some little town where we could sit in the sun and relax and recover.

There was a long pause, and then she told me she wanted to move to Adelaide, to be close to her sister who lived there. On top of that, she wanted me to sell the business and find another way to provide for the family so I could spend more time with her and Sofia.

That was a lot to take in. It was one of those sliding doors moments when your whole life goes down a different path based on a single choice.

I was wrestling with the guilt of having gone through one divorce and knowing how much that had hurt Ava. It was bad enough when Kelly and I separated and I moved out of the family home, so I was terrified that if I moved interstate Ava would feel abandoned all over again. At the same time, moving might help the marriage, and I owed it to baby Sofia to be by her side in these early years. I was torn.

There was no guarantee that Nadia and I would be able to work it out – we both suspected we were potentially doomed. I'd never been to Adelaide and didn't know a thing about it. But I was determined to make a last-ditch attempt to save the marriage, and if that meant going to Adelaide, I'd do it.

In 2009, Sofia and her mum flew to Adelaide ahead of me, and I packed up the ute and drove across the country to meet them. I'd done a lot of driving out into communities and had grown to appreciate the solace of a long overnight drive, so I drove the ute through the night and the sun was coming up again by the time I reached the city limits of Adelaide. By the side of the highway there was a huge billboard welcoming drivers to Adelaide with an advert for a popular local chain of Italian restaurants.

It featured a cheesy dude with a gormless grin holding up a plate of prawns to the camera – these tortured-looking prawns with the slogan, 'Prawns Gambero! $9.90! Pretty good eh!'

I slammed on the brakes and pulled over by the side of the road to better comprehend what I was seeing. It was offensive on so many levels. For one, 'gambero' simply means 'prawn', so this guy was trying to sell Adelaide 'Prawns Prawn'. And no self-respecting chef wears a black chef jacket – the jacket is spotlessly white, that's just the way it is.

I can't emphasise enough how demoralising it was to be greeted by that sign. This was my first hint at what restaurants might mean in Adelaide. It was like the start of a horror movie: I looked into that billboard's cold, dead eyes and saw myself plating up schnitzel and spaghetti for the rest of my life.

For some time afterwards, essentially I did nothing but try to repair my marriage. I got a job in a pub that a friend owned on Rundle Street, to put food on the table, but apart from that I stayed home and tried to be the best dad to Sofia and husband to Nadia that I could. We both tried so hard but our efforts failed again and again.

It reached a point where I just couldn't do it any more. We separated: I moved out, then in again – over the next few years we had several goes at trying to find our way back. I still loved her desperately: there was still a lot of love between us, but we just couldn't make it work.

I felt so much anxiety and guilt over leaving her and Sofia, because I did love her and I'd already fucked up one marriage. Now I was twice divorced, with a child from each marriage. It was my nightmare all over again.

I was miserable about never being able to spend enough time with my daughters. Sofia was so young that she had to spend most of her time with her mum, and our relationship was too volatile to provide much joy to her.

Ava had been devastated when I'd moved to Adelaide, because deep down she believed it was because I wanted to leave her. We'd had the conversation about how I was moving to a new city, that it was not her fault and I loved her with my whole heart. Maybe I didn't do it properly, or was unable to express exactly how I felt in a way she could understand at her age – she was just eight years old – but it gutted her, had a huge and detrimental impact on my gorgeous girl.

For a short time she flew to Adelaide from Sydney every other weekend to be with me, but it was never enough, and I was just a mess. I'd be driving her to the airport and just fucking sobbing from the time we got out of the car to watching her plane take off. Putting your daughter, an unaccompanied minor, on a plane without you? Doesn't feel great. Not for me, and certainly not for Ava.

Eventually even that fell apart. My relationship with Kelly didn't benefit from the distance, and there were some very strong, very protective women in her family who didn't think much of me. Between them, they decided that I was a bad influence in Ava's life, and not long after moving to Adelaide, they cut off my contact with Ava altogether. That, I've got to say, was gutting. I've been in chib fights that left me in better shape than I was the day I learned I wouldn't even be talking to my daughter any more. At first I spent a lot of time and money trying to get some kind of custody back, to get a message to Ava, but it's impossible and inhuman to try and really talk to somebody through a lawyer. I was distraught, but I called my family, and they advised me to let it go for now. 'She's your daughter, and she loves you. She'll find her way back to you when she's ready.'

That time was difficult and lonely. Then in 2010 I got head-hunted by Penfolds. They'd learned I was in Adelaide, knew my pedigree and that I was at a loose end, and offered me a job as executive chef at their flagship restaurant at Magill Estate. Very posh, very prestigious; ridiculous money.

I took a meeting and their pitch was essentially: 'We're the greatest Australian brand in wine, and we want to have the greatest Australian restaurant.' They wanted to know what I thought that would be.

I told them how for the past ten years I'd been thinking a lot about Australian food and what a true Australian cuisine would look like. It seemed to me that Indigenous ingredients, the history and story behind them, seemed like the true voice of Australian cuisine, or at least the root of something truly representative of this place. I was at my wits' end because nobody wanted to talk about it and I was at the stage

that I didn't want to cook in Australia if I couldn't make
food that at least attempted to grapple with the question:
what is the Australian cuisine?

At this point I'd spent quite some time in communities
and with each trip I'd become more certain that through
food Australia could start a different conversation with its
First Nations people, that sharing in culinary traditions
could be a respectful launchpad for a change in attitude.
As time went on, Noma happened in Copenhagen, with
René Redzepi carving out this new idea of what Danish
food really was. Alex Atala was doing the same thing in
Brazil, as was Rodolfo Guzman in Chile. Those guys were
all starting to articulate a new voice for their culture and
its cuisine. All I wanted to do was start that conversation
in Australia, a place I wasn't even from but had still seen
so much more of its heart than most people who were born
here. More than anything, I was incensed by Australia's lack
of acknowledgement of its First Nations people in general
and of their cuisine. The restaurant I envisioned would be
called 'Orana', named for the word for 'welcome' in several
Indigenous languages.

So that was my pitch (or my rant): basically that I wanted
to showcase Indigenous ingredients, and champion a new
cuisine inspired by our First Nations people, their unique
relationship with the land, and sophisticated knowledge of
traditional food culture. I fully expected Penfolds to show
me the door, but they were wild about the idea.

In October 2010 they hired me as executive chef for
their restaurant. I brought in a new menu, with a few native
ingredients on it, and shortly afterwards the *Advertiser*

named Magill Estate its restaurant of the year and *Gourmet Traveller* listed it in the top 50 restaurants of the year. Then we closed, shuttered it for a complete $3 million overhaul.

During the downtime I would develop a new menu that would showcase Indigenous ingredients, entirely bankrolled and supported by the Penfolds brand.

The endgame would be to make Magill a world-class restaurant. I wanted it to be a restaurant that people *must* visit when they came to Australia – for people to fly to Adelaide especially for the culinary experience, just as they visit D.O.M. in São Paulo, Brazil.

That would mean flying all over the world, which meant, once again, that I was putting work ahead of my loved ones, which was neither fair on nor appreciated by Nadia.

CHAPTER TWENTY-ONE

About a month into working for Penfolds, I was at some company dinner, talking to the guy seated next to me, telling him all about my passion for Indigenous culture and ingredients, how I'd been to all these communities, and the communities I was planning to make contact with next.

'You know, my mum's partner is a Nyul Nyul man. An artist and one of the most amazing people you'll ever meet,' he said. 'You should go up there and visit.' The Nyul Nyul are people of the Kimberley area of northern Western Australia, traditional custodians of absolutely stunning country.

'I'll take you up on that,' I told him and got the phone number for his mother, Marion Manson. I called and told her who I was and that I wanted to come up to the Kimberley, stay for a month and just sort of hang out and learn.

She said, 'Sure, just let me know when you're coming up', so I thanked her and hung up pretty chuffed. Everything was going great, all I had to do now was get from Adelaide to the Kimberley, about 3000 kilometres north. I decided to drive.

I looked at the map and saw that would mean travelling to Alice Springs and then up the Tanami road – 1000 kilometres of mostly unsealed road running from just north of Alice Springs in a diagonal line to the Kimberley. It crosses the Tanami Desert, goes past the Rabbit Flat Roadhouse and then on to Halls Creek in north-east WA.

When I came to work with Penfolds, one of the perks was a company car supplied, via a fleet hire service. The car was a Mitsubishi Outlander, which was a nice little all-wheel drive number, but having driven in the outback a fair bit over the years, I was more than a little worried about it being up to the task of driving to the Kimberley.

I rang the fleet-hire company, told them about the trip, and my concerns with the suitability of the vehicle. They told me they couldn't see any problem.

'Are you sure?' I said doubtfully. 'I don't think it's a great idea.'

'It'll be fine,' the lady on the phone said. I could hear her tapping away at a keyboard in the background, 'it's an all-wheel drive vehicle.'

'Yes, it's an all-wheel drive, but it's not really designed to go off-road, I don't think . . . '

'It'll be fine,' she insisted, so I asked her to make a note on my fleet account that I'd formally asked for advice about driving the car to the Kimberley, flagging that it might not be a good idea, and had been given permission. They were fine with that, so I was fine with that.

Now I was ready to go. This had all happened in twenty-four hours, and I was just about to leave Adelaide when

I ran into my mate Vince, who could be described as a four-wheel drive guru. I told him I was leaving for a month in the Kimberley.

'How are you getting there?'

'I'm going to drive that thing,' I said, pointing to the Mitsubishi, 'across the Tanami.'

'Mate, you can't take that car up the Tanami.'

'Why not?' In my mind I was already on the road.

'You'll fucking die, Jock. That's why.' So then Vince sat me down and explained that travellers who take on the Tanami can spend a year planning it: buying military equipment, radios, gas tanks, spare wheels, survival gear, a satellite phone and all the shit you need to survive when your four-wheel drive inevitably breaks down in the desert.

On top of that, November, when I was planning to drive up, is one of the worst times to visit. It's the build-up to the rains, with choking humidity and afternoon thunderstorms. If the roads didn't flood out, it would be a miracle. As if that wasn't enough, I now know there's all kinds of Indigenous lore carried out in that area at that time of year, which whitefellas have no business being anywhere near, and which it would be both insulting and dangerous for me to encounter.

All of this shit, he was telling me, and none of it had crossed my mind. I had been about to head out with a swag, a pack of biscuits and a map.

I went and got two spare wheels and some jerry cans of petrol, and thought to myself that would probably do it. I'd had enough of listening to people. Within forty-eight hours of deciding to go I was in the car, heading out.

In time the sealed road petered out, and as soon as I saw that beautiful red dirt road going on forever I just felt so much better. Every time I get on country I'm overcome by the landscape and the sense of freedom that sweeps over me; the sense of purpose. Every time I visit I come back a wiser person, grateful for the knowledge that my friends in communities have entrusted me with. Each trip is an education – but somehow, the basics of off-road driving had escaped me.

I drove through the night, nineteen hours, until I got to Uluru, about 450 kilometres south-west of Alice Springs. I stopped there, met some of the Mutitjulu community, and walked around Uluru at night, struck speechless by the magnificence of that sacred place, and by the kindness of the custodians who guided me on my walk. After a couple of hours sleep I rose to watch the sunrise, then got behind the wheel again and did another nineteen-hour drive, turning onto the Tanami road about 19 kilometres north of Alice and on through the guts of the country until I was close to Rabbit Flat, the midway point.

I flogged the shit out of that poor little Mitsubishi, and myself, downing Red Bull and No-Doz by the handful. By the end of that second drive I was exhausted, seeing double, barely keeping it on the road. Just before Rabbit Flat, I realised I just couldn't drive any more, and stopped for the night.

I got out of the car and unrolled my swag on the side of the road. Then I closed my eyes to try to sleep, but soon started to feel uneasy. It was dark though the moon was out, I kept hearing these weird noises out in the desert, and all these stories started coming back to me about the terrible shit that can happen to travellers out in the middle of Australia. A lot of dumb, reckless whitefellas just like me stumbled upon something they shouldn't have and vanished from the face of the earth. I got so unnerved that I gave up on sleep, got back in the car and kept right on driving until I got to Marion's house in Broome.

I'd called Marion just before I'd left Adelaide to let her know I was on the way to meet her, and she'd said: 'Great, looking forward to it, I'll see you in a week.'

When I turned up at her home in Broome having driven 3500 kilometres in two days, more or less, she was a bit shocked, because of course what I'd done was a bit crazy.

I'd pitched up at her home absolutely raring to go, I was ready to go out and start meeting people.

The car, however, was *not* ready to go. The car was in a fucking state. I'd just finished two sixteen-hour stints behind the wheel, and I had been driving steadily; some would say recklessly. The car had not been built to be anywhere near a road like the Tanami. Having done what is probably one of the roughest drives in the world I could now see why people really took their time and planned it out. I'd lost count of the amount of times that car bottomed out on the road because of potholes, or I'd tried to drive it through standing water and hit something under the surface.

I'd stopped in Yuendumu, a tiny community on the edge of the Tanami Desert and nearly been rolled. While I was waiting for the petrol station to open, kids surrounded the car and started picking bits off it, making off with the badges and mirrors and anything they could rip off. When the petrol station opened it stocked only diesel fuel, so charged me four times the going rate for petrol to fill up the jerry cans. I had no choice, as this was the only fuel before Rabbit Flat and it was not as if turning back was an option.

I'd had two punctures along the way, one of them a blowout which completely destroyed the wheel. I left it by the side of the road, saying a mental thank you to my mate Vince for his advice. The poor motor sounded like death – the amount of dust inside the engine was phenomenal. I crawled that car into Broome and it was just chugging along making these screaming, wheezing noises. It was a sick, sick car. If it were an animal, activists would be campaigning to give it a dignified and merciful death.

After I'd been to see Marion, I booked the car into the Mitsubishi repair place in town that the fleet service put me onto. I dropped it off, told them there were a couple of little problems that needed fixing before I went out into the Kimberley. They called me a little later.

'We've got a quote for the work to be done,' the mechanic told me. 'How quickly do you need it?'

'Well, I want to go into the Kimberley straightaway. So as soon as you can get it done.'

'We're going to have to order in some parts,' there was an awkward pause from the mechanic, 'there's a fair bit wrong with it.'

I told them no worries, and just to send the quote to the fleet hire place.

'Yeah. Sure, we can do that.'

'How much is it going to cost?

'All up, call it $17,500,' the mechanic told me.

So that wasn't great news. I called the fleet hire place to tell them what it was going to cost to get the car running again. They were surprised, to put it mildly.

'What the fuck,' the fleet hire guy yelled down the phone, 'have you done to our car?'

'I told you, man,' I said. 'I told you this was probably a bad idea. And you know . . . it was. What can I say?'

Anyway, they fixed the car, I went out into the Kimberley, and the car ran like a dream. At least, until it was time to drive it back to Adelaide, when I managed to rack up another $9000 worth of damage to the car on the drive home. But that was a little bit down the (Tanami) road, and ahead of me was a meeting with a man who would become one of the most important people in my life.

With Marion and her daughter Leah I drove north out of Broome towards the Kimberley. The road under our wheels turned to dirt, and Marion told me to take a turn off the road and all of a sudden we were in the bush. No signage, no infrastructure, just this track going into the bush which went for about ten minutes and suddenly we were in a camp.

Bruno Dann, Marion's partner and the elder I'd come to see, came out to meet us. A slim, softly spoken man with a smile that starts from the heart – a warmth that shines through which is all too rare in this world. Bruno did what all elders seem to do, which is, you know, size you up for a while; get the measure of you and what your intentions are.

After a couple of days, once we had some level of comfort, he started to share stories from his life: of being born on the land; stolen from his family and taken to a mission in

Beagle Bay; growing up and returning to country where he was now a leader of his community. He showed me all around Nyul Nyul country, which stretches from the Dampier Peninsula area in a sort of triangle out to Beagle Bay.

The more time we spent together, the more grateful I felt to have those kinds of conversations with this man, and for the trust he put in me by having them. It felt very special and honestly, it was just like meeting up with a really old friend, although we'd only met a few days earlier. I went up and down to the Kimberley many times (in more suitable vehicles) in the next decade, and Bruno taught me so much: about ingredients, foraging, farming with fire and the traditional harvests. And, more than anything, about friendship, and about myself.

At night, we'd cook in this makeshift bush kitchen in the middle of the camp, built of timber and corrugated iron and lit by the flickering flames of cooking fires and portable lamps. Overhead, lightning would crack through the sky as the humidity threatened to break into torrential rain. Those nights were the first time in a long, long period that I felt at peace. I'll always be grateful to Bruno Dann and his family for allowing me to share that time with them.

I could write a book just on what Bruno has taught me, which is only the barest fraction of his immense knowledge. He once described himself as a 'professor of the land' and he truly is. There is nothing he doesn't know about the soil, water and sky of his country. Above all, he reinforced what I'd learned in other communities, which is that sense of connection to the land, and the myriad things that meant. Bruno's connection to his land is inseparable from

his philosophy, family, people, culture and food. He has
no capacity for blind ambition, for keeping score or tit for
tat. He's a calm man whose gentle, soft-spoken demeanour
belies an iron will. He's a man who expects no respect from
a stranger, but earns it through his presence and integrity.

He took me out walking on the land, and showed me how
to forage for min min, a salty, sweet wild pea, in the dense
grey sand of the coast, over the middens carpeted with shells
where hundreds of generations of Nyul Nyul gathered to
feast on shellfish and crustaceans.

At low tide the water pulled back to reveal a secret
garden of black, craggy rocks where the Nyul Nyul main-
tained an intricate series of fish traps – an ancient and
ingenious method of natural aquaculture. A system of
different-sized ponds that trapped fish within them at low
tide, which I would never have seen or understood had I not
been educated in the practice. Further out was a reef where
oysters, sea snails and giant clams could be picked straight
out of the ocean.

When I complained about the insomnia that had plagued
me for years, Bruno brewed me a kettle of jilungin, a plant
the Nyul Nyul steep in hot water and drink.

'This is our dreaming tea,' Bruno told me, 'powerful
medicine.' Sure enough, two cups of jilungin later and I was
out like a light, enjoying the best sleep I'd ever known while
sober.

Bruno taught me everything there was to know about
gubinge, the original Nyul Nyul word for the Kakadu plum.
Bruno Dann introducing me to it was the first time I'd
heard its true name in language, and he was annoyed that

the whole world called it the Kakadu plum: 'It's not called Kakadu plum. It's not even from Kakadu! It's our name. It's our tradition. It's gubinge.'

That's just one example that reinforced something that was becoming crystal clear to me. There is obviously so much wrong with the way that we talk about Indigenous people, culture and food. For too many average people, Australia's understanding of First Nations cultures comes from a place of deep ignorance, which is at the same time rooted in a sense of misguided cultural superiority.

Since the early stages of settlement, the people who have settled in Australia have assumed that all the wisdom and all that information that Indigenous people had cultivated over 60,000-plus years of living in this land was a matter of simple survival, that it wasn't worth listening to, or believing in, or even documenting properly. To say nothing of the incredibly rich spiritualism, theology and environmentalism of Australia's First Nations. The arrogance and indifference of that assumption has never gone away.

I think Bruno was pleased by the fact that I wanted to know all this stuff; that I was desperate to learn everything I could about his traditions, because he'd almost given up trying to get white people to pay attention.

Even within the community, interest in traditional practices and culture was declining: the young people were moving away to big cities and getting into trouble as they grappled with the clash of culture, identity and expectations.

It was getting harder and harder for Bruno to convey the value of the culture to them because they saw no appreciation or representation of it in mainstream society. The sort of life that a young person could imagine themselves living in the cities, with cool music, clothes, cars – most of which ignored First Nations cultures – was too strong for many to resist. If the young kids aren't on country learning verbally from elders like Bruno then all of a sudden there's no more of that culture. It stops: the conversations, the doctrine, the songlines all risk being lost to time. I couldn't understand why every other person in this country wasn't horrified by that. I certainly was.

At the same time, I was overjoyed that I'd been welcomed into a culture that embodied my beliefs about food capturing moments in time and place. To find and be welcomed into a community that stood for that intersection of time, culture, and food so passionately that the traditional practices had survived all that genocide and repression could throw at it? I was like a moth to a flame, and wanted to know everything about it.

Bruno was so giving and generous both with his time and in sharing his stories and wisdom. He was able to verbalise the way the Nyul Nyul people saw themselves – as saltwater people, sunset people – not separate to or living on the land but as an integral part of the country.

Living on country, Bruno explained to me, was about knowing that there was a purpose for everything that was put there by creation. It's both the privilege and responsibility of humans to nourish, guard and care for the land and love it: 'Every tree, every plant, every bird, every creature . . . there's a purpose for everything that was put here.' Even as I write this, I can hear Bruno's voice carry the words through my fingers.

The fundamental truth of the traditional Nyul Nyul philosophy – that you look after the land and it takes care of you – is applicable to every person on this earth. Take no more than it can recover from, and give back, because you are part of the land you walk on, not above it.

The horrifying environmental catastrophes that are piling up all around us are only possible because by and large humanity has forgotten this and abandoned its responsibility to the land. Bruno Dann and his people never have.

Bruno has this incredible ability to build bridges between the two worlds. The way he speaks, his skill in storytelling, he manages to convey ideas and concepts in a way that anyone could absorb without sacrificing any of the integrity or power of them.

Being on the land with Bruno also made me understand in a tangible way how important spirits are to us. As we became closer each trip and the barriers between us started to fall; when we started to connect as friends on that level, on that land, our own spirits became integral to each other.

I feel very spiritually connected to Bruno, perhaps more than to anyone else I've met. We call each other 'brother' but I feel as though we are something more than that.

On the land, it becomes abundantly clear that nothing really matters in life except the spirits around you, the people in your life. Even more so for Bruno: the spirits of the ancestors are on country with him, watching over and protecting him, just as he does the land.

That balance, that complex symbiosis of human and spirit with every creature and plant on the land, is not something I think I'll ever really understand. It wasn't my land, my tradition. But what I could do was take inspiration from the ingredients, the flavours, the techniques that the Nyul Nyul people shared with me, and see if I could find a way to cook that honoured them. I hoped I could create dishes that celebrated the flavour, and so served as a gateway for mainstream Australians to celebrate Nyul Nyul culture, and its inextricable connection to country and the sustenance it provides.

This was something I did, not just because I felt I needed to, but because Bruno asked me to do what I could. He knew the value of chefs and the profile we had, and that I could use mine to try and start some small shift in the way Australians think about native foods. He shared with me not only his traditional knowledge, but his trust that I wasn't out to plunder or appropriate it to make myself rich.

As imperfect and unsuitable a person as I am to speak about many things First Nation, I knew food, and Bruno recognised that my intentions were good, and, beyond that, I think he saw that I had some healing to do that he could help with.

Being embraced by certain elders and the fact that I was trusted enough that they shared knowledge with me also went some way to lessening the pain of being away from my own family. Father's Day 2011 found me on the land with Bruno Dann, because if I couldn't see my girls that day, I could at least be doing something honest and true.

On Nyul Nyul country, where my phone didn't work and I could put aside the ego and the hurricane wreckage of my personal life, I found a kind of peace.

On my return, I found a way to reach out to Ava, and after a year without speaking, she was ready to forgive me, and we began talking, and to build on our relationship again.

For fifteen months I worked with Penfolds, alternating visits to communities all over Australia where I was educated by elders in their traditional ingredients and the way they cooked, then coming back to Adelaide and the kitchen.

Penfolds had closed their flagship Magill restaurant while it was re-fitted in anticipation of a grand re-opening with our Australian-cuisine-focused menu. I had a spectacularly talented team of chefs and sommeliers working with me, and they were all-in on what we were doing. We'd take jilungin or gubinge and really go all out to develop techniques and recipes that celebrated that ingredient, and in some way also conveyed the story of the place the ingredient came from as well as the traditional uses and preparation.

Everyone on our team shared the passion. Not just for these incredible ingredients that were blowing our minds every day with the potential for what they could mean to Australian cuisine, but for wanting to give back to the communities who had opened up to us and shared their knowledge. It was a profound responsibility, a great deal of trust had been placed in us, and we all understood we had a sacred duty to not fuck this up.

As passionate as our team was about Indigenous ingredients, chefs around Australia weren't really following suit. I figured the best way to get Australian chefs excited about them was to harness the curiosity of international chefs. If globally respected chefs were interested in Australian ingredients then the Aussies would have to follow. The cultural cringe again – it's a powerful thing.

Every year there's a big culinary hoo-ha called the Margaret River Gourmet Escape, a food festival that attracts chefs from all over Australia and the world. In any given year you'll find some of the world's hottest, most influential chefs there. In November 2012, Michael Hodgson, one of the directors of the Gourmet Escape, contacted me to ask if I'd be interested in curating some kind of Indigenous food tour for visiting chefs.

'I can do a lot better than that,' I said. 'How about I come down a few days early, go foraging with the local Wadandi people, get heaps of Indigenous ingredients and set up tables of produce that the chefs can get stuck into and play around with? And invite some Wadandi people to talk to them about the food, their country and culture.'

So I organised a little downtime for the chefs and select food critics – an afternoon off where we could gather, and I hoped everyone would show up with an open mind.

Josh, a Wadandi man from the Margaret River area, and I went foraging, gathered up all these incredible ingredients, then we set up these benches loaded with food: witchetty grubs, shellfish, berries, plants, shrubs, leaves, bark, sap, quandongs – you name it.

Josh introduced the food, and told the gathered foodies a little about his people; how they were people of the forest and of the ocean. He shared a bit of knowledge about the country by telling a couple of traditional stories, explaining the six seasons of the year observed by his people, and talking about Wadandi weapons and musical instruments.

Then we told them to go nuts and make their own lunch with whatever they wanted.

They loved it, because deep down every great chef is just a toddler with a giant knife who wants to experiment and play around and stick weird shit they pick up in their mouth.

As I anticipated, the international chefs were way more open-minded and into it than the Australian ones. David Chang of Momofuku and René Redzepi of Noma both blistered their hands trying to light a fire by rubbing sticks together but the gamest dude there was Adrian Gill, the food writer who'd given me my first amazing review back in Cornwall.

'Who wants to try a witchetty grub?' I asked, holding up a live fat white grub. Gill jumped at the chance, took it from me and popped it in his mouth still wriggling.

'Fantastic,' he said. 'Like a chicken crème brûlée,' which is, of course, exactly what witchetty grub tastes like! I've never met anyone who could articulate it so well.

He and I ended up becoming great mates as the years went on. We had a great deal in common: the love of food obviously, a mutual low tolerance for bullshit, but more than that. We both had a relentless thirst for new experiences and sensations, and saw beauty and deliciousness where others turned away in disgust. We went diving for scallops while great white sharks lurked about, then surfaced and slurped the molluscs straight off the half-shell. He balanced extraordinary refinement with actual good taste. I remember visiting a chippie in Scotland with him, and him having to argue with the fry cook that despite his posh southern accent he wanted the haddock – the pungent flavour bomb of the working classes and *always* the first choice of a proud northerner. In many ways, we were cut from the same cloth.

We'd both struggled with substance abuse and anxiety. Adrian carried worry beads with him wherever he went; I remember that he was flicking them in his hand the day I'd met him on that Cornish beach.

Eventually I inherited the habit from him, and began carrying a string with me while I went about my anxious way after the extraordinary Gill sadly passed away in 2016. When I next saw his wife, Nicola, she gifted me his beads, which I now take everywhere with me.

After Gill's adventurous start, it was a free-for-all. Everyone was cooking, tasting and comparing notes, and all those chefs and critics went away with the seeds of a new respect for the possibilities of Australian cuisine.

I wanted to get a handle on what like-minded chefs were doing abroad, so early in 2013 I flew overseas to consult with the leaders in the field. I *staged* for five weeks at Noma with René Redzepi – an amazing restaurant with a very quiet, dignified space. I spent those weeks soaking up everything they were doing in terms of cutting-edge service, food and identity in what was, and still is, one of the great incubators for culinary innovation in the world.

Then on to Brazil for a month in the Amazon to spend time with Alex Atala, a Brazilian chef who was doing astonishing things in the space. He works with native people in the Amazon, so I wanted to understand how he set up his non-profit and dealt with the inevitable backlash of being a non-native person working with native people and their ingredients; how to deal with all the hurdles I knew I had in front of me. Alex had been working with communities from the Amazon for some time, bringing traditional Amazonian fruits and staples like fermented manioc and Maniwara ants to fine-dining tables in Brazil. Naturally enough, he's been accused by various editorialists of plunder, cultural appropriation, theft, cooking with food that is not his to do so. But he hasn't stopped, and in doing so he's both revolutionised global cuisines, and raised awareness of the plight of people indigenous to the Amazon River, who have been disenfranchised and live under the shadow of the Brazilian state.

I was very aware I would face similar obstacles from mainstream Australia, but I didn't really give a shit. The only opinions that mattered to me were those of the elders and communities who had brought me into their trust. I owed it to them, and I would jump any hurdle that was put in front of me.

The first one I stumbled on, however, was nothing I'd anticipated in my worst anxiety-nightmare, which was in March 2013, when Penfolds called me on my mobile on a São Paulo street and told me there wasn't going to be a restaurant.

CHAPTER TWENTY-TWO

'd taken a couple of hours off in São Paulo on my way back from a trip to the Amazon with Alex Atala to check out the street art scene in that city.

I was in Beco do Batman (Batman Alley), a crossroads of three alleys where the best street artists in the world go to throw up pieces. Every inch of the walls, every garage roller door, is covered in amazing art.

I was staring, slack-jawed, at a mural of a bird, by a local street artist, when my mobile rang.

It was Penfolds calling with some news: they weren't going to go ahead with the restaurant as envisioned. I was gobsmacked. We were due to re-open with my menu in two months, and were already neck-deep in press coverage of the restaurant, most of it glowingly positive. We'd made no secret of the vision of the restaurant, so what was the story? What had changed all of a sudden?

'You hired me for a reason, and this restaurant and what it represents is potentially the best thing that's happened to the Penfolds brand since Max Schubert and Grange Hermitage,'

I told him (a bit fired up), 'and you're idiots if you can't see that.'

Basically, it appeared Penfolds was uncomfortable with the direction the restaurant was going in. So that was that – what was I supposed to say in the face of that line of thinking?

The call ended, as I stood there in Batman Alley, my head spinning, and my eyes fixed on the mural of the bird (in Glasgow culture, a symbol of freedom and change – traditionally you get a bird tattoo when you get out of prison and don't plan to go back). I could feel the dream of Orana slipping through my grasp, and I couldn't let that happen.

I realised that if the Magill Estate restaurant wasn't going to go ahead as I'd envisioned, I'd have to find another way. Too many people had put their trust in me, too many elders had shared their time and their knowledge. I knew that I couldn't give up now. There was only one way forwards, which would mean doing something which I had long ago talked myself out of, which I knew would probably end in destitution, financial ruin, heartbreak and madness. I had to start a restaurant. I had to start Orana on my own terms.

I'd have to sink all I had; every penny (which was not much at this point) and my reputation, into a fine-dining restaurant in the hope of said restaurant becoming so acclaimed that, on the back of its name, we'd be able to bring awareness to the wealth of food culture Indigenous Australia has to offer, and start to demand a little of the respect it deserves.

Rather, *we* – my team at Penfolds were as much a part of the dream as I was now – had to start a restaurant, and not only that, we had to make it the best restaurant in Australia. If we could make a world-class, three-hat restaurant that dragged fine-dining as a concept to the table, then Australia would have no choice but to take a seat and begin a conversation about greater respect for our First Nations and their culinary traditions.

It would showcase, celebrate and acknowledge Indigenous food cultures. There would be no compromise. We would do it right. That meant I needed the best people. My decision was made in seconds – it was barely a conscious decision, really – and a moment later, I put in a call back to Adelaide, and got my team together on a group call.

My head chef was Shannon Fleming, restaurant manager Aaron Fenwick and sommelier Joshua Picken. Chefs de partie Ryan Lenzi and Finton Rowe were also part of the team. Together, they represented some of the finest talent ever to bless Australian hospitality.

'This is what just happened,' I told my staff, 'and this is what we're going to do.' I told them that I didn't know what was about to happen, but Orana wouldn't be happening under the Penfolds banner any more. I was going to set out on my own, and asked who wanted to come with me. It would be risky; possibly career suicide, but I needed them. Without their talents Orana would never get off the ground, but luckily for me they were just as all-in on our mission as I was. They were unanimous in their support. Only one person was not in a position to sacrifice her livelihood on a possibly doomed quest, so remained at Penfolds but stayed a true and loyal support to us over the years.

I flew back to Australia immediately, and left Penfolds in April 2013. They didn't want me working anywhere else, so we reached an agreement in which I was put on 'gardening leave'. I wouldn't be allowed to work as a chef for three months, and they would give me a severance package on the condition I didn't go to a competing restaurant. For their part, they washed their hands of anything to do with Indigenous ingredients, which was made clear in the agreement we reached. Part of that severance package meant that the name 'Orana' would now be free for me to take with me and use down the line if I were to, say, open my own restaurant.

I didn't particularly want to open a restaurant in Australia, especially not an aspiring three-hat restaurant, because I knew full well how much money I was set to lose. At the same time, I knew it was what I had to do in order to bring Indigenous ingredients to prominence.

In the meantime, back to square one. Yet again. I was now living in an abandoned church in the hills, lonely again, just me and Clyde, my dog. Since I was contractually forbidden from putting on my chef's whites for a while, I made a living foraging wild mushrooms in the hills to sell at market. My old staff helped me to stay afloat during that time, coming foraging with me on their days off, which was really going above and beyond. It really was all for one, one for all.

There was one silver lining. The forced downtime meant that I actually had to stop, and breathe, and that let me really appreciate how dismal life was without my daughters in it. I missed Ava with every cell in my body when she was in Sydney but at least I got to spend weekends with Sofia.

Without my wage at Penfolds, I'd had to downsize from my home in the hills to a two-bedroom unit in Kilburn, which was just on the edge of roughness. The neighbouring suburb of Prospect was lovely yuppie-ville, but Kilburn was what you travelled through on the way there if you were a junkie looking to steal a stereo.

I'd just moved all my stuff into the unit, then went and picked up Sofia fifteen minutes away to show her the new place. She patted the dog, we locked Clyde inside, then went down the road to get a hot chocolate and a croissant. We were gone for five minutes, tops, and when we came back the front door had been kicked in, and Clyde was running around in the yard.

The house had been totally emptied out. Computers, tablet, phone, TV, my watch. Anything remotely of value just gone in the blink of an eye. Once I made sure it was safe for Sofia, I wandered through and discovered that everything that hadn't been stolen was wrecked – drawers tipped out, shelves ransacked; just a mess.

It was so unsettling that this had happened, and so quickly, when I was so close – just down the street. They must have been watching me the whole time I was showing Sofia the place.

On top of everything, I was trying to find a restaurant space. I didn't have ten cents to rub together, but my staff waited until I found someone who would lend me the money I needed for Orana. That wasn't easy. People weren't exactly lining up to invest millions of dollars in the tattooed, salty-mouthed, ex-bankrupt Scottish chef pitching an Indigenous food-themed restaurant. Eventually I managed to find Richard Collins, a diner who'd eaten at my restaurants over the years; an amazing guy with a good head for business who not only agreed to serve as guarantor for a bank loan but also personally lent me a considerable sum once I'd put together a business plan.

Just like at Pharmacy back in the 90s, we had the experiential fine-dining degustation upstairs, and downstairs we had Street ADL. A bar, basically, that served cool street food with native produce flourishes: pulled kangaroo shoulder on rolls; pork ribs glazed and fried in quandong and bush tomato, riberry cocktails. We knew Orana would be a hard sell for some punters so we wanted to serve accessible comfort food as a first taste of native flavours and ingredients without mentioning them explicitly on the menu.

That way we could make a ton of money at the bar downstairs, and it would make the fine-dining restaurant upstairs viable. But that meant a loan of close to a million bucks to fit-out both venues before we could even open. But together our team started the journey that would become Orana.

Penfolds were dignified in public, but I was told that privately they blew a gasket. A newspaper ran a story about how I'd 'stolen' the staff from Penfolds. It was all a bit over the top, really. As months went on, I kept hearing rumours circulating in the industry about how I'd stolen millions of dollars from Penfolds to secretly plan this surprise restaurant to ruin them. Utter bullshit, of course.

The fact is, I didn't have millions of dollars. I had enough money to pay the staff for two weeks after open. If we weren't making money by then, we'd have to close right back up again.

The staff were putting so much trust in me, which was a beautiful thing, but I didn't really know what I was doing, to be honest. They went above and beyond, and then some.

To furnish the place we bought furniture off Gumtree and even rescued dining chairs from hard rubbish on the side of the road to sand and reupholster ourselves because we couldn't afford to get them any other way.

It was the first restaurant I'd ever been involved in where there wasn't a millionaire standing behind us with a designer and an architect on speed dial. At the same time, ever since Damien Hirst showed me around Pharmacy, I'd gained a new appreciation of design and art and knew that ambiance could make or break a restaurant, so with First Nations guidance, I started thinking about art and artefacts from across Australia to fit the place out.

We were up to our eyeballs in it, to be honest. I felt such a crushing weight of responsibility. You do as any leader of a kitchen, but particularly at Orana, because the odds were stacked against us, and because my staff had given up secure jobs to do this thing with me, I felt obligated to lead them to be the best they could be. Which meant making sure that everything they did was better than anyone else in Australia.

Shannon Fleming, our first head chef, is a genius who found a way to turn my crazy ideas into actual dishes we could plate up. Wine waiter Joshua Picken matched drops to ingredients that were unlike anything diners had tasted.

Ryan Lenzi, Finton Rowe and Brittany Weckert came from Penfolds and rounded out an unstoppable team.

Aaron Fenwick came on as our restaurant manager, with Greta Wohlstadt, and without them we might never have lasted a day. In time, Greta became the restaurant manager. An absolute force of nature, a logistical and leadership genius, and more than a match for me.

I knew what it took to be the best, which was to do exactly what Marco had done to make a three-star restaurant.

You take a look at the best there is, how they're doing it, and then you do it better. If you do that, you get three stars. Simple.

I said to my staff, 'We're going to make a three-hat restaurant, we're going to make Indigenous ingredients the main focus of a restaurant and make it number one in the country.' Simple. This minimisation approach to the task at hand would come to be called 'The Jock Zonfrillo Reality Distortion Field' by exasperated staff in the coming years. I'd stand up the front of the room and tell the staff that we were going to win three hats, of course we were, it was inevitable, and Greta would take a deep breath and start to figure out how we were actually going to achieve that.

In the past year I'd visited all the top restaurants in Australia and overseas, had eaten at them several times, and had taken it all in: courses, style, flavour, texture, floor staff and their demeanour, what worked and what didn't, everything – and brought it all back to Orana.

The serving style at Orana would be very different from anything else in Australia. The chefs would bring each course out as they cooked it and explain what it was and how it was made. They were doing it at Noma back then, which was much talked about by food critics, and hailed as a sort of revelation.

I saw it as a throwback to a very old tradition called Guéridon service. In classic French restaurants back in the day, back before they were properly wait-staffed, the chef used to take food out all the time.

The chef would come out with a trolley and carve the beef, and talk to the customers, and they loved it because they got to talk to the chef, the creator.

It was still a thing at very old-fashioned hotels in Scotland, where these creaking old traditions linger. The chef would come out to do a flambé table-side, or bring out the Chateaubriand, simply to cut it in two and put half on each plate, and the punters were mad for it.

When I saw that at Noma it was like going back to the old days, I realised that people still love that shit. Of course it makes sense for the chef to talk about the food, because they were going to know more about it than the waiter. The message wouldn't get garbled in a game of telephone. It just made sense to me. So we did that. I didn't want to emulate what fine-dining restaurants did, which was have some stuffy chef come out and recite a shopping list of French gibberish at you.

If you ate at Orana, there was a good chance that not only would I bring your meal out to you and introduce your course, but also that I would start swearing in a moment of passion or frustration as I talked about the ingredients, where they came from, and their cultural importance.

'This is crocodile,' I would say, putting down the plate. 'It's fucking great, and this is why.'

The story was as much a part of Orana as the food, and we had an absolute guardian angel looking after us there. Monica Brown is a PR specialist who was based in London at the time, and who'd worked with Heston Blumenthal for years. I'd met her back in Margaret River, and we'd got along famously, chatting for hours about anything and everything to do with food. She offered to help pro bono before Orana opened, which I will be eternally grateful for.

We knew we were doing good work, but we had to find a way to cut through to ordinary punters. Getting a chef, particularly one as adventurous as Heston, to enjoy a plate of green ants is one thing, but finding a way to make that appealing to an average Australian who goes to a fine-dining restaurant as a treat was a challenge.

The critics we'd talked to had been generally unimpressed. They just didn't seem to get it. We realised that if we were ever going to succeed, we needed to cut through the cultural cringe.

'We need to go outside to come back inside,' Monica said. 'There are journalists all over the world who are dying to write a story like this.'

She laid out a strategy to win over the world first, and then Australia. She knew that if a respected international publication wrote about the work we were doing, then people in Australia would pay attention, and doors would start to open.

Sure enough, they did. Even before we opened, well-regarded food writers in Europe and America began to write about Orana, and my links with Alex Atala in Brazil and René Redzepi at Noma, tying us in with a narrative of a global food movement that was just picking up pace.

Monica was killing the PR, the media kept coming in, people were writing Orana up all over the world, which was wonderful, but it still wasn't paying the bills.

Then one day Monica rang me with an offer.

'The Discovery Channel want to talk to you about doing a TV show with them,' she said.

'No way,' I said. We were in the midst of trying to get the restaurant ready by opening night, and I was only getting about four hours sleep a night. 'No way am I doing a TV show.'

We said no, they came back again, and Monica sent me the 'bible', the pitch and outline for the program.

'Just take a look,' she urged. 'It's the real deal. It's you, pretty much what you do with Indigenous communities here, only it's worldwide.'

I opened the file, and read the pitch for a show called *Nomad Chef* that looked really cool. I'd go into ten different communities with fascinating cuisines around the world, learn from them, and take the knowledge they'd shared with me back to the restaurant. Then I'd whip up a couple of dishes inspired by where I'd been and feed them to ordinary Australians. It actually looked really exciting.

I closed that email and opened one from my accountant, which spelled out the payments to the bank for Orana: what the payments would be and the interest on top of that, plus working capital, plus . . . plus . . . plus – a terrifying document.

I rang Monica straight back. 'I've read the pitch. Yeah, it looks great. But I've got a restaurant to run. I just don't have time. But out of curiosity, what's this sort of thing worth?'

She told me a figure and that changed my perspective a little bit.

'Well,' I said. 'That would be helpful.'

I agreed to do the show. The producers were stoked, and were talking about how excited they were to film in my restaurant.

'Me too!' I said. 'But the thing is, the restaurant isn't quite . . . built yet.'

'That's fine,' they said. 'We've got two weeks of filming in Vanuatu before we even need it.'

So off I jetted to Vanuatu to film the first episode. For two weeks I was jumping in and out of boats, and learning how to act on camera when there's a great big fuck-off Steadicam in your face. I'd be killing chickens with a stick, acting like this was all normal and everyday for me, then racing up the volcano because it was the only place I could get phone reception.

Whenever I got a signal, hundreds of messages would drop in, with photos of door handles and signage for the bathroom and all the stuff I really needed to be there for. Shannon was in the kitchen trying to work out the fermentation on some ingredients we were using for the first menu, and I was trying to design a restaurant over the phone while clinging to the edge of a crater and covered in chicken blood.

We finished up in Vanuatu and I raced back with three days to go before we were meant to start filming and the place was still not done. Nothing was finished, it was still clearly a building site, and the producers started freaking out.

They had crew flying in, diners booked into the restaurant, and they were not pleased.

'It'll be fine. Don't worry, it's fine,' I told them. 'These things all come together on the last day. Haven't you ever opened a restaurant before?'

We'd flown in Never 2501, a Brazilian street artist whose intricate artworks adorn Batman Alley, to paint a mural on the wall. He was taking his time too, because his creative process seemed to involve sitting around smoking or coming out foraging with us, but very little actual painting. Then one day I came in and he had created this stunning stylised mural of a chocolate lily that stretched all the way across the hallway to the door and around the corner into the restaurant.

We were frantic but somehow we managed to get the downstairs bar, Street ADL, open in time to film. On the day of filming there were still tradies and labourers crawling all over the place, so we put nice jackets on them and made them extras on the background footage we shot. There's this amazing photo of the bar on opening night, looking stunning and full of all absolute randoms.

A few days after that, Orana upstairs was finished and we were ready to open to the public.

We printed no menus. Orana would be a tasting menu designed to showcase and honour Indigenous Australian food. On opening night, the sitting would start with sticks of raw damper served on a twig, along with a bed of glowing coals. The diner would have to cook their own amuse-bouche of bush camp bread on coals. It was an authentic taste of the outback, but also a statement of intent. A meal at Orana would be like no other fine-dining experience they'd had.

We wanted to open minds, for people to eat with their fingers and try things they'd never dreamed existed. A punter would sit down, and when they stood up again they would've had an unprecedented experience, tasted fifty things that were entirely new to them, and walk away with new knowledge and understanding of Australia and its people.

Spencer Gulf prawns dressed in Davidson plum. Pearl meat, diced and marinated, on a spoon with Dorrigo pepper. We served fried saltbush, which tastes like nothing you've ever had, and at the same time like salt-and-vinegar chips – a taste which hits even the most hardened critic or food snob right in the nostalgia.

Bittergrass puree dressing on perfect bites of Wagyu intercostal. Coorong mulloway with native cherries and sea parsley, with starchy blond folds of white yam arranged in beautiful ruffles on the fish. Kangaroo with native pepper. Coconut with coconut ash and native currants. Riberries with frozen gin. Chocolate lily for dessert. Matched wines from Beechworth, Adelaide Hills, Coonawarra.

We did a 'soft open', a private service for friends, family and press the week before, and it went flawlessly. People embraced the food wholeheartedly. The diners were just as passionate and curious about our cuisine – and the culture that inspired it – as we were. The Orana family were overjoyed.

Then we opened the restaurant on Friday 9 November 2012, proud and gleaming and ready to show the world what Australian cuisine could be . . . and Australia ignored it. Nobody came on opening night. Not a soul.

CHAPTER TWENTY-THREE

There were no bookings, no walk-ins for the opening night. We were sitting there waiting, and waiting, and waiting, and finally we closed without serving a single cover. Just crickets.

You can't imagine how terrible that felt. Everything was on the line: my reputation, my name, every dollar I had and, worst of all, the weight of the trust put in me by the Indigenous community I was trying to acknowledge was on my shoulders. I felt like all these elders had shared their knowledge and culture with me, really trusted me to give something back in return, and it was all for nothing.

Saturday: same story, no diners, no interest. Then there was the financial reality, which was that the clock was ticking and the rent was due, the bills were due, we had fresh food in the fridge, ingredients that we'd paid for that had come out of communities, and we'd been fermenting stuff as well. I sat there flicking my worry beads until the stones flew off the wire in my fingers.

It was horrific. We knew the food was good, but the people just weren't coming. The week earlier, during the soft open, the food reviewers Terry Durack and Jill Dupleix came in and left with tears in their eyes. In their review, they wondered why a restaurant like this hadn't existed for years, and questioned what the concept of Australian food meant.

Which was nice, and genuine, but didn't translate to covers. I still wasn't exactly fending off a horde of punters with a pointy chicken-killing stick.

One of the very few who came in the opening days was Heston Blumenthal, who loved it. If Heston, mad fucking genius that he is, is impressed, you've got to be doing something right. You can't put a price on that.

Of course, you could put a price on everything else about Orana. All our creditors did.

It was so expensive to run. The problem was I didn't have any capital. All I had was a shitload of credit cards that I kept maxing out and then transferring over. I'd see an advert online for a credit card balance transfer with zero interest for six months and I'd grab one. All the Australian banks, and wherever anyone would give me one anywhere in the world. I had one from fucking Dubai – whatever it took to keep the restaurant going until people in Australia started talking about it and realising what we were trying to do.

It was such a risky game to play. As the debt racked up, the cost of running our restaurant racked up, because of having to carry those massive debt repayments. A restaurant is always a black hole for money in its first couple of years, and it was made so much worse by paying 27 per cent interest on some predatory fucking line of credit from the dodgiest corner of the banking world.

If we'd had a partner in the first place, it would have been so much easier. If someone had invested in us from the beginning, our break-even point would have been much lower than it was, and we probably would have saved a good million dollars along the way.

Our accountant was just mortified: 'I'm giving you all the advice in the world and you're ignoring it,' he said to me. 'I couldn't sleep at night if I was in the kind of debt you are. There's no way out of it. I mean there is *no* way for you to recover.'

He'd plead for me to stop, because he could see I was headed for ruin and I insisted we'd keep on going. In the end, he gave up and walked out, and we hired someone who was better suited to the risks involved. The new guy was happier to see the money flying out the window. In the first year alone, we ran at a loss of $360,000.

It was a tough first twelve months of our life as a restaurant, because in order to find a way to make Orana work, I couldn't actually work there hands-on much in the first year, which was all kinds of fucked-up irony. Throughout that first year, I had to go away for blocks of two to four weeks at a time to film *Nomad Chef.* I was flying off to Ethiopia, the Amazon and Belize, filming, sending an invoice so we could put the money into the restaurant, then jumping on the phone between takes because my guys were back home freaking out.

It was a bit fucking chaotic, me trying to stay on top of everything while smiling for the camera and eating bats or piranhas or raw cow stomach. That last one made me so sick I lost 8 kilograms. I got sick just about everywhere I went.

For the whole of 2014 I grew thinner and thinner, and my profile grew and grew. I've been known in the food world since I first worked for Marco, when I was still a kid, basically, so I was used to being recognised here but when *Nomad Chef* went to air, I was completely unprepared for the level of exposure that being on the telly brings.

Nomad Chef was so big, the sheer size of the Discovery Channel meant this huge international burst of exposure. I wasn't ready for it at all.

Then in 2014 I was on the front cover of *Fool* magazine, the equivalent of *Time* magazine, but for food. It was probably the hippest publication in the world at the time, produced in Malmö, Sweden by art director Lotta Jörgensen and her partner, photographer Per-Anders Jörgensen. Their pitch was to send me into a community I'd never visited before, the Nauiyu community from Daly River. The idea was to document the process of growing trust, asking respectfully for education, and cultural exchange I went through in a remote community. Everything they touched turned to gold, and they shot an absolutely stunning photo essay to accompany a story about Orana by Australian writer Zane Lovitt that actually got what we were about and could explain it to the world.

After that, the international profile of Orana blew up, and the bookings sheet for the restaurant began to fill up.

At the same time, bullies started to come out of the woodwork, and people I'd always thought quite pleasant began to undermine me in the industry, on social media, in the papers.

It was my first real exposure to tall poppy syndrome, which is a uniquely Australian affliction. As an immigrant, it still seems weird to me that there's this national mani-festation of envy and jealousy. It's so odd that the public reaction to hard work and success is scorn: 'You know that thing you did? It's great! Therefore we hate it and we fucking hate you.'

If I had understood the flipside of that level of exposure, I might never have done *Nomad Chef,* even knowing all the good it did me and Orana.

It is perhaps a measure of my utter naivety of that world that I did all this press and media and a global television show without even considering that my sordid past might come to light. In retrospect, the astonishing thing is that it took so long to happen.

In 2014, a journalist in Adelaide named Michael McGuire actually did some proper journalism and spoke to some people I used to work with in the UK rather than just the names on the press releases. Which means that he called people who knew me prior to 2000, when the fact that I was a heroin addict was scarcely a secret in the inner circles of London's hospitality industry.

Next he called me up and told me he was going to break the story that I was once a heroin addict.

'Can you, umm . . .' I was in shock, trying to work out what to do, or say, to fix this. 'Can you . . . please not do that?'

'Why?' he said. 'Do you think I'm going to be the only person to find this out?'

He told me he was sorry, but he was going to run the story. I can't say I blame him. It was a reasonable article, and it was truthful, and that's what a journalist does. I had to respect somebody who was good at their job, even if that meant blowing my life into little pieces.

Until that moment, outside the company of other junkies, my addiction had been this dark little secret. My parents didn't know; Kelly, my ex-wife and mother of my oldest daughter, had no idea. Sure, she knew that I'd taken drugs, but heroin was something else entirely. In most people's minds, a heroin junkie is the dirtiest, skankiest version of an addict, and now everyone I'd ever known would know that about me. The fact I'd been clean for fourteen years felt irrelevant.

Having all my dirty laundry dragged out for the world to see was hard. It was and still is a really humiliating moment that was so public.

It meant Kelly found out not only that I'd been a junkie for the first years of our relationship, but worse, I'd kept a secret that massive from her. She wasn't too pleased about it.

Mum and Dad were the most embarrassed. My mum in particular was very upset that people she knew would know that her son was a junkie. To this day, it's the first line in every story written about me: 'former heroin addict Jock Zonfrillo makes a caponata' or whatever, and each time, Mum will call me, distressed, and ask, 'Why do you have to talk about that all the time?'

'I'm not talking about it, Mum!' I protest. 'That's what the media does, to get people to click on their story. Do you think I want to talk about it?'

The hardest part of all was telling my girls that I'd been a heroin addict. Sofia wasn't even eight yet, probably a bit too young to understand what it all meant, but Ava was thirteen, which is old enough to know what heroin was, and for all her friends to read the article and ask her about it.

That's an impossibly difficult and shameful conversation to have with your teen daughter, telling her about your heroin addiction and then having to answer her questions, the way a child does about anything. Long ago I'd made a parental pledge of always being truthful with my children, and I couldn't back down from that now.

'What is heroin? What does it do? Do you swallow it?'

'Actually, you cook it on a spoon so you can inject it.' Not my proudest moment as a father. I felt sick, watching my girl's innocent face trying to picture her dad shooting drugs like she'd seen in all these gritty movies.

I'm not ashamed of having been an addict, but I will never forget how painful that conversation was. I know that every time my daughters watch a movie where there's a junkie character shooting up in the street, they'll know that that was something their dad used to do.

At least, since it came out into the open, I could be completely honest with them about my past. I hope that if the time comes when they need to talk about substances and addiction, they'll know they can talk to me.

At the end of the day, my life is my life. It is what it is. It's been what it's been. Post that story breaking, there's nothing I needed to hide any more, and in a strange way it set me up for what happened next, which was finding the love of my life.

CHAPTER TWENTY-FOUR

B eing outed as a former addict wasn't the happiest day of my life, but it could have been worse. Eventually the hoo-ha died down and it didn't dent the growing reputation of Orana, and it didn't stop organisations and brands reaching out with those lucrative offers that were vital to keeping the lights on at Orana while we lost money by the truckload.

In 2014 I was an ambassador for Krug champagne, and I was doing an event in Sydney where I had to design a 'guilty pleasure' dish to pair with the champagne. From memory, it was a scallop and pancetta roll with HP sauce. Lovely little dish: you pull a scallop up from the ocean floor, with just the freshest, most elegant natural brine, expand the depth of flavour by grilling it with some really good pancetta and a cheeky little kick of HP cut with silky crème fraîche. Not very posh, but extremely tasty.

So there I was at this event in Sydney, doing the schmooze thing, shaking hands, when a woman came up and introduced herself to me. She was very nice, chatty; we took a photo together, then she disappeared. Didn't think much of it at the time.

Unbeknown to me, however, wheels had been set in motion. She was friends with Lauren Fried, a businesswoman and panellist on the ABC show *Gruen*, who was in Europe on holiday recovering from a relationship gone bad. Lauren got a message from her friend with a picture of me and a sales pitch: 'Loz, I've found the perfect guy for you. He's European, he's got an accent, he's a chef. He's everything you want in a man. He's even a champagne ambassador!'

The mutual friend was meant to introduce us when Lauren got back to Sydney, but it never happened. Then one night Lauren was going through her phone deleting old photos, and it threw up the photo her friend had taken. If she'd simply hit delete, that would've been the end of the story, but instead she stopped, and thought: 'Oh, it's that chef, Jock.'

She followed me on Twitter. I followed her back because I recognised her from *Gruen*, which I liked, so I thought she'd probably do some interesting stuff on Twitter and then . . . nothing. We just went on with our lives.

That might have been that, but then one Saturday night that October, she'd had lunch with her family and had a few champagnes.

On the way home she was killing time by clearing out her email on her phone, and she went into the spam folder, where she found the Twitter notification that I'd followed her.

Neither of us used Twitter very much, so it was two pretty lucky coincidences that brought us there. She was a bit tipsy, felt chatty, and sent me a message. 'Hey, my friend met you at an event a few months ago. She said you're my kind of guy.'

This was around 11 pm on a Saturday night back in Adelaide and I was cleaning down the kitchen with my team. I wrote her back, and we started a conversation that went on all night, until 8 am basically. We only stopped talking because the sun was coming up and I had to go get breakfast ready for the girls – Ava was over from Sydney for the weekend. Before I signed off, I asked if I could call her later in the day. We chatted and eventually I asked her if she wanted to have dinner with me.

'Don't you live in Adelaide?'

'I'll come to Sydney, that's fine,' I said, and booked a flight. So after the kids had left, I went up to Sydney on Tuesday 21 October 2014 for a date that afternoon.

We planned to take a water taxi to a restaurant on the harbour for lunch, so we met in the bar of the waterfront hotel I was staying at. I was very nervous beforehand, really working myself up with a fair bit of anxiety, so I had a whisky to calm down. That didn't work, so I had a martini. I had one waiting for her when she came in, which she appreciated, so I knew from the start she had good taste.

When she walked through the door she smiled, and I just knew. We were going to be a thing, and it was going to be wonderful. It was as simple as that.

We just got along really well from the first words we ever exchanged. The food at the restaurant was shit, so we ended up ignoring the meal and just ordering a really nice bottle of champagne. We shared our first kiss on the water as the boat took us back.

Loz lived in the Rocks, so we went out to dinner that night at her local, an Italian restaurant where she went

several times a week, and she had been on a lot of terrible
first dates there before. All the waiters knew her and were
really protective of her, and were so rude to me. The waiter
came, took her drink order, brought it back, and I was like,
'Mate, could I get a drink too, please?'

Apart from that, it went really well. We went back to
her place, then out for a midnight walk through the Rocks.
We strolled along the seawalls and through all the little
sandstone alleys. It was a beautiful spring night: sea breeze,
moonlight; very romantic.

Shortly before meeting Loz, following a string of disastrous short-term relationships in Adelaide, after which
I realised I was actually a fairly shit partner to women, I'd
finally put myself in therapy to try and sort myself out.

So that night in the Rocks, I found myself spilling my
guts, just telling her everything I didn't want her to find
out later on: the drugs; the failed marriages; my daughters.
I basically dumped six months of concentrated relationship
on her in a couple of hours. Looking back, I was maybe a bit
too intense about the whole thing, but, as I said, I somehow
already knew that this was the real thing.

I was meant to go back to Adelaide the next day but
pushed back my flight so the date could continue on the
Wednesday. Thursday morning I did that again, so I ended
up staying for three days before I absolutely had to be back at
Orana for service on Friday and I just couldn't skip it.

On Friday morning I was at the airport, just about to fly
out, and I realised I really didn't want to get on that plane
without Loz. So I called her from the airport, asked her to
come to Adelaide, and she got the last flight out that night.

I picked her up from the airport that Friday night after work, and we went back to my place in the hills where I had a fire going, champagne on ice and a carbonara ready to roll. And so the date continued, four nights and counting, and we haven't been apart for many nights since.

In between me going to the airport and Loz flying to meet me, she went to work and wrote her sister an email telling her she'd just been on a date with this guy and she knew it sounded crazy, but she thought that she might be in love with him.

At my end, I knew for certain that I loved her. How that love-at-first-sight thing works, I don't know. I didn't believe in the concept until it happened, but there was no denying it.

By that weekend, we were telling each other that we loved each other. And it was just on from then, building steadily. It was immediate, but no less deep and real.

The whole thing was very romantic. Kind of old school, but also new school, in that it wouldn't have happened if it weren't for a fair few intrusive phone apps that seemed determined to make it happen.

It was completely unexpected. I'd sort of given up on ever finding somebody. It's already sort of difficult to build a life as a chef. The hours, the drugs, the burnout – it led me to two divorces, and very few close friends, because there was just no time to nurture relationships. The growing profile of being on the telly and outed as a junkie in the media hadn't helped.

Being well-known really makes it harder to trust people. You have a few bad experiences and you start to question why people are talking to you and wanting to be around you, particularly in relationships, which is difficult when you're single and looking for someone to share your life with. You just want to meet someone without all the hoo-ha.

Then, all of a sudden, there was Loz.

After that first date the relationship deepened pretty quickly. There was definitely a moment of understanding about what we wanted, and we were old enough to know we didn't want to mess around.

We'd both been restless for so long, unable to stay in one place or in one situation without getting the urge to roam. Honestly, I was a bit lost, and Loz was as well. We'd both been married twice before, had been lonely for a while, and reached the point where we had given up on finding someone who held our interest so completely. Then we met, and we were at that stage of life when we were ready for each other. Ready to be happy.

At the end of 2014 we went to Europe for a month, and while there we started to discuss the possibility of having children one day. When we met, Loz had already decided she was going to freeze her eggs. She'd already had all her appointments and tests, and was going to have the procedure when we got back from Europe, and she was telling me all this over dinner one night.

'What if you didn't do that?' I said. 'What if we started trying for a baby?'

'That,' she said, smiling, 'sounds great.' This was after we'd spent just eight weeks together.

For a while we were bouncing between Sydney and Adelaide, spending alternate weeks in each city. I had Orana, and Loz ran her own marketing agency so we were both just crazy busy, and we realised pretty quickly that it wasn't sustainable, and so we moved in together in Adelaide. We met in October 2014 and bought a house together in April 2015. Loz could continue her career from Adelaide, but the priority at that moment was starting a family.

We had so much in common. Both of us were hugely competitive, highly ambitious and pretty much incapable of backing down from a fight. In previous relationships, I think blokes had struggled with her strength, intelligence, and ambition, so she'd had a bit of a rough trot.

I told her in the first few days that I wanted to show my girls what a happy home looks like, and what a good relationship looks like. I hadn't managed that with their mothers. I hadn't provided the model of a relationship built on respect where you can have an argument in a respectful way. It was important to me that they saw this because the relationships kids are exposed to growing up will be the model for what they expect in the future. I needed to do better than in the past.

Around this time, things grew more difficult with Nadia, my second wife, and I lost contact with Sofia. It was heartbreaking, but part of me understands. I was not a good husband to her. I knew that I could throw a shitload of money and lawyers at the rift, and try and force her to let me see Sofia, but I knew that would only make things worse. I love Sofia so much, and I'm so proud of her, but I don't want anything but the best for her, and dragging her through the courts while she grows up will not help anyone.

The critical thing is that she works out the relationship that she wants with me, one that's not dictated by either me or her mother. All I can do now is hope Sofia finds her way back to me the way Ava has, and work to be a better father and husband.

And Loz expects the best. I'm a better man, father and husband when I'm around her. I don't really have a choice: she's an epic, fierce businesswoman and leader and I'd follow her anywhere. I'm also so grateful she followed me to Adelaide and Orana. She was a blessing to me personally, but my staff were just as grateful she'd come into their life.

She came into the kitchen at Orana and basically tamed the chaos.

I'd become obsessed with some new ingredient, with mastering the absolutely perfect recipe to do it justice. For a while I became obsessed with making a Malteser from scratch. I don't know why, I just had to prove to myself that I could do it. Lauren would find me up at night trying to find a way to inject air through malted milk, and she'd go off: 'Why do you need to make a Malteser? You can buy a whole packet literally anywhere!' That's not brilliant.

She had a way of making me see sense, even in my own behaviour and obsessions, which no one had ever been able to do before.

For example, I was smart enough to marry her. I would have loved for my girls to be with me at my wedding, but it was not to be.

We eloped to Mnemba Island in the Zanzibar Archipelago, Tanzania, and tied the knot on New Year's Day 2017 at a private ceremony by the beach. Afterwards we walked barefoot into the water – Loz in a gorgeous wedding gown, me in a kilt – kissed, and we've never looked back.

CHAPTER TWENTY-FIVE

Loz was amazing with my girls. It wasn't long before Ava, who was fourteen at this point, was like a sister to Loz as well as a daughter. She was so good with kids, and we couldn't wait to have more.

We tried for a baby for six months, but it wasn't really happening, so we decided to go the IVF route.

It worked straightaway. Of fourteen eggs fertilised, one was genetically perfect, so the doctors popped that one in and away we went. It would be two weeks until we found out if the embryo was viable, but we never doubted it. We just knew it would work out for us. Loz wasn't scared at all, and sure enough the embryo took. We were going to have a son – Alfie.

We had all the scans, everything was going fine, until we got to the twenty-week mark, which is when the doctors called us in and gave us some news.

Scans showed that Alfie had a talipes equinovarus, or club foot. After birth he would need to wear a cast for six weeks to reshape the bone, then an operation in which his Achilles tendon would have to be severed, broken, then held in a cast until it regrew. On top of that, he'd need to wear a boot contraption to bed until he was four.

It was a real punch in the gut, to know that our son's first experience in the world would be such an intense medical ordeal. He wasn't even born yet and we were already seeking treatment for poor little Alfie. Already this excitement we had about him, the euphoria of knowing we were bringing life into the world, had been impacted in a major way.

Obviously, we went into overdrive, and went out to find the very best specialist for this condition in Australia, who reassured us that what Alfie was facing was nothing out of the ordinary, the treatment was good, efficient, and standardised worldwide. So, not ideal, but we'd deal with it as a family.

Then we got to the 28-week scan, and there was more bad news for us: 'It's not looking good. His nose bone isn't as long as we'd like it to be, and one of the femurs is not the width we'd like it to be,' we were told.

Apparently the nose bone was the main cause for concern. It was a red flag for several genetic disorders.

We rushed over to see Loz's obstetrician, Sabrina, who grew to be a good friend to us, and she told us that at twenty-eight weeks we were really hitting a crunch point. Potentially, as early as Tuesday next week after another scan, we'd have to make a decision about whether to terminate the pregnancy.

As white as a sheet, Loz and I asked what that would involve.

We were told that a needle would be put in through her stomach into the baby's heart. Then the baby's heart would stop beating, and birth would either be induced or Loz would have a caesarean.

Fuck me. It was so heavy. That was gutting, this revelation so quickly after the other. I was still reeling from the reality of Alfie's foot, and now this impossible news. We were inconsolable, both of us crying hysterically as we went out to the car.

I had to work that night. We had a food reviewer coming to rate Orana and the restaurant was hanging by a thread already. It was a real make-or-break kind of thing, but I couldn't leave Loz at home alone with this.

'Go, go to work,' she told me. 'I'm fine, I really am, this is important. Go take care of Orana.'

I dropped her off at home and went down the hill to the restaurant. I got to the door of the restaurant, walked in, unrolled my knives and then just had a moment of clarity, staring down at the steel while the kitchen bustled all around me.

'I'm going home,' I told my team. 'This one's up to you,' and I ran back to the car.

Lauren was still on the couch when I got back.

'What are you doing here?' she said, through tears. 'What about the review?'

'It doesn't matter. Not compared to this,' I said. 'These might be the last few days that we've got with this baby. So let's just be in that and stay close, stay home and just try and stay calm until Tuesday.'

So that's what we did. We stayed home and basically held each other until Tuesday, when we were to go in for another scan. It was awful, the longest few days, just the parenting orientation from hell.

But then we went in, got the scan, and mercifully the nose bone was fine. We were in the clear.

Two weeks later, I had an event in Europe, followed by an episode of *Four Hands Menu* with Poul Andrias Ziska to film. Loz was thirty weeks pregnant at this stage, and planned to come with me for a little holiday in Italy.

She booked a doctor's appointment the day we were flying out, where her obstetrician, Sabrina, had some concerns and wanted to run some tests.

'You can fly to Melbourne to catch your connecting flight to Italy,' she told Loz. 'But if the results aren't what I want them to be, you have to guarantee me you'll fly back here.'

Loz gave her word, and called Sabrina from Melbourne airport, who gave her the go-ahead to fly at the last minute, and we were able to spend a magical week in Italy.

Afterwards, Loz flew back to Australia and I went on to the Faroe Islands where I was filming the TV show. An absolutely spectacular part of the world, a really special place for me; very, very isolated. I was out all day fishing and up and down mountains, and was only able to get phone reception back at the hotel. A few days passed like that, I was having a lovely time with the locals, eating fermented meat and all that good stuff, and then I got back to the hotel where I had a message from Loz. The baby was coming right then, two and a half months early, and I was on the wrong side of the world.

What had transpired was this: while I was fucking around on the Faroe Islands, Loz had flown home, gone to sleep and the next day gone to her doctor for a scheduled appointment. She was on her way home from that and the doctor called her and told her that she needed to come straight back and be admitted into hospital right away. That baby was coming out in the next twenty-four hours.

She couldn't get in touch with me, and went into full-blown panic mode. She was alone in the Adelaide Hills and you couldn't even get a taxi out where we lived. Sabrina, her doctor, was amazing, calmed her down and talked her through the whole thing, got her to the car, to the hospital and into the maternity ward.

By the time Loz finally got onto me, she'd sorted everything out, changed my flights, and would get me home by 9 pm that Saturday night. But that was well after the baby was due, and we were both devastated I wouldn't be there.

In my absence, Loz's best friend Joey, her mum, brother and sister all flew in from Sydney on the first available flight.

They all came into the ward, where Loz was lying with all these monitor straps around her stomach. An issue with the placenta and umbilical cord meant the baby was in danger and had to come out via caesarean as soon as possible. At this point, I was on a plane with no hope of getting back in time, and Loz had to decide who was going to come into surgery with her.

Sabrina told her that she was going to hold off performing the caesarean as long as possible. She was making the decision to go into surgery on an hourly basis as the scans came through. Pushed it back an hour, then another, and another, long enough that my plane touched down in Adelaide.

I landed right in the nick of time, called Loz and found she was still in her room, abandoned my suitcases and raced straight to the hospital. I only stopped to get some Oporto, because I was hungry and I figured Loz would be too, and we both love Oporto. I rushed in, all sweaty and jet lagged with a double Bondi meal and Loz was like, 'Honey, you know, we're in a bit of a rush here.'

As it turned out, however, I could have taken my time, and even gone for a side of fries. Loz stayed in the ward for two more weeks in an uncertain condition. What went from Loz having a baby within twenty-four hours became two weeks of tests every four hours, waiting until the last possible moment to induce labour.

In that two weeks, they walked us through the neonatal intensive care unit (NICU) where Alfie would be spending the first part of his life. Part of it was to show us the standard of care he would be receiving, and part of it would be to take the sharp edges off what we were about to experience.

It was clear that we were going to have a very small baby. When it looked like he would be born without me there, he weighed just 900 grams, which was way too small.

Alfie was finally born at three in the afternoon on 12 February 2018, well shy of his April due date. He was 1.2 kilos, which was a relief, but wasn't ideal. Many full-term babies are more than three times that size.

He was put on Loz's chest for literally a two-second cuddle with him in the birthing suite, then he had to be taken away and put straight into an incubator in the NICU, so Loz didn't get to really hold him for some time. I didn't get to hold him at all, and a very capable, no-nonsense Scottish paediatrician took him away for specialist care. I followed in hot pursuit. Loz couldn't walk because of the caesarean and we had to fight for her to be put in a wheelchair and pushed down to the NICU to see him.

They'd wrapped him in a tiny baby nappy but had to fold it again and again to try and make it fit. His head, the size of a tennis ball, was covered with a tiny cap, and tiny goggles covered his eyes to protect them from the incubator's heat lamp. There were feeding tubes and oxygen tubes coming out of his body all over the place, and electrical monitors clamped to his feet. With skin covered in fine hair, it was clear Alfie wasn't meant to be in the outside world yet. That was heartbreaking, but though so small at least he was whole – ten fingers, ten toes; a perfect little baby boy.

We couldn't cuddle him. The slightest bump can cause a premature baby pain, and Alfie couldn't afford to cry. He could only take in a few millilitres of milk per feeding, so he just couldn't spare the calories that crying would cost him. For an infant so small, it could be life-threatening. It was such a vastly different experience from the birth of my two daughters, and it felt like fate was robbing us of this most precious moment in my son's life.

We stayed with Alfie all night, and in the morning Ava arrived to meet her new brother. Loz and I had agreed that she should be the first person who got to hold him, because it was important they bond. Looking back, I think it was in the back of my mind, in the dark part of the mind where the unthinkable fears live, that it was vital Ava meet her brother in case he didn't make it. So she was the first to hold him, and it was a very special moment. As wonderful as it was, it broke my heart a little that Sofia couldn't be there as well.

In the first few days after birth his weight dropped to 937 grams. I feared the worst. We didn't get to hold him for another thirty-six hours. Loz went first, then I took the next opportunity, but we could barely touch him with our fingertips. When my girls were born, all I wanted to do was cuddle them close, but poor Alfie couldn't be touched at all, and babies really need that. He couldn't even be swaddled or wear clothes, because there were too many tubes running in and out of his tiny body. It's such a hard way to begin life.

It went on like that for five weeks. Five horrible, shitty weeks. Those days were spent by Alfie's side, listening to the beep of the heart monitor, with the buzzing and lights of the NICU all around us. Just hellish. Alfie was in a sealed humidicrib, so we could only touch him if we sanitised our hands, and reached through little arm holes in the side of the crib. For those first weeks, we were separated, and could only watch him through the transparent roof of the crib as he struggled to breathe.

Every time we left for the night, I just wanted to stay with my boy. I knew that every time I walked out that door I might not see him alive again. There was never a guarantee he would make it through that night. I knew I had to be the strong one for Loz, and would insist that we go home at night and rest for the day ahead of us. It seemed to me that if I succumbed to the fear and depression that threatened to overwhelm me then all would be lost. I had to keep it together, but I was barely managing. After each sleepless night, we called the hospital staff for a detailed update: Alfie drank a little milk, he's put on 13 grams, he's doing really well for a baby his size. They were amazing. Genuine heroes.

Then one morning we went in and something had changed. Loz and I looked at each other in wonder.

Alfie was in a crib. He'd been in a little sealed incubator chamber from birth, and now he was just lying there in a normal little bed, just like any baby. Now we could touch his little face and his hair without going through the sterilisation procedure. We could pick him up, take him for a little walk, and put him down again.

Two days after that, his oxygen and feeding tubes were gone. All that was left was a monitor clipped onto his foot that we were allowed to take off to pick him up.

One day, just like that, he was our little baby, our little boy who we could pick up and cuddle and bathe and change his nappy and all that basic stuff we'd been so badly missing. It was just the most amazing milestone. Looking back, it makes me a little sad that that was such a huge moment for us, but at the time we were just ecstatic.

When we finally got him home, he was such a calm baby. The poor little guy was so used to pinging machines and alarms going off and people poking him day and night that when he came home he just seemed so relaxed and resilient. He never cried or grumbled, content just to smile and look into our eyes. A perfect little gentleman, our Alfie, from day one.

Alfie was so laidback that he even came to work with us: for seven months he was at the restaurant with us day and night. We'd prop him up in his bassinet and he'd just happily pass the time kicking his little legs in the air and laughing. The best front-of-house manager I ever had – this portable little dude who was happy to chill wherever he was. There's plenty of photos of me in the kitchen in my apron, cooking with one hand and cradling Alfie with the other. Now and then I'd go out and introduce a dish to a diner still holding Alfie, and you'd see them do a very alarmed double take that I'd walked out of the kitchen holding a plate of goanna in one hand and a baby in the other.

It was such a relief, and it meant most of the pressure points of a relationship that can come with a newborn were taken away. Despite the incredibly stressful start to his life, I don't think we had it as hard as a lot of other parents, so it gave our relationship the oxygen it needed to continue and strengthen. We both recognised that the very worst thing we could imagine had almost happened, so anything that happened afterwards was a blessing. For the first time since that worrying scan all those months ago, we realised we were truly happy again. We didn't have to try to be happy, or stave off depression. There was too much good in our life. Our baby was home, and healthy, and happy. And so were we. After that, we knew we could handle anything, whatever the future had in store for us. We'd handle it together.

CHAPTER TWENTY-SIX

Loz and I fit together so perfectly. After we met, every-thing in my life started to fall into place. She was this calm, moderating force that brought out the best in me and tempered my worst instincts and propensity to be a maniac about whatever was holding my interest at any particular moment.

Most importantly, Loz understood my passion for a true Australian cuisine; my drive to honour Indigenous people and their culture through food, and she turned her talents towards making it happen.

I dreamed of using my profile as a chef and the good standing of Orana to introduce the incredible native ingredients of this country to the world while celebrating Indigenous culture and supporting Indigenous communi-ties. How exactly that would happen, I didn't know.

But with Loz's help, the Orana Foundation started to take shape, going from a passionate but chaotic initiative into something more focused that could actually achieve our goals. Our mission was to shine a light on Australia's

Indigenous food and assist our First Nations to protect and preserve their cultural heritage through research, innovation and enterprise. Restaurant Orana was designed to start a conversation about the acknowledgement of Indigenous culture through food. The Orana Foundation's mission was to continue that conversation.

As I'd been asked to do by so many elders, we wanted to work to help develop industry and Indigenous enterprise, so that ingredients could be sourced directly from the traditional custodians, and restaurants pay a fair price for them. Restaurants would benefit from unique produce and some of the communities we work with desperately needed money for medications, schooling, fights for land rights. We wanted the food we served to be an act of honesty, from community to the dining room of Orana. Which was all well and good in theory, but we didn't really know what we were doing, until the right person walked into our lives.

In 2017 Loz and I were eating a quick lunch before dinner service at our downstairs restaurant (which we'd renamed Bistro Blackwood) when a very distinguished, very classy-looking American woman at the next table leaned over. 'Excuse me, are you Jock?'

This was Dena Kaye, philanthropist daughter of the great actor Danny Kaye, who had read a profile of me in the *Wall Street Journal* and had flown over to check out the restaurant. Now that she was here, she couldn't stomach the thought of a twenty-course tasting menu, so told us she was just eating in the bistro. I urged her to come to dinner and she relented, and came in for dinner that night.

At the time I didn't actually know who she was, or how important and connected she was in the world of international philanthropy. I just genuinely wanted everyone in the world to eat at Orana, and so cajoled her into it. I'm glad I did, however, because afterwards she approached us, and told us that her Danny Kaye and Sylvia Fine Kaye Foundation searched the world to invest in people with purpose, and she'd sussed me out and wanted to help.

'What help do you need?' she asked.

'I'm just a chef,' I said, 'I have no idea how to set up a foundation.'

Dena told me she could see I had passion and drive, but passion and drive alone wouldn't get me there. I needed the right people, so that's how she would help. She wasn't going to give me money. She was going to give me the people I needed to make the Orana Foundation possible.

Dena Kaye offered us expertise and vision. She also introduced us to Norman Gillespie, an Australian finance and philanthropy powerhouse who would become executive director of the Orana Foundation.

He made us sit down and define our clear goals and tasks for the Foundation. What we wanted to do fitted into three key buckets.

The first was to partner with the University of Adelaide, with government funding, to create a compendium of native ingredients because at that point only twelve had ever been researched by the government. This information would be protected according to the protocols of the Indigenous custodians – no language group would have access to the knowledge or lore of another, and information not meant for non-Indigenous people would be protected from them. Once the database was complete it would be handed over to the appropriate Indigenous custodians. What happened to the information from there was entirely up to them. Whether they use the information for commercialisation and to develop enterprise, or keep it as a time capsule for future generations would be a decision entirely for the elders and custodians of each language group.

For the entire time I'd been visiting communities, whenever I asked what I could do to help the community, the one thing elders asked for time and time again was help to preserve knowledge of the plants and animals on their country, and to protect the intellectual property that rightfully belongs to their people.

The second goal was to research and then develop ingredients such as Geraldton wax, as no manufacturer is ever going to put an ingredient in a lotion or food without at least a toxicity report. The third was to create an enterprise culture around food for these communities. How could we make the process – from foraging and harvesting to commercial sale – easier and more profitable for the communities, should they wish it?

If we could use scientific research to codify the unique properties and benefits of traditional ingredients, it would help make them less confronting to the mainstream. Once top chefs in Australia and abroad got excited about them, they would appear in menus, and slowly start to trickle down into more common use, and the industry would grow. After all, tea was once an exotic, unheard-of idea to western consumers – the way I saw it, the same could be true of jilungin, which tastes a lot like green tea, minus the bitterness. When we had it tested by RMIT it was found to have a hundred times the antioxidants of green tea. We should all be drinking it, every day.

Through the Foundation, we wanted to set up initiatives in which communities could harvest the natural food resources on their land, store them viably then take them to the fine-dining market, even if the Orana restaurant was the primary customer in the beginning. Each community we worked with would be in control of their own autonomous production process and the intellectual property of their traditional foods.

We needed a great deal of help to navigate cultural protocol and boundaries, so Jo Willmot joined as board director. Jo is a Wakka Wakka woman, born and raised in Queensland's Cherbourg Aboriginal mission, who has intricate Indigenous cultural literacy, and a lifetime of experience in organising and training, and in diplomacy between State and Federal governments and Aboriginal nations.

We were also joined by Dr Philip A. Clarke, an ethnobiologist with vast research experience in Indigenous plants and their uses in food, medicine and creating artefacts. Bruno Dann provided guidance and insight to the Foundation, as well as acting as an ambassador for what we stood for. Without his invaluable support, nothing would have ever got off the ground.

One of our first initiatives was in Winawarl on Nyul Nyul country, where in May 2019 Bruno helped us to establish a solar-powered packing shed in which the community could wash, freeze and store freshly harvested gubinge, jilungin and native lemongrass. Since its establishment, the packing shed has provided clean water, electricity, internet connectivity, and become a significant source of income for the community. Since its advent the community has been able to invest in a new truck, vastly improving their foraging range, and encouraging people scattered across Nyul Nyul land to come back to community and take part in the growing enterprise.

Loz and I brought Alfie, just four months old at that stage, along with us because Bruno wanted to meet him and perform a smoking ceremony for him. After the ceremony, Bruno told Alfie that he considered him like his own son, and would protect him as though he was, and all Bruno's ancestors would also look after him and protect him.

It was an incredibly powerful, emotional experience and one of the most special moments of my life. I truly believe, too, that the Nyul Nyul ancestors watch over my son like their own and that he is protected.

Afterwards, we sat around the fire and Bruno told me he considered me to be a brother, and loved me like a brother. It was another frog-in-the-throat moment, but of course I already knew that. My relationship with Bruno is probably one of the longest I've had in my life, and definitely one of the most precious to me.

When we're together on the land we can just walk for hours without saying a word – which is very rare for me, as there's rarely a moment I'm not jawing away about something – and that's when I'm the most at peace.

I don't know how much time we have left together, which makes me deeply sad, but I have treasured every moment I have been privileged to spend time with him. Deep down, I truly believe that he will stay with me forever, long after we have to part ways on this earth.

We wanted to share something of what visiting country and being on land had meant to me as an outsider. As part of that, we produced some videos that introduced Indigenous ingredients and the communities they came from. In one of the very first, we featured Bruno, who we knew would be able to reach out to ordinary people. Just as he had to me.

I wanted people to look at the videos and question their knowledge of Indigenous people – to meet an elder like Bruno Dann, who was eloquent, and funny, and wise – and start to rethink assumptions they may have made about Indigenous communities.

You can relate to the video Bruno shot for us even if you're a white person without much knowledge in the space. Every time I watch it, I'm reminded of the value of this country we all live on, and the responsibility that comes with that. And that was what was so important. I couldn't have got just any elder to do that video; it was such a contentious and difficult task that many elders would have been rolled for being part of it. I needed somebody that could bridge the gap a little bit and Bruno was that guy.

I'd spent a lot of time on country with Bruno. Without him, there would be no Orana, so everyone on my staff knew who he was, but hadn't met him, and everyone was really nervous.

There wouldn't have been a moment in Orana's short history when we wanted to make a better impression than when Bruno walked in the door on 13 September 2017. Forget about opening night or food critics or any of that shit, Bruno Dann was coming to dinner, and that mattered. He was a great man and an important person to all of us and we were naturally shitting ourselves.

Then Bruno walked in, and something amazing happened. It was small, but it meant so much to me. The restaurant was packed, and when Bruno walked in – wearing a ski jacket, as he thinks any place colder than Broome is freezing – one tableful of diners called over a waiter and asked her eagerly, 'Is that Bruno Dann from the video?'

Those videos were made as much for an Australian audience as an international one. We weren't sure at that point how much impact they'd had, so the moment he was recognised as soon as he walked in and sat down, two things struck me. One: that someone out there had not only watched the video but paid attention, and two: that they cared enough to be able to recognise Bruno Dann as a Nyul Nyul elder and respect his knowledge.

That table got up and went over to Bruno's table to shake his hand and tell him what an honour it was to meet him. Then another table did the same then, one by one, the whole restaurant of diners from all over the world filed over to pay their respects.

I had tears in my eyes. I get a fucking frog in my throat thinking about it even today. That's why we did it; that acknowledgement was what we were trying to do with Orana and it had worked. That ordinary Australians *were* curious about our First Nations' food, culture and people; they *were* willing to listen and to learn and to open their minds and acknowledge Bruno Dann and his people. That's very fucking powerful. It's so much more powerful than a score out of twenty in a fucking newspaper. And it meant more to us as a team than anything else we did, or any of the awards and accolades that would follow.

It meant that the driving passion and constant pushing and the need to make it work were worth it, that our efforts had started, in whatever small way, to bring some respect and acknowledgement to our first Australians.

As the years went on, the Orana Foundation continued to steadily work towards our core goals We teamed up with universities around Australia, particularly the University of Adelaide, to undertake research projects and build a native food database to collate knowledge of Australian plants, help Indigenous people protect that knowledge, and investigate traditional and innovative culinary uses. All of it was incredibly expensive but the team were fantastic at sourcing revenue and government grants, and every dollar we got was invested back into the mission to bring Indigenous food to dinner tables worldwide.

One of my favourite ingredients in the entire world is the cherabin, the giant freshwater prawn native to the Top End. Lovely, delicate meat, and I would choose one over a dragnet-harvested ocean prawn any day. A good-sized king prawn will come in at 80 grams, but a fully-grown cherabin can reach 300 grams, which is insane value.

There are already aquaculture places hatching and growing them, but the harvest is the greatest problem standing in the way of a viable industry. Cherabin start losing their freshness the second they're pulled out of the water, so if you can't eat them on the spot you need to freeze them immediately. That's not easy when they only grow out on wild land.

The Orana Foundation sought advice, and hit on the possibility of a mobile processing facility – basically a machine you could truck around to freshwater aquaculture tanks or even wild ponds as needed. The cherabin are harvested, loaded into the machine, and come out the other side processed and frozen, ready to be shipped to restaurants anywhere in the world.

As a first step, we talked to a professor at James Cook University back in 2016, and the possibility of a mobile processing plant was floated. Over the next eighteen months, we worked with him on an overarching plan to start developing wild freshwater grow ponds which could be used to cultivate and process cherabin within local community enterprise.

There were dozens of initiatives like that driven by people much smarter and more talented than me. I wasn't doing any of it for glory, or for my ego or profile. More than anything, I was driven by a sense of despair that so much incredible potential was going to waste. That and the knowledge that I was living on stolen land, and that as a white guy I had certain privileges and a debt I could never pay back. But I still had to try and do something, to give something back. Sovereignty was never ceded, and if you're living on someone else's property, you pay the rent.

I got, and continue to get, a lot of grief about working in the Indigenous space – most of it from white guys – and accusations that I'm trying to be this white saviour. That's not what I'm going for. Being any kind of saviour isn't really in my wheelhouse. I know what it looks like from the outside, but I'm a chef, and I hate to see what I believe is some of the best food on the planet going unappreciated, aside from everything else.

Little by little, we stopped losing money. In 2014, we lost only $270,000. By 2017, we were almost breaking even, when everything started accelerating exponentially. In October, the Orana Foundation was awarded the *Good Food Guide*'s Food for Good Award, and the following year I was awarded the Basque Culinary World Prize for a chef whose work has a wider socio-economic benefit. A public-private initiative that is funded by the Basque Government and judged by a jury featuring some of the world's most influential chefs and experts, this prestigious award came with a purse of 100,000 euros (about AUD $156,000), which went straight into the Foundation.

Restaurant Orana was also named 2018 Australia's Restaurant of the Year by *Gourmet Traveller* magazine, and that same year *The Australian* named me as Hottest Chef.

The *Good Food Guide* named us 2019 Restaurant of the Year, and awarded us the three hats I'd promised my staff right back at the beginning. It's nice to be acknowledged; it never hurts to be recognised for the hard work and vision of your entire team – and it meant the world to me that they were recognised. But that's not the most important thing for me. Don't get me wrong, it was wonderful for the staff to be part of a three-hat restaurant, because that's great news for any chef, sommelier or waiter's career, but that's not what any of us were in it for.

Our goal was acknowledgement of Indigenous people through food. That's what we cared about. But having three stars, and the respect of the entire hospitality industry didn't hurt. It wasn't a bad bonus. Winning awards does feel fucking great.

As the accolades and awards piled up, the thing we'd always wanted to happen began to manifest. In the space of a few years we went from begging critics to have a conversation with us about green-ant sorbet to being considered the best restaurant in the country, and we were booked out for months on end by serious foodies who were travelling to Adelaide specifically to celebrate Indigenous food. And that was pretty amazing.

Then in October 2019 I got another one of those dramatically life-changing phone calls I seem to get with alarming frequency. It was from the team behind *MasterChef Australia*, and they wanted to chat about maybe having me on as a judge.

CHAPTER TWENTY-SEVEN

I told them I'd have to call them back. My mind went immediately to 'No'. It's not that I didn't enjoy the show. I watched it, and I'd been on it as a guest chef, and I remember watching the British version with my parents decades earlier. I was sitting on the carpet in front of the television and Loyd Grossman was playing to the camera with a glass of wine: 'One for the pot, one for me.' It looked like a load of fun.

What I was wary of was the level of exposure that would come with it. I'd already been through the wringer with the publicity I'd experienced after *Nomad Chef*, but the level of exposure of *MasterChef*, on the telly every night in a million homes across the globe, would be magnitudes greater. I had seen what famous mates went through, and I didn't love it: people staring at you when you go out to eat, taking pictures of you when you're in the park with your kids – none of that appealed to me.

I'd also just seen George Calombaris, a previous judge and a mate, shafted and humiliated very publicly through trial by media. I knew that going on the show would be painting a big neon target on my back for every armchair pundit remotely attached to the industry. I didn't really want to put myself or my family into that situation.

At the same time, the general premise of the show really appealed to me. The thing I enjoyed most was that you had enthusiasts from all kinds of careers and backgrounds who really wanted to follow their dream of a career in food. It's a real privilege to watch people's journey from being a green-around-the-edges amateur cook, to getting their apron, then going through the competition and beyond. If you look at the restaurant and food mediascape now compared to ten years ago, it's undeniable that *MasterChef Australia* has unearthed and nurtured a lot of talent.

Not only that, but it has really helped elevate the basic level of food literacy in Australia. People who might other-wise be feeding themselves and their kids fish and chips or microwave dinners because they don't even know how to boil an egg, can sit down in front of the TV and learn some-thing that encourages them to try cooking a dish they'd previously thought was beyond them.

I've known many chefs who have gone the haute-cuisine route – worked in Michelin star and three-hat restaurants, and done the hard yards in gruelling apprenticeships and twenty-hour workdays – who think that's the only way to become a chef. Yes, that's one route to becoming a chef, but it's brutal and traumatic, and it teaches you how to execute a certain kind of cuisine perfectly. But that's not the only way to become a magnificent cook.

Chefs hate on Jamie Oliver because he's best known as a TV guy. I don't. I fucking love the guy. I've known chefs with three hats who loathe TV cooks. They hate them because they're getting paid shitloads of money to do what is a fairly easy job compared to being a hands-on chef, but if they're teaching somebody a little bit of good nutrition or how to feed their kids then what's the harm?

Marco Pierre White taught me and a handful of amazing chefs how to make the best foie gras terrine in the world, but Jamie Oliver has taught millions of people how to make an omelette. Because of him, tonight hundreds of thousands of people are cooking dinner for their kids because they were given the skills and encouragement to give it a go. That's not nothing.

As a chef, it's natural to want to teach people. As selfish and bloodthirsty an industry as it can be, I've never met a good chef who didn't want to show people how to cook better food. That's a given. We all feel an obligation to give back to the industry. And with *MasterChef*, I'd be working with people who were completely focused on learning about food; human sponges eager to learn whatever you've got to share. That's a nice thing to be around.

And then there was something else to consider. As one of our advisers at Orana pointed out, if I was true to my word about trying to acknowledge Indigenous people through culture and food, I'd be fucking nuts not to accept this opportunity. It was a chance to get into the homes of a million people, casually in a way that suited them, five nights a week. I wouldn't be standing on a soapbox and ramming it down their throats along with crocodile meat like I'd been doing for years. If I could meet people halfway, didn't I have an obligation to do that? So that was my big demand in the negotiations – we would have to include Indigenous ingredients in the cooking aspect of the show, and at least once a season we would feature Indigenous voices and culture on country.

I'd already been on the show a couple of times as a guest judge back in 2014, and twice in a row in 2017 and 2018, so I had an idea of how it would be on set.

So I said yes . . . and immediately started freaking out. It was probably two weeks from the first meeting to it being announced to the media. Things moved very quickly. Once it was announced to the public that I'd be one of the new judges, alongside Andy Allen and Melissa Leong, my anxiety really started to kick into gear.

Outwardly, everyone in my circles was talking about how the three previous judges had been on it for over a decade and really *were* the show. And here were three new judges daring to take their places. Inwardly, I was just as racked by doubt. I kept thinking of *Top Gear*: it had been one of the most beloved shows in the world, then they changed the cast and it flopped disastrously.

I loved being on the show, but crashing the party for a day is a whole different level of responsibility to being one of the hosts. I sat at home absolutely hammering away at my worry beads, imagining the stage lights in my eyes and a hundred crew standing around waiting for me to perform.

We had a wardrobe fitting the first week of November 2019, where they measured me up for all these posh suits I was to wear. I saw them and thought that at the very least, I would look a million bucks. I weighed 82 kilos, a weight where suits hang off my frame well, so that was one thing I could relax about.

I wanted so badly to be good at it, and I had no idea if I would be. There is nothing I'm more frightened of in life than doing something badly, and so doing it in front of a television audience of millions was not top of the pops for me.

Mel, Andy and I hadn't screen-tested, so we had no idea if we would work on camera or even get along. That only added to my hypertension, because I could just see us turning up and having nothing to talk about, the show flopping, and all of Australia talking about how we killed *MasterChef*.

That was my mindset up until the day in December 2019, just before the holidays, when we actually got together to get all dolled up and do some rehearsals for two days. We'd go over some lines, do a little bit of cooking and judge some dishes so we could get an idea of how the three of us would work on screen. I was very nervous – I imagine all three of us were. It felt a bit like the first day of school, when you don't want to ask anyone where the toilets are, and I half-expected the big kids to start spitting on me from the studio balcony. So that was a tough day, but that was as hard as it got.

The crew were amazing. There are about a hundred people who work on that show, and most of them have been working on it for years and years, so they're a really tight crew, and just fantastic at what they do. I saw them in action and realised that this was an environment every bit as clockwork and professional as a kitchen brigade, but a lot friendlier. For the first bit of shooting, I had it in the back of my mind that I was this meat puppet that they'd propped up and the show went on regardless of who that was, and once I leaned into that, I started having a great time.

I quickly learned to trust the crew, and that if what we were doing in front of the camera was a bit shit, a hand would go up from somewhere off camera, 'Sorry, Jock, that's a bit shit, what you're doing. Let's try it this other way?'

I felt like I was in safe hands, but I was still a bit freaked. After those two days of rehearsals we paused filming for four weeks over summer, and I went on holiday with Loz and Alfie where I was so anxious I could barely eat. Whenever my anxiety gets bad, I automatically start shedding weight, and in the two months between wardrobe testing in November and when we started filming with our contestants in January, I'd dropped from 82 to 70 kilos.

It was a massive problem for the wardrobe department. They'd been expecting this strapping, couture-dressed TV-ready judge and when I came back in I was basically this skeleton swimming around in his suit and rattling worry beads at them. The poor wardrobe department had to scramble to design me a whole new set-up, and as the show went on, I just got smaller and smaller. If you look back at those early episodes, you can see me shrinking away week to week. I'd come in and the crew would be like, 'Get into hair and make-up quick and see what you can do about this.'

It was 90 per cent my own anxiety. Mel, Andy and I got on like a house on fire, and we all bonded very quickly. The fact we got along so well – onscreen and off – is a bit of a miracle. The three of us had all done television in one form or another before, but never together, so I guess the executive producers and directors of *MasterChef* understood our demeanour and personalities better than we did. At the end of the day, once we started working together, we were mates, and it was all easy.

The first episode was a bit of a challenge, as they informed me the guest judge would be Gordon Ramsay, a man I'd had little to do with aside from us slagging each other off in the press for twenty years. Before we began filming, I went and saw him to make peace.

'Hi Gordon.'

'Jock,' he said, 'how long's it been?'

'Twenty-four years . . . ' I said, searching for the most diplomatic thing to say, and coming up with, 'You were a bit of a dick back then.'

He laughed then. 'So were you. I don't think either of us were the best version of ourselves back then.'

So we started to reminisce about how crazy things were back then, how dysfunctional all those kitchens were, how lucky we were to survive it. By the time we were ready to film, we were mates again.

The crew took a load of pressure off, and the producers of the show had the foresight to bring in a series of all-star former contestants to compete for the title that year. It took a lot of heat off us as new judges, and allowed us to settle in a bit and feel more comfortable.

The all-stars had all done a series before, knew the ropes better than us, and knew exactly what to do on camera, which camera to look at, and how to do an exit interview. We didn't have to tease out their opinions or their style of food, because they were all legends Australians already knew.

You didn't have to coax them into studying a bit more, or trying a little harder in the kitchen, because they were already skilled cooks, working in some capacity in the industry, and had come into the competition with all the fire and passion it requires.

As we went on filming, I learned to manage my anxiety. I'd come in early to set and make everyone coffees, because at the end of the day, feeding people and showing hospitality is what I love, and one of the few things that relaxes me. Nobody expected that, and I think the crew thought it was a bit weird at first, for the judge to be taking coffee orders, but now they expect it, more or less, everyone waiting around for their short macchiato before they start the shoot.

Of course, I'm still a bit of a joker. I can't help it. I spent a lot of time dicking around in the first season, and playing practical jokes on the crew. For a week running, I'd wait until Mel took off her shoes between takes – it's painful to wear high heels and we're standing around all day long – and I'd grab one and hide it behind a range hood or the fridge. I think she doesn't mind too much, and my jokes are all harmless these days. Maybe, deep down, I'm capable of learning my lesson after all, but I'm not the only one who clowns around on set.

I more than met my match the day Katy Perry came in. She sings the theme song to the show, and apparently the producers had been trying to get her on for ages, and it just happened to happen on my watch.

She was *wonderful*. Just this being of pure chaos, bouncing around the set sneaking up behind contestants in the middle of the cook. She didn't seem to understand what show she was on, but that only made it better. *MasterChef* has a 'solid fourth wall' – you pretend the cameras aren't there unless you're doing an interview outside a cook or after leaving the competition. Katy either didn't know or didn't care, and started talking to the cameras the second she walked on set, and didn't let up the entire day. The energy level just never dimmed, and she seemed to be having a marvellous time.

At one point, she was served a steak, and couldn't cut it because she'd sprained her thumb, so she asked me to cut it up for her as if she were five years old, then started singing 'Put it in my mouth, daddy!'

Now, I didn't know what that meant, but I could tell by the reactions from the rest of the cast that it wasn't PG. My family was on set that day, so I looked over to Ava, who was standing at the side of stage, and who, then aged nineteen, knew exactly what young people meant by that. She just had her hand over her face, and looked utterly shocked and embarrassed, and then suddenly so was I. For the first time in my life, I was speechless. What *do* you say to that?

Apart from that, Katy was amazing. She was pregnant, and a very hungry lady who just hoovered up all the food in sight, game to try anything – a trait I admire in a person. In between takes she would hang out and talk to the contestants, and was really just a genuine and lovely person.

When we'd wrapped for the day we went backstage where Loz and Alfie were waiting and when she saw Alfie Katy immediately knelt down and held out her arms for a hug, and little Alfie ran up to get one. I think that speaks pretty highly of her character. I've met a lot of celebrities who will give you the time of day if there's something in it for them, but hugging a toddler backstage on a film set in Australia isn't for the benefit of anyone but that child. It's just a nice thing to do, and despite being one of the most famous women on the planet, that's how she carried herself. A class act.

Meanwhile, back in Adelaide, Orana was going strong – we were finally in the black, and because of the boost from *MasterChef* when it aired we were booked out for six solid months, and we were looking forward to the best six months in the history of the restaurant.

At the same time the Foundation was going from strength to strength and my new role on television was set to introduce a new global audience to the wonders of Australian cuisine. Best of all, Loz was in the first stages of pregnancy with our beautiful daughter. After decades of struggle, and butting my head against a brick wall, life was unreservedly beautiful – which is, of course, when the world ended.

CHAPTER TWENTY-EIGHT

During those first uncertain weeks in early 2020, as the COVID-19 pandemic started to worsen around the world but before it became clear just how bad things would become, reliable information was still light on the ground. We had no idea what the effect of contracting Covid might be on a pregnancy, or if it could threaten the life of our unborn daughter. I had to be in Melbourne to film, but until the last possible moment, Loz and Alfie stayed with me to help me through the anxiety of filming. To my great joy, Ava was with us too. When *MasterChef* started she'd moved to Melbourne to live with us, the first time we'd lived full-time under the same roof since she was a baby.

Like everyone else, we were watching the daily press conferences, trying to work out what was going on. By March, it was clear that it was all about to kick off, and we decided that Loz, Alfie and Ava should return to Adelaide, where we felt our house in the hills should be safe no matter what happened. I would stay behind in Melbourne to finish the series.

But first, I'd have to do something I'd fought tooth and nail against for seven years. Covid was looming, and there was the possibility we'd have to temporarily shutter Orana.

We had no idea how long it would take for the world to recover from the pandemic, but we ran on such tight margins that having to pay rent, suppliers and staff was untenable for very long.

On Thursday 19 March, Loz flew back to Adelaide for an appointment with Sabrina, her doctor. I flew over and joined Loz the next day, suddenly realising that the Saturday service at Orana would be the last for some time. The government had just announced that from 22 March a major emergency would be in place, and restaurants would have to close to comply with restrictions to stop the spread of the virus. That meant our last service would be on Saturday 21 March.

With lockdowns looming, we ran the numbers, and realised that even if we could open again in a few months, we'd have to sell out every sitting at every service in order to break even and it was clear that wouldn't happen for a long time. The decision to shutter was gut-wrenching.

We called a staff meeting on the twentieth, the night before the last service, and broke the news to the team. I said, 'I don't know what's happening, or when we're going to be able to open again, but we will, and in the meantime, I'm going to look after you. Until this is over, keep your heads up, keep in touch, look after each other. We'll get through this.'

It was really emotional. It felt like a funeral to have to close the place. Everything we'd fought for had been a struggle; not one thing about that place had ever been easy, and this was the hardest thing we'd ever had to do. We'd been through so much, and we were like a family.

For our final service, the whole staff came in. Even staff who'd left came back because they wanted to be a part of the final day. Andy got time off from the set and flew over with me from Melbourne to be by my side for the last day of this thing that was so much more than simply my restaurant.

We all felt that it was one of the most important things we'd ever been a part of, and might ever do. It was a bitter-sweet moment, and just so difficult to say goodbye. In the kitchen, we served our tasting menu, dish after dish of incredible food sourced from communities all around Australia. We had come to rely on each other, those communities and I, and now I had no idea what would happen to the promise I'd made to them. As I cooked, I had to fight to keep the tears from dropping on the plate.

Tears were everywhere. People who had come in to eat were crying at the table, because this might be the last time they would experience anything like this for who knew how long. Other people were angry. We'd had to cancel hundreds of bookings, and furious people were ringing up demanding a seat at the last service.

We pooled all the money we had in the war chest and kept staff on payroll as long as we could, and paid out annual leave and benefits for as long as we possibly could. The Orana team was family, and we would look after each other. Loz and Andy were both crying at the table. Greta had to keep avoiding our table because every time she met my eye she burst into tears. It was a heart-wrenching night, but we were sustained by the idea we would reunite on the other side of the pandemic. At that point we had no idea that it would be the last ever service.

When we closed in March, we held out hope we'd be able to return, but in October we had to put the business into voluntary administration, end our lease and close the restaurant permanently.

That was the end of the seven-year Orana journey. What we achieved there as a team remains the thing I am proudest of in my life, outside of my children. The Orana Foundation remains in place, in a holding pattern until such time as we can travel safely and freely again to our friends in communities. Our database is nearly complete, and I look forward to the day we can hand it over, in its entirety, to the rightful owners and custodians of the knowledge.

When we started Orana, nobody in fine dining was talking about Indigenous food, much less mainstream Australia. And for seven years, people could come from the other side of the world, or just from down the street, and taste sixteen dishes they'd never imagined existed, that were all from this beautiful country, and they could get a true taste of an Australian cuisine that I hope to see again one day.

It's my dream that, in twenty years, I'll be able to go to the cafe down the road and see cherabin and quandong on the menu next to avocado toast and pulled pork burgers. If that happens, whether Orana gets a nod or not, I don't really care. The important thing is that we started the conversation. Whoever jumps in next, I can't wait to see it.

*

I was absolutely gutted about the forced closure of Orana, but the show had to go on. April and the television premiere were right around the corner and I had to be in Melbourne for *MasterChef*. I flew back to Melbourne into the state of emergency, and Loz stayed behind at our house in the Adelaide Hills with Alfie and Ava. I thought we would be apart for a few days at the most. The idea of a three-month lockdown separated by state borders was unthinkable.

At this stage, Loz was twelve weeks pregnant, and it still seemed like the pandemic might blow over before too long. And if it didn't, well, there wasn't a safer place in the world than our property, which was a tranquil haven that never saw anything more dangerous than a kookaburra. Whatever happened, I felt Loz, Ava and Alfie would be safe there. But while I was happy they were secure, we didn't realise how hard the separation would be.

On 13 April we watched the first episode of *MasterChef* together on Zoom; Ava, Loz and Alfie on one end drinking water, me alone on the other drinking whisky. Alfie had left his favourite toy, a stuffed Elmo doll, behind in Melbourne, so I propped Elmo up next to me so that Alfie could see that he and I were having a lovely time in Melbourne. A very surreal experience to watch myself on television, so far away from the family who had supported me the whole way to this point.

It turns out we weren't the only ones watching *Master-Chef*. When the ratings came out, I got a text message from the producers giving us the figures. They were healthy, to say the least. The ratings were amazing, absolutely through the roof. In all fairness, there were lockdowns rolling across the country, so we pretty much had a captive audience, but I was still pretty chuffed. *MasterChef Australia* was an absolute juggernaut, and now the team that I was part of had more than acquitted ourselves. I was pretty proud to be on it, I've got to say.

That was amazing, but in Melbourne, lockdown started to wear me down. I missed Loz and my kids so much, and while Zoom was fine for a while, it got tired very quickly. As the weeks passed, it was so hard to be in different cities. Since we'd met, Loz and I had rarely been apart for more than a night, so the weeks ticked by and I got lonelier and lonelier.

Loz's bump got bigger and bigger, she was going to appointments and scans by herself, and it was killing me that I couldn't be there to support her and feel the baby kick. I was alone in Melbourne, and every morning I'd have to try and perk myself up to go in and perform for the cameras.

It was a pretty dark period. At night, to cheer myself up, I'd work on perfecting recipes and make videos of them, while trying to ignore the whisky bottle.

In the end, I pretty much set up a home studio in the lounge room, because (of course) I became so obsessed with getting the videos just right. Once they were absolutely perfect, I would upload them to Instagram, and then stay up all night planning the next one

At the five-week mark, we knew we couldn't stay apart much longer, it just wasn't going to work for us. If Loz went into labour early, or something went wrong and we were locked down again, it meant I wouldn't be able to be there for her.

So Loz and Ava packed her car with overnight bags, propped Alfie up in his child seat, and drove across the border to be with me. Didn't tell me she was coming, just jumped in the car, drove all day, and knocked on the front door. I'd tried calling her a couple of times, and was a little worried I couldn't reach her. It turned out she was out of range because she was making a mad dash to rescue me.

When she walked into my rental apartment, she held me for a long hug, then her face sort of fell, because I'd turned the place into this crazy man cave with recording equipment everywhere.

Apart from that, it was just the best surprise. I was with my wife and our three kids, born and unborn, and that was all that mattered. Our 111-day lockdown would come and go after that, which was a nightmare, but at least we had each other.

It was early July 2020 and I was lying on the floor with Alfie, pushing toy trucks around, the sort of play you do with a two year old on a Sunday afternoon, when I got a call from a journalist at *The Australian* newspaper who wanted to talk about the Orana Foundation.

We started chatting, and I was explaining what we did, and what the goals were, a little distracted because at the same time I'm playing with my son, pushing toy trucks around on the floor, looking for a toy that had rolled under the couch. The journalist kept me on the phone for ages, asking detailed questions about finance and funding, specifics of the plane trips taken by board members: really specific, granular inquiries, and I gradually realised this was something bigger than just a general chat about the Foundation.

'Look, you're asking for a lot of information here that I don't have to hand,' I told her. 'Can you email me the questions and I'll get right back to you?'

'Sure,' she said. 'Print deadline's five o'clock.'

That was at 3 pm. When the questions arrived, there were so many, all impossible to answer without looking up a lot of information, that I texted her we'd need more time to get the data she was asking for, then Loz and I set to work answering them. Loz was thirty weeks pregnant and it was painful to sit up for any length of time, but she powered through them.

We were still typing our response when the journalist's story went live online at 10 pm that night. The first I knew about it was the email the paper sent out advertising the front page of the next day's paper, and I was on it.

That article was pure character assassination, basically accusing me of being this foreign chef who'd come in and was plundering Indigenous culture; exploiting communities to make myself rich. It alleged that I'd misused a $1.25 million government grant intended to produce a database of Indigenous food. Grossly unfair, as not only was the database still under construction, we'd already conducted some ground-breaking research and were reporting on a six-monthly basis to the South Australian government, which seemed happy with our progress.

Worse than that, it misrepresented the work of the Foundation and our partners in communities around Australia. It was a devastating article.

Clearly they'd been working on the story for some time and while they had contacted me for quotes, they did so without giving me time to respond. Now we didn't know what to do. It was clearly defamatory, full of falsehoods, assumptions and lies, but we had no idea how we would go about correcting the record. We called a friend who's very experienced with publicity and a cool head in a crisis, and they told us to sleep on it.

'It's never as bad as you think. Say nothing, give them no comment, give it no oxygen. Just let it be and you'll be fine.'

Well, we tried to for a while, then got up and started dealing with the fallout.

Through the following day we got many calls and text messages from communities and Indigenous people that we were working with. They were really upset. On one level they were upset because we were good mates and I was being slandered in the national press. On another, they were worried that this would mean the end of the nascent food-production industry in communities. Would this mean the top chefs in Australia and internationally that they were supplying would be scared off? At this point, food produced by Indigenous people was on track to grow into a billion-dollar industry over the next decade, and our partners on country were concerned this would kill it. Many thought this was just another way for white people to oppress them.

It was disastrous for the Foundation, and not great for me personally. This was in the middle of *MasterChef* season one, and I was deeply anxious about how this might affect my career. We'd just moved our whole life to Melbourne, a new city we had no roots in, in a pandemic, and we were about to have another baby. But Channel 10 and the production company, Endemol Shine, were great about it. They knew the accusations were bullshit, and advised us to ignore it all and carry on.

What we felt by the time we went to bed, twenty-four hours later, was very, very hurt. But we also felt strongly supported by the people around us, and that was enough.

The paper, however, had not had enough. That was day one. Day two they ran another article.

Day three, they interviewed the Bush Tucker Man as an expert on Indigenous culture, with his own online database of over 180 items. He didn't have finger lime on there. Mate, you can buy finger lime at Coles. The Foundation database had catalogued and analysed 1443 ingredients. At that point all I could do was laugh, because it was so ridiculous. Then Chris Kenny was on *Sky News* reporting on the Bush Tucker Man 'controversy'. After that there was another story about the Bush Food Alliance demanding that I apologise for stealing traditional knowledge and hand over the database.

For weeks it was a series of media hits that just kept coming and coming and we felt there was nothing we could do. None of what they were saying was true, but without becoming entrenched in a messy legal battle, there was little we could do except watch as this massive media company calmly destroyed the legacy of the Orana Foundation and everything so many people had worked so hard to build. We'd lie awake at night, just holding each other in the dark, dreading what the next day would bring.

Finally, there was a bit of a breather, then on Saturday 9 August, at lunchtime, the same journalist called again, seeking comment on yet another story.

Again I told her to email me the questions and I'd get back to her.

And again I was given till 5 pm.

The Australian sent through questions about the Foundation's research into freshwater prawns, we responded, and the next day the article came out.

We really didn't want to go to court, because I'd already spent too much of my life there, either defending myself against my own stupid actions, or fighting for custody of my daughters, but we couldn't see any other way to make it stop. On 23 September, shortly before we were set to go to Federal Court to take on *The Australian*, *The Advertiser*, another publication in the News stable, ran an exposé on the incident when I accidentally set an apprentice on fire with an idiotic prank all those years ago. Not much of an exposé, really, since the whole thing was already on my Wikipedia page, but I took it as an intimidation tactic designed to scare us into dropping our defamation action. Naturally, it got picked up all over the media, so now there was a whole other angle to the whole 'Jock's an arsehole' discourse.

Once again my mother was reading about me in the newspaper and once again it was causing her a great deal of shame and hurt. It was bad enough for her to live through the disaster with the apprentice back in the day, but to revisit it now that I had a television profile was just the pits. I've never stopped feeling guilty about that. It was a dumb prank that went horribly wrong and could have been even more disastrous than it was. All that remorse that had been stewing away at the back of my mind just came pouring out as I was confronted – yet again – with my own reckless past.

Then, of course, social media got onto it. There'll always be trolls on social media, but there were a couple of repeat offenders who seemed to have nothing in their lives except an urgent need to ruin mine. These trolls were running hectic campaigns: tweeting that I shouldn't be allowed to work with children in the middle of *Junior MasterChef*; calling journalists and making shit up; writing to Channel 10 and our sponsors telling them that I wasn't of good character and should be fired.

The idea that a person might grow into a different disposition and world view twenty years after they've achieved renown as a reckless fucking idiot seemed to be beyond the scope of these people's understanding. But then so is the basic ability to run a restaurant that people want to eat at, so I'm not going to judge them too harshly.

The case settled, and the upshot included articles being taken down and *The Australian* publishing a statement to the effect that it acknowledged that the Orana Foundation had complied with the conditions of the government grant for the development of an Indigenous database, and that I had donated the funds from the Basque Culinary World Prize as I had submitted I would. I'd donated them straight into the Foundation.

Some damage you can't undo. No 'acknowledgement', no amount of money, is going to undo the stress and harm caused by printing those lies in a national paper with a global readership. The damage done to the cause of the Orana

Foundation, our dream of sharing the incredible Indigenous Australian food with the world, and to the dignity of our friends and collaborators on land and in communities was devastating. That's unforgivable in my book. The damage done to our good name and those of our partners across Australia remains unclear, but I fear it will take a great deal of work to repair.

You can't undo it and it won't take back the sleepless nights for my mother, or for my pregnant wife who fought the battle by my side. But it's something, and it's something I would fight for again, and again, and again, because if there's one thing I've learned from a life packed with every mistake a man can make, it's that if someone threatens the wellbeing of your loved ones, it's your responsibility to hound them until they regret the day they were born. That's just common sense, the way I see it.

Remembering Alfie's birth, we were worried that the intense stress of that period might mean complications for Loz's pregnancy, and we basically had a panic attack going in for her next check-up, but everything was fine.

'Yep, everything's cool,' confirmed the ultrasound nurse. 'She's a great size; healthy little girl; see you in a few weeks.'

After all the challenges with Alfie's birth, this was a walk in the park. Loz couldn't believe how wonderful and joyful the whole experience was.

We welcomed little Isla into the world that October, right in the middle of a global pandemic, a 111-day lockdown, a brawl with a vindictive media conglomerate, and a million other problems. But on that day, none of that mattered.

Loz was just crying with pure joy. The doctor put Isla straight on her chest and Loz held her for six hours straight, until I had to tap her on the shoulder, and ask, 'Do you think I can have a turn, please?'

'Yeah, okay, sorry. Here you go.'

It was pure joy to hold my fourth child, but I don't think even I was as over the moon as Alfie. He loves his little sister so, so much. He gets upset if she goes to sleep before he's given her a goodnight kiss. He'll walk up to her cot and kiss her little forehead, and she'll smile up at him and God help me, it's overwhelming that there is something as beautiful as that moment in the world. I held her head and sang to her as she cried her first tears in this world. I had so much to show her. There are so many tears to be cried in this lifetime, but also such joy. Who would have thought I would ever hold so much happiness in my arms?

EPILOGUE

Food saved my life. If I hadn't found cooking as a career path, I would have ended up just another statistic of the Glasgow heroin epidemic. It's a thankless drug, one that takes everything from you, but when you're an addict there's very little more compelling than heroin. The only thing that will stop you doing heroin is something more compelling than heroin. Luckily for me, I somehow found cooking.

That gave me some kind of rope to grab hold of, rather than spiralling into certain death or jail time. Having a career working for amazing people, in outstanding restaurants that demanded everything of me, meant that there was something heroin couldn't take from me. Without the drive and passion of all the chefs who inspired me along the way, if I hadn't become obsessed with the quest for excellence, and the drive and passion that requires, I would have been dead long ago. Because I was already on that path when heroin began to take over my life, I was able to hold on.

Somehow, I managed to find my way to kitchens where masters of the craft recognised my talent and nurtured it.

Talent left unacknowledged turns into resentment and dies, and if that had happened to my love of cooking, I would have died along with it.

I was thrown into a kitchen where extremely passionate, motivated and focused individuals were having conversations about food that were as intricate and technical as anything you'd find in a NASA lab: about the size of a pot to reduce a sauce, or how many trotters is enough gelatine to get the perfect consistency. It was sink or swim, and I've been swimming ever since.

To walk into that environment, to be inspired when you walk through the door; how many people get that opportunity?

Addiction constantly needs something more interesting, more exciting, more fucking real than that intangible thing that drugs offer you. Otherwise you can't get out of it. You just can't.

Food has been my anchor. It's always been there, my entire life; the one constant. Whether it was looking forward to eating clootie dumpling at Nana's house or lasagne at Uncle Tony's, meals were the highlight of my day, and a very grounding thing.

But then it became my career, and when that career became all-consuming, food was still my anchor. All through the ups and downs; the triumphs, the losses, food was always that base anchor point that I could check back in on and reorient myself with reality.

That was something I needed, especially as my career progressed, because as I advanced and my profile grew I became more and more obsessive, to the point where my obsession became the reality-distorting field that consumed my whole life. The paradigm of what I considered normal, whether it was a recipe or a particular career path, shifted on its axis. Whenever I was in danger of spinning off the planet entirely, food brought me back down.

It was the anchor to my life, but it didn't give me happiness, or peace, or solace. Only one thing has ever done that for me, and that's my family. For most of my life I thought I could only bring perfection into the world through food, but I was barking up the wrong tree. The only perfect thing I've ever created is my children.

Once, back in 2016, I was flying to China to film an episode of *Chef Exchange* for Quindao TV, and Ava, who was about fourteen at this point, came with me. She loves travel and was always down to come on some daft adventure with me. A very cool young woman, my Ava: resourceful, tough, just rolls with whatever. Loz was in Sydney and picked Ava and me up from the domestic terminal, to drive over to the international terminal.

On the flight there, Kelly, Ava's mum, had let me know that Ava had been a bit down in the dumps lately. 'I don't know what it is, but Ava's been a bit sad lately. She was looking through some family photos. I'm not sure what's up.'

Loz asked Ava if everything was okay. 'Yeah, I was just feeling a bit sad, like, maybe it was my fault Mum and Dad broke up? I know I had colic as a baby and screamed a lot, and it must have been really hard.'

'No, Ava, no, never think that,' I said. 'I was just so high all the time. When I proposed to your mum I was tripping on acid. I never should have done it. She never should have said yes. But we were young, so we did. We were just kids, and that's why we didn't work. It wasn't anything to do with you, but we both love you more than anything.'

'Oh,' Ava said. 'I didn't know that, Dad.'

'We were too young to have that kind of relationship. When your mum broke it off I was really devastated because I didn't want to lose her or you. But now I realise she was right, and made the best, hard decision for both of us, I just couldn't see it at the time . . .' and so on.

Meanwhile, Loz was looking on horrified that I was being this candid with my fourteen-year-old daughter, but it actually closed it off for her, this worry that had been causing her a great deal of angst for a while now.

I'll never lie to my children. I figure I owe it to my kids to be honest because I want them to have the best in life, because they gave me the best in life.

With my kids, there's no hiding who I am. With young children, who know nothing other than what you put in their brain, you have to be so careful about what you do with them, what you say to them, how you treat them, and what you teach them.

There's nothing as profound as that responsibility and privilege. As my life got weirder and weirder, the sanctity of my kids remained the only thing that could cut through. Whether I was losing my shit in a kitchen because my green ant sorbet wasn't working out right, or because I'd gone out to buy milk and seen my face whizzing by on a TV advert on the side of a bus, it's easy to lose perspective, but when I come home with Alfie and he runs across the room to yell 'Ciao!' at his little sister, that's more thrilling to me than anything I've cooked in my lifetime.

It does give me a great deal of joy that Alfie is very much my son. He's got an adventurous palate and will try anything. The other day, I was making a barberry and chilli sauce for chicken, very spicy, and Alfie found the cup and happily took a big gulp. It didn't faze him one bit.

'You all right mate?' I asked him. 'That's not going to be too much fun coming out the other end, but I'm glad you're trying new things.'

In the absolute chaotic fucking hurricane that is my life, the kids are in the eye of the storm, where it's calm. The time we have together is real, and the world shrinks down to the size of a room, and there's nothing that matters but that moment. Unfortunately, at some point I have to walk out the front door again, and straight back into the storm.

The storm is calming down a little, but not that much. There's always something to work for.

The same relentless inability to let things go, that powered everything I've done to this point, came from the same self-destructive place that made me an addict. Whether it was to get my first Michelin star, or my three hats, or to make Australia pay attention to the incredible food of Indigenous Australians and respect the culture – I went the long way around. If there's a harder way of doing something, I'll fucking find it. And I'll conquer it every time.

I've never backed down from a fight, even when it's with myself. In many ways, I'm my own worst enemy that way.

I know this, because I've had it carefully explained to me by very capable and patient therapists.

I went through three therapists before it started to work for me. I went to one the first time and told him a bit about myself and he went: 'Oh, you know, it sounds like you've got OCD.'

'Bullshit,' I said. 'I do not have OCD!' I walked out and never came back.

The second therapist talked to me for a while and then listed all my symptoms and chronic behaviours, and told me I had functioning OCD.

I wasn't having that. 'I don't have fucking OCD,' I insisted. 'I don't go around checking the locks three times or turning the light switch on and off or any of that. Come on now.'

Then the third therapist basically took a look at me and diagnosed me as having OCD on the spot.

'Maybe there's something in this,' I thought, and started listening to the therapist. She explained that I had a classic case of OCD with a highly binary world view where it was hard for me to see anything less than absolutely perfect as worthwhile. That it was probably a learned behaviour over a long period of time rather than something I was born with, and that you saw it a lot in people who are in highly professional jobs or are at the very top end of their industry, where perfection is necessary.

Then she just rattled off all these different things in my life: girlfriends, money, cars, houses, possessions, workplaces, friendships, relationships. 'Either it's really good, perfect, awesome, or it's absolutely worthless. There's nothing in between. And that's how your brain works. There are no shades of grey as far as you're concerned.'

She was right, obviously, and once I was aware of it I could start working on it. It's something I still struggle with. There are shades of the old me around still: like, why should I have something in my life that's not the best it can possibly be? But that's just not how life works, which is the bit I had to understand.

Life is not perfect. If it were a dish, it would be one that despite your best intentions didn't end up anything like you envisioned while creating the recipe.

Sometimes life is hard, and wrong, and you just have to learn to deal with that. People will let you down; they won't reach your standards; they'll disappoint you or break your heart – or put cream in a pasta carbonara. As hard as it is to accept, that's not something I can control.

I found my way there through therapy and talking about relationships more than anything. The therapist got me to look at relationships with friends that had gone bad over the years, and that's what helped me recognise that pattern of behaviour. Like Bob, who's the classic example.

He was an amazing guy, my best mate for a long time. We went to Australia together, and he was best man at my wedding to Kelly. We were inseparable. And I told him to fuck off out of my life because I didn't like how he was cooking fish.

Looking back at that is what made me really see what was going on.

It was a hard realisation for me, that there are shades of grey in the world. My best friend in the world should be able to plate up a not-quite-perfect sea bass without me ripping his throat out and casting him to the side. I've called him since and apologised, and he was very chilled-out and good about it, all things considered.

Bob, mates, girlfriends, my marriages: I would test everyone around me all the time, and in the process I lost some amazing people. All because I held them to a standard that was completely arbitrary because I'd manufactured it in my fucking head.

Now that I'm aware of it, I can catch myself doing it, and check myself and think *why am I talking to this person like this?*

It helped me understand a lot of how I've behaved since I got off the gear. I love cars, motorbikes, jumping out of aeroplanes – anything that gives me that adrenaline rush.

It happens a lot with ex-drug addicts, apparently. Our brains have been rewired. You just can't seem to get as excited about certain things as non-addicts; what works for normal people doesn't work on me to the same extent. Most people get great excitement and pleasure from having a birthday party but if you've reached the stupid highs from drugs, something like that's a yawn.

When you've blown the excitement fuse in your head, scientists call it 'dysphoria'. When my therapist explained that to me, it blew my mind – again. You'd think there weren't that many fuses left to short out in my skull, but there you go.

For me, it was understanding and actually acknowledging that I was not like most people: happy to go for a walk in the park or along the beach at sunset holding hands with their partner. Because I blew my fucking brain cells out for such a long period of time, it takes a lot more than a sunset for me to be excited. The threshold is different. Sure, I like watching a sunset, but I like a sports car more.

But now, with Loz, with my kids, that's slowly starting to change. That part of my brain, absolutely battered by narcotics, is coming alive again, and life is just so much more real than I'd been able to experience before. I can walk along the beach, holding Loz's hand, and actually, for the first time since I was a child, appreciate the sunset. And if I can drive home in a sports car afterwards, well, that's even better.

At the time of writing I am, much to my shock, happy; absolutely content with life. The borders opened, and Ava was able to fly down from Sydney and be with us for Christmas 2020. Alfie, now three, took her hand in his little one and gave her a tour of the house, excited to show off his room, his toys, his baby sister. Life is not perfect – I miss my Sofia every day, but I know we'll be together again in time.

I've spent my entire life fighting, and now for the first time since I was old enough to pick up a chef's knife, I don't feel like fighting any more. When I look into Isla's eyes and she flashes her smile at me, that's all the happiness I need. The difference is, now I have someone to fight alongside me. Loz kept her career, and made my dream for Orana her own, so we share that, as we share everything. The weight of the world, the stress of the job, the work that needs doing – we face it together. She is my other half, the calm, sensible, logical ocean to the wild, reckless fire that's driven me my whole life.

So that's it. That's the story so far. I may not know shit from clay about so many things, but there's a few things I do know. I know food. I know that if you try something new – a dish, a recipe, an experience – you probably won't regret it. At least not for long.

Every day I get into the *MasterChef* studio, Loz and the kids drop in, and I'm struck anew by how amazing my life is, that I have the privilege to share my love of trying new things and exploring all food has to offer with the world.

Can I tell you the part that makes me happiest? When I go into the *MasterChef* garden. It's brimming with native Australian plants that weren't there when the show started all those years ago. Then when you open the studio pantry, there's a whole section of native ingredients there: eighty fruits, vegetables, edible plants and spices for contestants to use in a cook any day. Just the other day, one of the contestants whipped up a dessert with a saltbush tuile, which you can imagine I was a bit excited about, even if I try to tamp it down for the camera.

I knew from the start that if we did Orana properly people would start looking at these ingredients with fresh eyes. Chefs who are much better cooks than I am will be inspired, make better dishes than I ever could, and hopefully start visiting communities and making new dishes. Eventually, I hope, we'll have a really amazing, unique cuisine in this country.

That won't be me. I didn't go on this journey to stand on a soapbox and say, 'Here, I've invented Australian cuisine. We're done.' That's not going to happen till long after I've gone. I've done what I can, and that's what the Foundation is all about, to make sure that happens. It's so important that we have representation of First Nations food, culture, and voices on shows like *MasterChef*. It will help ordinary people to open their minds, and to learn, and acknowledge the incredible culture that was here for at least 60,000 years.

My voice isn't the most important one in that mission. Every voice matters, so look around you, get to know the people on whose land you live, and what they stand for. I guarantee you'll become a richer person.

Bruno Dann taught me that as long as you walk this earth, you are responsible for it, and I really believe that. Care for the place you live and the people around you. Make sure you look after the people in your life, your community, your children and your elders. Give something back, and try to leave the world a better place than when you came into it. If there's one thing I've learned in life, it's that.

Oh, and if you only take one thing away from my story, please, I beg you, don't put cream in your fucking pasta carbonara.

ACKNOWLEDGEMENTS

This book, and anything covered in it, would not exist without the help of so many people. It would take a whole other book just to thank them all properly, but here goes . . .

The inspiring, incredible, resilient elders, leaders and legends from Australia's First Nations and allies – some of whom have passed – who opened my mind, opened their homes, and trusted me with their knowledge. I can never repay what I owe you, but I will never stop trying: Bruno Dann, Cynthia Dann, Robert Dann, Jesse, and Marion, Leah, Ali, David – and their families. Albert Wiggan, Richard Gandhuwuy Garrawurra, Mary Nulumay, Daisy Burarrwanga, Timmy Djawa Burarrwanga, Timmy Galalingu, Oscar Gararrwicha, Buku-Larrnggay Mulka, Will Stubbs, Sienna Stubbs, Dhalulu Merrkiyawuy Ganambarr, Gunybi Djambawa Marawili AM, Gurrundul Marawili, Ishmael Marika, Patrina Munuŋgurr, Gutiŋarra Yunupiŋu, Bec Charlesworth, Joseph Brady, Djalu Gurruwiwi, Larry Gurruwiwi, Wukun Wanambi,

Patricia Marrfurra McTaggart OAM, Kieren McTaggart, Aaron McTaggart, Miriam Rose Ungunmerr Baumann AM, Susan Nurra, Therese Daly, Bikhita Dora, Glen Wightman, Daniel Motlop, Narelda Jacobs, Keith Jeffrey, Stephen Goldsmith – Kaurna, Peter Watts, Uncle Derek Walker, Arthur and family, Kevin Kropinyeri, Ngopamuldi Aboriginal corporation and the Beagle Bay Rangers.

The Orana Foundation team: Lauren Zonfrillo, Norman Gillespie, Bridgette Hunt, Joanne Willlmot, Dena Kaye and Dick Fallin, Pamela Ryan, Anika Valenti, Terri Janke, Jason Karas, Skip Lipman, Phillip Clarke, Phil Weinstein, John Carragher, Jim Deed, Renate Faast, Kate Delaporte, Bianca Dunker, Michelle Waycott, John Conran, Vlad Jiranek, Ken Chalmers.

The founding team at Restaurant Orana: Shannon Fleming, Aaron Fenwick, Joshua Picken, Brittany Weckert, Ryan Lenzi, Finton Rowe, Terry Intarakhamhaeng, Peter Hardwick, Justin Healy, Kane Smith, Greta Wholstadt, Sarah Feehan, Emily Kinnear, Alex Thomas, Angus Love, Paul Cleary, Amanda Hughes, Amanda Renoso, Amber Gardner, Jack Wilkes, Amy Dunleavey, Arash Arashdeep, Singh Randhawa, Audrey Menz, Beowulf Downing, Blake Drinkwater, Bethan Chaplin Dewey.

Brent Mayeaux, Charlotte Martin, Chris Greentree, Della Goodfellow, Elliot Vials, Georgia Murray, Georgie Davidson-Brown, Harrison Gloyne, Hayley Elkins, Imogen Clarke, Jade Lach, Jason Coltan, Jack Winfield, Jill Chimielewski, Jonothan Brook, Joshua Cooke, Sam Christopher, Joshua d'Ambrosio, Kate Ozolins, Kathryn Simmons, Kelly McMeeken, Kiana Crook, Kyle Poole, Louis Schofield,

Mark Reginato, Louise Daily, Maddie Skippen, Madeline Deans, Marcio DaSilva, Mark Kamleh, Marco Vigorelli, Ivy Tran, Mimi Lauritsen, Nic Wong, Nicola Jacobs, Oliver Edwards, Brianna Smith, Nicholas Chapman, Nathan Fallowfield, Paul Cleary, Richard Henshke, Sam O'Reilly, Samantha Payne, Vincenzo la Montagna, Lara Marro, Max Sharrad, Laura Sharrad, Shaun Lau, Simon Ruiliang Ming, Stefano Magrofuoco, Steven Seng Meng Che, Sue Hana, Susman KC, Tess Jackson, Xavier Figier, Natto Wei Hao, Misty Yi Rou, Joshua Donk, Jae Wilkinson, John di Pinto, Zac Markov, Simone Panayiotakopoulos, Zelimir Harasty.

To Alfie's medical team who bought our little boy home to us: Sabrina Kuah, Geoff Mathews, Michael Stark, and all the midwives at the Adelaide Women's and Children's Hospital – thank you.

Davie Auchie, Mark Bull, Marco Pierre White, David Cavalier, Dietmar Sawyere, Simon Bryant and so many other chefs and mentors along the way.

Paul Robb, Richard Turner, Jimmy and Jane Barnes, Joey and Nath Sculthorpe, James and Bronwyn Taylor, Mark Carnegie, Kate Thompson, Carolyn Sutton, Mark O'Brien, Monica Brown, Jeanine Bribosia, Shannon Blanchard, Nicole Foster, Naomi Watson, Michael Hodgson, Per-Anders and Lotta Jörgensen, David Sly, Pat Nourse, Jill Dupleix and Terry Durack.

Andy Allen, Melissa Leong, Marty Benson, Jodi Crawford-Fish, Tim Toni, David Forster, Simon Child, David Bocca, Charmaine De Pasquale, Megan Thompson, Maureen Moriarty, Lee O'Keefe and all my *MasterChef* crew. There's not enough space!

The team who worked on this book: Emma Nolan, Liam, Anabel Pandiella, Dan Ruffino, Katie Stackhouse, Meng Koach, Tina Smigielski, Brendan Fredericks, and the whole team at Simon & Schuster.

Most all, for their love and support through the years, my family. My parents, Sarah and Ivan; and Carla, Grace. Jack, Patty, Lani, Joel, Manno and Jakey.

And the great joy of my life, my little ones: Ava, Sofia, Alfie and Isla.

Thank you all.